CATHARINA

Black & White & Very Little Gray

George Frederick Brauer Jr.

 FriesenPress

One Printers Way
Altona, MB R0G 0B0
Canada

www.friesenpress.com

ISBN
978-1-03-913929-9 (Hardcover)
978-1-03-913928-2 (Paperback)
978-1-03-913930-5 (eBook)

1. BIOGRAPHY & AUTOBIOGRAPHY, PERSONAL MEMOIRS

Distributed to the trade by The Ingram Book Company

TABLE OF CONTENTS

FORWARD

Within the pages that follow are my life, my story, my experiences, good and bad, my successes as well as my failures. It is my sincere hope that you find some of the lessons I have learned in my 90 years helpful to you on some personal level. The more serious mistakes we can avoid, the better. Decades pass, even centuries, but many of the fundamental lessons in life never change. They are timeless. Life is challenging enough without causing ourselves additional pain by inviting unnecessary complications and obstacles into our existence!

They say with age comes wisdom. As you read through these pages of my life, I sincerely hope you find that particular adage to be at least partially true for me as well.

My motto has always been "nothing is free" and with hard work, strong morals, and self-discipline, I have enjoyed a beautiful life. I am a proud immigrant who came to America through legal channels. I strongly advocate for people to immigrate through lawful methods! I love the USA and wave my flag proudly.

As you no doubt recognized immediately from the cover, this book is a combined effort. Although I have been an American citizen for over 50 years and speak English very well, I don't write it well enough to author a magazine article, much less a book. My son is the writer.

Several years ago, Freddy and I started discussing the idea of a book of my memoirs. I had joked about writing a book about my life for years. Since the passing of my husband in 2000, there is literally no one on Earth now that knows me personally, who I am in my soul, and the details of my life better than my son. So, together we sat on my big glassed-in porch for many hours a day, for many days, and sifted through my life, year after year, in chronological order as Freddy asked questions and filled several notebooks with notes of every pertinent detail I could recall. I can tell you that it was a long process! I was amazed at how challenging it was at times to remember certain details. Most of my first four or five years were told to me by my parents when I got older, of course. After 54 years of being my son, Freddy knew a lot about my life. Of course, he knows most of it starting from the mid-'70s because he was there to witness it. It was the first forty years of my life that he needed to pick from my memory one detail at a time.

Certain people, places, and events that had some impact or significance in my life, good and bad, remain clear in my memory. After all, those are the things that stay with us, that we learn from and in part, make us who and what we are as we grow older. We are truly the sum total of all of our experiences. Everything we see, smell, hear, feel, do . . . it's all there. Specific dates and times from the past elude me more often than not so many decades later. That's what diaries are for and, I never kept a diary. Maybe I should have.

My life is in your hands, so to speak. I thank you from the bottom of my heart for having the interest to take the time to read it. I've lived a good, full, eventful life, and I'm still going! In my 90 years I have run the gamut of emotions, from overwhelming joy to absolute terror, love, hate, hope, and despair and one way or another, I've embraced them all. I had to. I think it is crucial that we do. As human beings, we are the entirety of our experiences, thoughts, and emotions. Ultimately, I think we must embrace the events of our lives, good and bad, so we can learn from them and use them to grow emotionally, spiritually and improve ourselves and our lives. I think it is invaluable for us to remember the important events of our lives, good and bad.

Remember, not dwell! Never dwell in past resentments but rather use them as lessons to move forward and grow. To dwell in the past is to miss the present. Be like fine wine, get better with age!

We all have a story. I sincerely hope you enjoy reading mine. More than anything else, I sincerely hope that while you read my life story, something from my life has a meaningful and personal impact on you and in some way, enriches yours.

Freddy: thank you from the bottom of my heart for writing this memoir! I appreciate the time and effort it took to create this book. Both Freddy and I are grateful for Claudia Seelig and Suzanne Odell for their assistance with this project.

God bless America!

Catharina Brauer (Toosje)

PROLOGUE

We crouched silently in the dark, dank, dugout shelter, muscles frozen in fear, staring upward into virtual blackness. Even though I was just a young girl at the time, the absolute terror of that moment is still such a vivid memory, I can still close my eyes, almost eighty years later, and recall it as if it were a few weeks ago. Just a few feet above us was the cacophony of countless Nazi boots thumping the ground in unison, Nazi officers shouting orders back and forth, and loud, heavy military vehicles, artillery, and equipment rolling through our brick and cobblestone streets. The Dutch security officers had sounded the evacuation siren that a Nazi Panzer battalion was approaching Asten. "Panzer" is the German word meaning armor vehicle, specifically tanks. We had managed to conceal ourselves within the shelter no more than twenty or thirty minutes before they reached our location. That morning we had awoken to a light but steady rain and the soft dirt floor of the shelter had become a few inches of cold mud. The shelter was nothing more than a covered and camouflaged dirt trench approximately five feet deep, three or four feet wide, and maybe twenty feet long. My Father and a few men on our street had dug it out by hand with shovels weeks before. At one end of the shelter was a young man with a rifle and at the other end was another young man, not yet even 18 years old, with a revolver. There were a few young men that lived on our street hiding in the shelter with us for good reason. The Dutch made every effort to hide the older teens and younger men in their families. In Asten, my father was one of the leaders of the now somewhat famous Dutch Resistance. He had learned early on that the Nazi Reichskommissar, whom Hitler had appointed and stationed in Amsterdam to oversee the German military occupation of Holland had issued a decree. By order of "Der Fuhrer", Hitler, all Dutch men between the ages of 18 and 45 would be conscripted as needed to work for the German military as laborers. After the war, we learned that over half a million Dutch citizens had been forced into slave labor, housed in horrid conditions by the hundreds and thousands in large concentration or labor camps, most of which were located within Germany, within walking distance of war production factories. Thousands of even less fortunate young Dutch men were forced to endure grueling manual labor working dawn to dusk every day, rain or shine, in the summer heat and in the freezing cold winter on Hitler's many construction projects. Many of them perished from overwork, malnutrition, and injury. Young healthy Dutch women were not exempt from this decree either. Thousands were used as laborers on assembly lines in German factories as well. In the years to come after the war, the world would learn that by September of 1945, Hitler's Nazi war machine had conscripted over twelve million European civilians and POWs from twenty different European countries into forced slave labor.

For hours we waited, silent and motionless, huddled in the cold, damp darkness of our dugout trench shelter while the Nazi's bustled about above us when suddenly, the ground all around us began to tremble and we could hear what sounded like a very large, squeaky vehicle with an enormous engine.

Bits of soil fell from the sides of the shelter as the sound of this lumbering vehicle grew louder and louder until it was directly above us. The bitter taste of panic rose in my throat, and I clenched my hands together in front of my face and swallowed hard.

Every part of my being wanted to scream, but I knew I dare not. The engine revved loudly several times and then fell eerily silent. Moments later there was the sound of several pairs of booted feet hitting the ground and then steps, walking away. The painful lump in my throat subsided a little and I slumped against the wall of the trench as tears of despair began to well up in my eyes. I heard my younger sister Annie whisper, "Mommy, I have to pee-pee." "Don't talk darling, just pee, it's ok", my mother hastily whispered back. In time, we all succumbed to the same urgency Annie had.

Eventually, after how many hours I couldn't tell you, most if not all in the bunker, simply passed out from fear-induced exhaustion, aka adrenal fatigue. I know I did. Despite the fear, the cold, the mud, and the cramps in my legs, I fell to sleep. The mind and the body can only endure so much stress. After so many hours of my body and mind both clenched in the grip of fear bordering on panic, my body and mind just shut down and I simply passed out. I don't know how long I was out. Unable to see outside the bunker at all I lost all sense of time. I didn't know if it was day or night. I awoke sometime later, shivering terribly from the cold. In my sleep, I had slumped down into the mud and from the waist down I was soaking wet and caked with mud. The bunker was noxious with the acrid smell of urine. I remember having a fleeting, morbid sensation of being in a large, freshly dug grave. Annie was still asleep, snoring quietly with her head and shoulder resting against my back and I recognized my mother's familiar quiet snoring. It was deathly quiet. There was not a single sound coming from above us. Aside from the rhythmic breathing of the others in the bunker still fast asleep, the only other sound was a couple of the young men whispering behind me, discussing what they should do next, wondering if the Germans were gone. We had no way of knowing. Since there was nothing but silence above us outside the shelter, one of the men suggested sliding back the small trap door of our hiding place to sneak a look above.

A match was struck, and the interior of the shelter became dimly lit with a single candle flame. I shifted my legs in the mud and repositioned myself just enough so I could watch the young men tentatively slide the trap door back. The men looked at each other with fearful apprehension, nodded in agreement and the one closest to the trap door reached up, put his hand on the door and the candle was snuffed out. Ever so slowly, a small sliver of daylight pierced the blackness of the bunker, getting a bit brighter with each inch of the door being slid back. When it was open just enough for the young man to poke his head through, he looked at us, crossing the fingers on both of his hands, and proceeded. I closed my eyes and held my breath. In my mind, I prayed, "Please God, let the Germans be gone!" When his eyes were just above ground level, I saw his body freeze in position for several moments. Then, ever so slowly, his torso rotated left, then right, then slowly he lowered his head back into the bunker. The daylight from the slightly open trap door illuminated a horrid look of abject despair on his ghastly white face, his eyes big as saucers. We stared at his wide-eyed face for a minute until one of

the fellows broke the silence and whispered hoarsely, "What do you see?!" He continued staring wide-eyed toward us, mouth agape and speechless, his countenance paralyzed. Finally, after what felt like an eternity, he blinked several times and then whispered in a flat monotone of utter disbelief . . .

"There's a Panzer tank parked directly on top of us!"

CHAPTER 1

MY EARLY YEARS

....

I was born into a large Catholic family on August 28, 1931. Consequently, I have a Catholic name, Catharina Martina Johanna Hazenberg. My parents were Catharina and Willem Hazenberg. My mother had four sisters, Mia, Marie, Ida, and Nell, and my father had five brothers, only two of whom I remember at all, Janes and Schane. I remember Schane as being a very kind man. I have memories of sitting on his knee while he sang to me. He brought me a present once, a brightly colored tin spinning top. I recall really loving that toy and having it for many years. All I remember about my grandparents is that my mother's parents were simply horrible, which is probably why we hardly ever saw them. Her mother was a mean-spirited and judgmental woman, and her father was a complete drunk, probably because his wife was so controlling. My father's parents were very nice as I recall but lived far away. The only thing I remember clearly about them is that they had a big house, beautifully furnished, and had a lot of artwork. The rumor was that my father, being the baby of the family and born with a bit of a silver spoon in his mouth, was quite the spoiled brat when he was young, due to his mother catering to his every whim.

One of the family stories was about how my grandfather had sent my father to a military academy in his youth to toughen him up but within a few weeks, my father wrote to his mother crying about how awful it was and how harsh the instructors were, so she boarded a train immediately and rescued her baby boy from that horrible military academy.

We lived in a small municipality called Blerick in the city of Venlo, the Netherlands. Venlo is a small city in the province of Limburg. The Netherlands, or "Holland" as commonly known in the USA, has 12 provinces. Limburg is the furthest southeastern province and is located right on the border with Germany. The name "Holland" refers to a former province that was located on the west coast of the Netherlands. The popular usage of the name Holland used in place of the Netherlands is generally accepted in most other countries and is even quite often used by the Dutch themselves. Since it is so widely known and accepted and a tad easier to type than "the Netherlands", I'll use the name Holland here.

While I'm on the subject, I'd like to explain that the Amish popularly known as Pennsylvania Dutch are not actually of Dutch lineage. Their ancestors did not emigrate to the US from the Netherlands. The Amish in the US originated from Germany. The German word for Germany is "Deutschland". Somehow in the US, Pennsylvania Deutch became Pennsylvania Dutch.

I know when I was two, my parents moved us from Blerick to a slightly more affluent neighborhood in Roermond, another small city 27 km south of Venlo on the east bank of the Meuse River. My father was an electrical engineer, among other skills, and had found a rather well-paying job in Roermond with an electrical company of some sort and subsequently had rented a residence close to his new job. This residence doubled as a small Inn of sorts with rooms to rent on the second floor and a small bar on the ground floor. Most people in those days tended to live as close to their job as possible. There was very little commuting from the countryside to the city for work. In those days very few families in Holland, including mine, owned a car so it was necessary to live as close to your place of employment as possible. Only the very wealthy had cars. For most of the population, transportation was provided by trains, streetcars, and bicycles. In addition to his own source of employment, my father had rented us a two-story residence that was built to serve two purposes. Most of the ground floor was a bar, with two small bedrooms in the back. There were separate bedrooms upstairs that could be rented by traveling guests. This was quite advantageous for us economically as supplemental income. My parents were a little more business savvy than most people.

According to my mother, I became terribly ill at 9 months old and then again with the same exact symptoms again around the age of three. According to my parents, the town physician had diagnosed me with polio and instructed her to burn everything that had touched my body, all my clothing, and my bed linens. He prescribed antibiotics and gave her a specially medicated soap to sterilize me with when she bathed me. From what I know about polio today and the horrific effects it so often has on the nervous system, I think it is quite possible that the doctors misdiagnosed me at the time, not once, but twice.

I might have been quite ill with some kind of nasty virus, however, I never suffered any of the numerous, potential debilitating effects on my body or nervous system whatsoever that are so common to polio victims. Did I fully recover from polio twice? Honestly, I don't know. I was too young to remember, but research tells me that scenario is not very likely.

I have one sibling, my younger sister Anne, "Annie", or "Anika". She was born in 1934 when I was three. When we were kids, Annie was "the cute one". I say that because that's what I heard over and over all through my childhood. Annie was the cute one and Toosje was the ugly duckling. They thought it was funny. I didn't! Once, when I was around five or six years old, my father needed someone to take Annie and me in for a while and I overheard my Aunt Mia tell him she'd be happy to watch adorable little Annie, but he'd have to find someone else to watch the Toosje. Joking or not, it wasn't funny to me. It was very hurtful, and I never forgot it, clearly.

You might be wondering where the name "Toosje" came from with a name like Catharina Martina Johanna Hazenberg. "Toosje" is a nickname I got when I was still in diapers, and it has stuck with me to this day. My Mother's first name was Catharina as well. Toosje, pronounced (Tose Ya) is Dutch for "little Cato". Little Cato means little Catharina. The pronunciation for Toosje became (toe-sha) in the US. To this day, everyone I know calls me Toosje.

My parents were a very outgoing, charming, gregarious handsome couple. My mother was a homemaker. Women weren't educated to go into the work world in Holland in those days, at all. After the basics of reading, writing and some arithmetic, girls were sent to what was known then as finishing schools, where they were educated in etiquette and every aspect of tending to a home, a husband, and children. In those days, a wife was the backbone of every home and family. There were no "latchkey kids". Mom was home, always. Husbands may have brought home the money, but wives oversaw the home and managed everything within it. My mother was an attractive woman, quite intelligent, and had a head for organization, business, and money. She also liked to drink, a lot . . . and smoke. Of course, indulging in booze and cigarettes was quite common in those days and my parents were definitely no exception. My father was a tall, handsome, charming, intelligent man and very well educated. He was skilled in electrical engineering and was cunning with current politics. He was very well-liked and respected and had a solid reputation in the community. My mother was held in high regard in Roermond as well. On several occasions in our home, my parents entertained local politicians and the Deacon of the Catholic Church in town that we attended and where I made my Holy Communion.

Although my father was an educated, attractive man of many talents, he was also somewhat of a womanizer, terrible at business, and even worse with money. Money simply slipped through his fingers, probably a personality trait he developed from being born with a silver spoon in his mouth. I discovered later when I was a little older, that he spent a fair amount of his earnings pleasing girlfriends. He was, however, a wealth of knowledge in numerous subjects such as history, politics, engineering, mathematics, and literature but he was a habitual procrastinator and, as far as managing a business or tracking finances and expenditures he was completely incompetent! Had it not been for my mother's instinctive business and finance savvy, we all might have been put out on the street more than once!

What little I recall, life in Roermond was okay. My father was earning a fine living while my mother managed the home and the Inn business she ran within it. It was busy enough that my mother needed to hire some part-time help. There were two young ladies that worked for her for a short time, one to serve as a nanny and take care of my sister and me when needed and the other to clean and help her in the kitchen when it got particularly busy. The ground floor incorporated two bedrooms, one for Annie and me and the other for my parents, a very spacious bright, clean, and tastefully decorated dining and lounge area for the guests, and a large, well-equipped kitchen. There were four elegantly set dining tables in a row, one for each of the four bedrooms on the second floor that was available for guests. In the center of the room was a reading table stocked with current newspapers, magazines, and comfortable chairs where guests could relax and read, have coffee, smoke etc. On the side of the room opposite the dining tables was a small counter with several stools. By day it served well as a lunch counter where people could walk in from the street and get a small lunch of whatever soup my mother had ready or possibly some bread and cheese. By night it served even better as a bar where the locals could come in and have a drink. My mother kept Heineken and Amstel beer stocked, a few whiskeys, brandy, and of course, Dutch gin. In those days in Holland, any Inn or pub stocked with a sufficient quantity of Dutch gin and Dutch beer was considered ready for business!

According to my parents, I was quiet and withdrawn until about the age of five and spent a lot of time sitting on the floor in the corner of the room, sucking my thumb. I don't have a clear recollection of this. I vaguely remember sucking my thumb, but why I was quiet and withdrawn, I couldn't tell you. Perhaps it was a result of the illnesses that were diagnosed as polio.

As I have mentioned, my younger sister and only sibling, Annie was born in 1934 when I was three. My sister really was a beautiful child, adorable like Shirley Temple adorable. That was the most favorite comparison as she did look like Shirley Temple. All through our childhood Annie was the pretty one and got all of the attention. Regardless of having Shirley Temple's Dutch twin for a little sister, my father made up for it. He was always very attentive to me, much more than my mother. You could say I was a Daddy's girl. He was always mindful of my mood and my frame of mind. Whenever I was unhappy, he was usually quick to find out why and do what he could.

Being from a Catholic family, naturally, I went to a Catholic school for girls staffed entirely with nuns. School wasn't a completely horrible experience, but it wasn't any fun either. The school was an old, dark stone, foreboding-looking building that always felt damp, dark, and chilly inside. The classrooms were dreary and uncomfortable with hard wooden desks and hard wooden chairs. We all wore a specific uniform that consisted of a jumper-style dress and a white top, knee socks, and polished shoes. Our uniforms were required to be perfectly clean and pressed including shoes polished to a shine. If our uniforms were not perfect, we were promptly sent home. After all, cleanliness was next to Godliness! The nuns were what you might expect in a Catholic school in Europe in 1935. They hardly ever smiled. They were very strict and regimented and would not hesitate to smack us on the back of the hand with a wooden ruler should we so much as make a sound without being told to.

None of us dared misbehave in class. I remember saying something out of turn once by accident and one of the nuns did just that, smacked the back of my left hand with a wooden ruler, hard! My hand was sore for a week. When weather permitted, we were marched out into a dingy, drab concrete courtyard with stone benches to sit on and eat lunch, bagged lunches of course. Schools did not provide lunch back then, even in the US. There was a well in the courtyard where we could get a ladle of water out of a wooden pail.

It was around the age of six, I think, that my world changed dramatically. I didn't know why at the time but, tensions between my parents began to escalate. All I knew was, they began fighting all the time and my father was doing most of the yelling. The comfortable serenity in our home gave way to violently loud, verbal attacks, door slamming, and hours of arguing back and forth. I loved my father but, he was quite capable of being one heartless S.O.B. when he lost his temper. I remember the moment when tensions between them completely boiled over.

It was the middle of the night, and I was still awake because I could hear them arguing. We must not have had any guests at the time because I clearly remember hearing my father screaming at the top of his lungs. For some reason, I remember the next thing he said as if it happened yesterday. He screamed, "I hope both of you die, you and that brat growing inside you!", and then stormed out of the house, slamming the door so hard that the windows rattled in their frames. What brat? I didn't know but, the problem was that my mother was pregnant again and he was furious with her as if she had gotten pregnant all by herself, right? My parents had never fought like this. They'd had arguments but never violent, ear-splitting, dish-throwing brawls! That's terrifying to a six-year-old child!

The next thing I remember was a vision that I have never been able to forget. Eighty-four years later I can still close my eyes and see it. To my young mind, it was an absolute horror, and it had a lasting traumatizing effect on me.

I woke up the next morning on my own and the house was deathly quiet. That was very odd because my mother almost always woke me up and it was never quiet. I got out of bed and walked through the kitchen to the dining room. As I was standing in the dining room area, I heard footsteps on the stairs and turned to see my mother, slowly coming down the stairs, a horrid, blank, almost dead look on her face. The front of her nightgown was completely soaked through with blood. I was old enough to know what blood was. Panic rose in my throat and all I could do was stare as she descended the staircase.

Of course, I had no idea what had happened to her, and the story was that she had suffered a miscarriage. She told me in detail many years later, after my father had died, how she had induced abortion by herself. I won't go into the details. The infamous stories of self-induced abortions by desperate women to end pregnancies are not silly rumors or old wives' tales. It's been done many times, more than anyone cares to admit. Women couldn't simply run down to the local Planned Parenthood in Holland in 1937! When I learned the truth, I was angry with my father for many years. I couldn't believe he could be that cruel and put my mother in such a stressful position where she felt desperate enough to do that to herself and her unborn baby.

My mother told me I stood there, looking at her, my eyes big as saucers until she got to the bottom of the steps and then just collapsed back against them. Then I ran out of the house.

Neither one of us knows what happened next. I must have gotten help for my mother somehow because my father wasn't home, and my little sister was still asleep in bed and only 3 years old anyway.

I'm pretty sure my mother was in the hospital for about a week after that. Because he still had to go to work every day, my father sent Annie to stay with my Aunt Mia and I was sent to stay with my Aunt Marie, which only served to traumatize me further. That was the time I mentioned earlier when my Aunt Mia said she would take Annie because she was so cute, but not me. Aunt Mia may have thought Annie was cuter, but she wasn't anything like my Aunt Marie. To be perfectly honest, my Aunt Marie was a cold, hard, nasty, self-serving bitch. No need to sugarcoat it now. She disliked children immensely and never had any of her own. She was far too selfish to ever care for a child. After a two-hour train ride north to Marie's house in s-Hertogenbosch in Brabant, my father had to pay her $50 a week to take care of her own niece while her own sister had nearly bled to death and was in the hospital! Can you imagine? It's not as if she was poor. Her husband, Gerret, had a good-paying job as a foreman in the shipyards. The minute my father left to walk back to the train station she threw a dingy, old hand-me-down house dress at me and snapped at me to get out of my fancy clothes because she wasn't going to wash them anyway. She took all the clothes out of my suitcase and threw them into a drawer and then gave me back the suitcase. I had brought a toothbrush, some of my picture books and maybe a doll, I think. She was always a terrible cook, but I remember she and Gerret had eggs, bacon, and warm biscuits with butter for breakfast. Not me. No, the only breakfast I was allowed, and not until after they had eaten, was a ladle of some kind of slimy, starchy tasteless porridge. In the evenings, after she and her husband had eaten a nice dinner, she told me I could scrape whatever was left at the bottom of the pot, which usually amounted to not much more than a few mouthfuls. I can't remember what lunch was, probably because I didn't get one. Aside from mealtimes, she locked me in my bedroom all day! I could get through the days because the room had a window facing the street. All-day long I could occupy my mind a little because I watched the goings-on in the street . . . people walking by, riding by on bikes, horse-drawn carts, the occasional car but, it was at night that I was really scared and miserable. For a week I cried myself to sleep every night and it took a long time for that to happen because I was so hungry! Were it not for the tiny bit of light coming from a streetlamp, the room would have been totally dark. I was more scared than I'd ever been. I had never experienced this kind of treatment. I didn't know where my mother was. Was she even alive? All I could do was think. Over and over my mind played the images of my Father so furious and screaming at my mother and the vision of her standing on the stairs in a bloody nightgown. I don't think I could have been more distraught and the only person in my life at that very moment, my Aunt Marie, was treating me like an unwanted, mangy dog! What had I done wrong? Why did she hate me so much?

Finally, my father came to get me and take me home. It had only been a week, but it had felt like an eternity to me. Aunt Marie made sure I was cleaned up and wearing one of my dresses I had brought with me before my father arrived. They exchanged pleasantries and we left. As soon as we got to the sidewalk, I said, Poppy, can we get something to eat?" It was mid-afternoon so asked me if I could wait for dinner. I couldn't. I started to cry and pleaded with him to get me something to eat. He knelt and wiped my face with his handkerchief and asked, "Didn't you have lunch?" I shook my head no and before I could say anything else, he said quickly, "OK, let's go." Right away he took me to the nearest cafe. There was one less than a block away. I wolfed down two sandwiches and a glass of milk within minutes. As soon as I was finished, he asked me what had happened at Aunt Marie's. I spilled it out! I told him everything. He believed me without question, always. I never lied to my father, never. Not only was I a Catholic girl, in a Catholic school. I never really had the need to lie to my parents. I rarely misbehaved, on the rare occasions that I did do something "wrong", it was never anything that required a stern talking to. Aunt Marie treating me in such a way was bad enough. That in itself was unforgivable. What was really the icing on the cake was he had given her $5 for anything I needed. Back then, $5 dollars was a lot of money. An average weekly salary in those days was something like $50. A pound of flour cost 20 cents!

We left the cafe and walked right back to Aunt Marie's house. When we got there my father told me to wait for him on the sidewalk, probably in hopes that I wouldn't hear the verbal wrath that Marie was about to receive. He banged on the door and when Marie opened, he didn't wait one second. He barged in, shoved her out of the way and slammed the door behind him. I could hear him. I'm sure a lot of people heard him because Marie had a window open. For several minutes my father verbally tore my Aunt Marie to shreds, hurling a select list of profanities at her. He never liked her to begin with but, her treatment of me was simply unacceptable. He never forgave her for it and neither did I. During the 2-hour long train ride back to Roermond, my father must have sensed what emotional turmoil I was in because I remember all the way home he had his arm around me and held me close, and I'm pretty sure I fell asleep. My father and I had a special bond until the day he died. It was as if he could read my mind sometimes. I've always been aware of the effects that the atmosphere around me had on my overall psyche and my father was sensitive to this. Throughout my childhood and into my adolescence my father would base many of his decisions on how I felt, especially where we lived. Once, when I was a young teenager, my mother was going to look at a house that was for rent and my father told her to take me with her because if I didn't like it, he wasn't renting it.

The next day, after my father had rescued me from Tante Marie, he took me to a very nice place. My mother was still in the hospital, he had a full-time job that he had to get back to, and he was very concerned about my well-being. He took me to what must have been a kind of sanitarium. It was a very large colonial style house with green lawns and gardens with wooden benches. Inside the floors were clean, shiny black and white linoleum tiles like a checkerboard. I remember speaking with a kind faced doctor that asked me several questions. I can't remember exactly how long I stayed there, but I do remember it was nice and I felt safe. It was a pleasant place, clean and colorful with soft white cotton sheets and big fluffy pillows on the bed, sunny rooms and good food. Years later my mother told me that the doctor had determined that I was suffering from a form of post-traumatic stress and was in a kind of dissociative fugue state and needed a calm and relaxed atmosphere for my mental health for a few weeks at the least. I must have been in some sort of fugue state indeed because my mother told me that even when I finally came home, I looked at my little sister Annie and asked my parents who she was! Apparently, I had kind of mentally checked out for a little while.

I did recover, obviously, and life went on normally. I went back to school; we went to church every Sunday. When I turned seven, I made my holy communion. I seem to remember it as a kind of a big deal, at least it seemed to be to my parents and their friends. Everyone, including the Deacon of the church, gathered at our home afterwards to celebrate the occasion with music and food and of course, plenty of Dutch beer and gin.

Some time when I was around the age of 7, my father changed jobs and became a sales manager for a washing machine store in downtown Roermond. This I do remember. I remember him being very excited about it being a fantastic, lucrative business opportunity. It was walking distance from our home, and I would visit him at work often and play in a grassy yard that was behind the store. My father gave me one of my favorite toys then, a little toy oven with a little teapot and little pots and pans. I played with that little toy oven cooking set for hours! I remember the showroom of the store being very impressive. It was brightly lit with white walls and dozens of bright, shiny white washing machines with one situated in the front of the store used for demonstration. Among his several talents, my father was a gifted salesman as well and did a fine job as a one man show in that store. I watched him interact successfully with customers many times. He definitely had the gift of gab. My father was happy with the increase in his income, which was all commission, and was even able to purchase a BMW motorcycle.

Yes, all was well in our world, for a while, until disaster struck . . . again.

At the end of every month, after the close of business for the day, my father had to add up all the sales and calculate the net profits for that month and bring the cash and sales records to the owner of the shop in person. One night, well after sunset, while my father was driving toward his employer's home, two thieves had strung a rope across the road and my father was pulled off the back of his motorcycle and the two thieves beat him and robbed him of every penny. Even though my father was beaten and bruised with a bad black eye and his motorcycle was badly damaged from slamming into a brick wall, he was mercilessly fired. Despite all the evidence to the contrary, the owner insisted my father had concocted the whole scheme in order to keep all his money. Not long after that, we learned that the owner of the washing machine shop had filed an insurance claim and recouped all the money lost. Several other businessmen in town that respected my father and knew his boss to be of unscrupulous character confided to my father that due to his unusually high volume of sales and profits for that month, the owner had not only paid a couple of thugs to stage the robbery and steal the money for him but swindled the insurance company as well by falsifying sales documentation and filing a claim for much more money than was actually stolen. Naturally my parents were very upset, and I remember feeling very sympathetic towards my father then. Even at the age of seven I understood that he had been horribly cheated and swindled by a greedy man with no conscience. My father had his faults, but he was a hard worker, a stand-up guy in his business affairs and he was never, ever a thief! Not only had he lost a great job, but he had also lost a whole month's worth of income in commissions. With winter approaching, business at the Inn would slow down considerably. I remember my parents becoming more and more worried and solemn by the day. Winter runs between November and March in Holland and is typically very cold, wet, snowy and foggy. The streets got very quiet in the winter and travelers renting our rooms were very few and far between, not enough to live on, that's for sure. Without travelers renting rooms and my father out of a job, money got tight, and it wasn't long until we were forced to move.

Sometime in early 1940, February I think, when I was 8, my parents sadly informed me that we had to give up the Inn and move to a small, much cheaper apartment in Tegelen, a small town 20km northeast of Roermond. My father assured me that it was just temporary and we wouldn't be there long.

He was certainly right about that. We only lived in Tegelen until May 10, 1940.

CHAPTER 2

THE WAR

· · · · · · · · · · · · · · · · · · ·

In the wee hours of Friday, May 10, 1940, I was abruptly awakened by a cacophony of noises the likes of which I had never heard, starting with a constant, droning humming sound that seemed to be coming from far away. I didn't realize it right away, but it was planes, hundreds of them. Shortly after that I began to hear a rhythmic sound, constant and increasing in volume. As I sat up in bed, staring sleepily into the nearly pitch-black darkness of my bedroom I heard . . . CLOMP, CLOMP, CLOMP, CLOMP, CLOMP, CLOMP! As the sleep cleared from my head and I became fully alert I was able to single out other sounds like men shouting in German, rumbling on the street, squeaking metal and engines, large, powerful engines, as if hundreds of very large trucks were approaching nearby.

I sat on my bed for a few more moments, staring anxiously at my bedroom window while the last of the sleepiness cleared my head, completely baffled as to what could create such a massive conglomeration of such noise! Ever so slowly I pulled the bed covers back and as I swung my feet to the floor a sudden wave of dread and apprehension shuddered through me. Immediately my mind recalled what my father had spoken of so often in recent months and had described as inevitable and imminent repeatedly. "Oh, NO", I whispered loudly. I sprang to my feet, ran to my window, and peered through the darkness at a horrific spectacle. A seemingly endless parade of helmeted German soldiers armed with rifles and machine guns were marching right down our street along large, armored vehicles with big machine guns mounted on them, dozens of tanks followed by dozens of trucks towing cannons and artillery! During previous months I had pored over many of my father's newspapers and the dozens of black and white photos in them of the Nazi army and their tanks, planes, artillery and armored equipment they had already unleashed on other countries so, I was quite sure of what I was looking at. For many months the newspapers and radio reports had been inundated with stories about Hitler and his maniacal rantings, his "Blitzkrieg" (German for lightning war), his invasions of Czechoslovakia and Austria and then his attack on Poland. Of course, television hadn't been invented yet, so the main sources of information was the newspaper and the radio, if you owned one.

I stood there for the longest time, my body rigid in utter shock, looking down from my bedroom window in horror and disbelief at the seemingly endless columns of men and machines passing right by our home! I vividly remember the whole scene being so overwhelmingly intimidating, so daunting that I wondered how anything on Earth would ever be able to defeat them.

I had heard my father's numerous rants, on almost a daily basis for at least a year that sooner or later, treaty or no, the Germans would invade Holland, and he was right! They were here! Marching down our street! Questions raced through my young mind. What did this mean? Why are they here? What did WE do? What are they going to do to us?! Imagine what the sight of thousands of Nazi soldiers in full battle uniform with all their machinery looked like to an 8-year-old. There really aren't any words. Eventually, I snapped out of my shock, jerked my bedroom door open, and sprinted to my parent's bedroom.

My parents had gone to a party earlier that night and, as usual, had consumed entirely too much Dutch gin and beer and were in a deep, alcohol-induced slumber. I grabbed my father's shoulder with both hands and shook him, saying several times, "Poppy wake up, the Germans are here. Nothing. He was out like a light!

I shook him harder and yelled again, "Poppy, WAKE UP! The Germans are HERE!"

Still mostly unconscious he finally mumbled something to the effect of I was dreaming, and I was just hearing thunder, go back to sleep, something like that. Becoming more distressed by the second, and a little angry, I began punching him repeatedly in the upper arm and screamed at the top of my lungs, "Poppeeee! I'm not dreaming!" "THE! GERMANS! ARE! HERE! That got his attention! My Father's eyes snapped open, wide as saucers and clear as a bell as if he hadn't had a drink in years! He propped himself up on one elbow, listened intently for a few seconds, then popped out of bed like a jack in the box and ran to the window. "I knew it!" he said aloud, sounding almost proud that he'd been right in his assertions but, then mumbled a long string of profanities under his breath as his fist banged the windowsill in rhythm with each profanity. He stood there for the longest time, staring down at the German military column advancing down our street, all the while mumbling more profanities quietly to himself. My mother had awoken as well and shouted, "What is it?" Seconds later she stood motionless next to my father, staring out the window in wide-eyed horror. She slowly put one trembling hand to her mouth and whispered, "Oh my God, they're here."

As alarmed and furious as my father was, I knew he wasn't the least bit surprised. Willem Hazenberg had never been as gullible as many of the Dutch were. Millions of Dutch citizens naively had faith in not only the Dutch policy of neutrality declared by Queen Wilhelmina and the Dutch Parliament but also the guarantee of neutrality Adolph Hitler had promised Holland just eight months earlier in September of 1939. My Father had never been a fan of the Dutch monarchy and had no faith whatsoever in either Queen Wilhemina's judgment or Hitler's verbal guarantees of neutrality for Holland. I must have heard my father exclaim a hundred times to friends and family what a maniacal and psychopathic liar Hitler was and that he would invade Holland sooner or later, treaty or no, and probably sooner. He was right, of course, and it was much sooner than later too, just eight short months after invading Poland.

I have to say, my father was an extremely politically savvy, intelligent man, well informed, and keenly aware of the current political atmosphere and of all the socio-political issues of the moment. He was quite outspoken about it too and his dislike for the Queen was no secret. On more than one occasion he was chastised for being so outspoken about his dislike for the Queen and the monarchy. The police had even threatened him with arrest several times and on one occasion, did jail him for a few days for speaking publicly against the Queen. I suppose one could describe my father as a political activist of sorts. He was well aware that a portion of the Dutch citizenry were Nazi sympathizers, believing the Dutch should cooperate, thinking that it would be advantageous to align with Hitler and the Germans. Some Dutch acquiesced that the Treaty of Versailles following World War I was too harsh on Germany. Others were motivated by money, thinking they could turn a handsome profit by cooperating with the Nazi's and some were just plain cowards.

My Father's oldest brother, Hendrik, lived in Amsterdam, the capital of Holland. He came to visit us in Tegelen once, with his three daughters whom he had enrolled in Hitler's "Jungsturm". During the war, Hendrick curried favor with the Nazi's by having all three of his girls entertain Nazi SS officers at parties and dances. I was only eight years old and too young to fully realize it at the time, but the main purpose of his visit was to size my Father up and see what side of the Nazi fence my Father stood on, so to speak. My savvy Father, of course, knew right away what Hendrik was up to. When he asked my father if he intended on enrolling Annie and me into Hitler's Jungsturm, he said that he was certainly looking into it. We heard that after the war, Dutch citizens in Amsterdam dragged Hendrik's daughters out of the house, shaved them bald, painted swastikas on them, and displayed them in the town square as punishment for having collaborated with the Nazi's. This kind of punishment was common for Dutch women that had cozied up to Nazi officers and some suffered much worse than that. They were lucky that's all their punishment was. Many people were killed after the war for collaborating with the Nazis.

Fortunately, for our family, I had a smart Father that was not only a patriot but planned way ahead. He was well aware of the fact that the whole area where we lived was in a very geographically precarious position, stuck between the Meuse River and Germany. Much of Holland is a complex system of rivers and canals. In those days, all goods that were shipped to towns in Holland that were east of the Meuse River, like Venlo, came by way of boat or bridge. Those goods, of course, included food. My Father had already considered the possibility of bombed-out or impassable bridges and had planned ahead to evacuate immediately in the event of war to my Aunt Mia's house in Deurne on the west side of the Meuse River, 23 miles away. He had predicted that in the event of the German invasion of Holland, getting across bridges would most likely prove to be impossible, if there were any bridges left at all. In a nutshell, no bridge, no food. In the years to come during the war, especially in the latter years, over four million Dutch suffered severe malnutrition and starvation. Thousands of Dutch starved to death. In order to stop or slow the enemy, the Germans systematically bombed bridges. As quick as the allies would rebuild them the Germans would bomb them and vice versa.

Venlo, Tegelen, and Blerick were just a few of the municipalities that would experience widespread hunger and even death from starvation in the latter years of World War II. The winter of 1944 - 1945 would come to be known and remembered by the Dutch as the "hongerwinter", literal translation, The Hunger Winter. Towns and municipalities in Holland that experienced famine during the war would hoist black flags up their flag poles to indicate to passersby that they were desperate for food.

My parents turned from the window, looked at one another, spoke quietly to each other for a moment, and then sprang into action. My Mother got dressed and promptly went to the kitchen. My Father turned to me and very calmly said, "Toosje, go wake up your sister, then pack a few changes of clothes for both of you, and be sure to bring sweaters and a blanket but, only pack as much as you can carry, OK? Be sure you don't forget sweaters and a blanket."

I asked my father, "Where are we going?" He said, "We're going to walk to your Tante Mia's house, ok? Now go, quickly, pack as I told you and help your sister!"

My Tante (Aunt) Mia lived 23 miles away in the town of Deurne on the west side of the Meuse River, which is exactly why he stressed the need for sweaters and blankets. He knew we would need them for at least one night during the 23-mile walk to my Tante Mia's home. It would be foolish to expect two small girls, one 8 and a half years old, and the other only 5 years old to walk 23 miles without stopping.

I went back to the bedroom I shared with my little sister and woke her. She was a sound sleeper, and it took me several minutes to awaken her enough to explain to her what we needed to do and why.Being only 5 years old, Annie didn't completely comprehend the gravity of the situation, but she was old enough to know the noise outside was anything but ordinary. I could tell by the worried look on her little face she could sense the tension in the house and the urgency in my voice. I did my best to calm and reassure her just enough to keep her anxiety at a minimum so I could accomplish the task of getting us both packed in short order as my father had instructed.

Meanwhile, my mother was busy in the kitchen, packing the food that would sustain us for the 23-mile walk that awaited us. She packed as many apples and Gouda cheese sandwiches as she could and filled a few bottles with water. We had meat to put on the sandwiches, but my mother was smart enough to make only a few with meat lest they spoil, and we get sick. She had no way of knowing how long the trek would take us or what we may encounter on the way.

I overheard my father telling my mother it was far too dangerous to leave now in the dark, especially with thousands of heavily armed Nazis right outside. We wouldn't leave until dawn. He only had one old flashlight anyway and it didn't work very well at all. It wasn't much brighter than a candle flame. My Father was counting on his calculation that the German column that was marching past our home at that moment had a destination far from our home and would be well away by dawn so we could begin our journey to Deurne with much less likelihood of encountering Nazi soldiers.

Apprehension and insecurity of a dangerous, uncertain future engrossed us. The world that we knew had literally changed overnight. We had gone to bed relatively content and at peace just hours before and had been awakened by war!

Daylight began to shine into our home shortly before 6:00 am, and as my father had predicted, the Nazi army column had completely passed through Tegelen and was gone, most likely headed for Eindhoven, he said. Eindhoven is one of five major cities in Holland and was of military importance industrially. After making a few final preparations and gathering some paperwork and documents he needed, my father announced loudly that it was time to go and ushered us out the door. We took one last mournful look at our quaint, comfortable little home, gathered the few belongings we had packed, and shuffled solemnly and reluctantly out the door, leaving everything behind. I had liked our little home in Tegelen. Even though it was smaller than what we'd been accustomed to, it was clean, warm, comfortable and had felt safe, to me. Leaving it felt like leaving safety. Outside, my father turned to us, and with a brave smile said quietly, "Ok, let's get going." We set out on our journey on the first day of our lives during World War II, for a 23-mile walk to my Tante Mia's house in Deurne.

It's difficult to describe, but I remember feeling a kind of psychological numbness as if I were stuck in some sort of surreal nightmare with no way out. I stared ahead blankly, instinctively placing one foot in front of the other, mile after mile, whilst searching for some real cognizant ability to grasp the situation or normalize it somehow and being unable to. I resigned myself to just keep my body moving forward. It was all I could do. How often in our lives we find ourselves utterly confused and bewildered with no immediate recourse but to keep moving forward. Looking back, I think what I was feeling at that moment was the first time experiencing the same exact emotion that I have experienced again and again throughout life when the current situation is so bad, so ugly, so helpless feeling that all you can do is put one foot in front of the other, keep getting up each morning and breathing. How often in life do we reach a point where we want to just lay down and cry, just throw in the towel and quit?

Within an hour we were outside of Venlo city limits, entering the countryside, walking past farms along a dirt road that would lead us to Deurne. Occasionally we could hear, far off in the distance, what sounded like ominous rumbles of thunder, sometimes in rapid succession. Annie didn't really take notice, but my parents and I were fairly confident we knew what was really creating such an ominous, repetitive rumbling since it was only partly cloudy. We walked all day, stopping only to relieve ourselves when necessary behind shrubbery alongside the road.

My Father was insistent we go as far as possible before dark. We even ate our lunch while walking. Annie did well, but short little five-year-old legs can only go so fast and so far, so we only made it a little more than halfway to Tante Mia's before the sun started to set. With twilight approaching my father began to look for a good spot off to the side of the road and as out of sight of passersby as possible where we could bed down for the night.

Several times my father hopped across the gully on the side of the road to inspect potential hiding spots behind tall grass and foliage until he found one he felt confident would conceal us sufficiently from the road for the night.

My mother spread out the blankets we had brought, unpacked our provisions and we had a dinner identical to our lunch, gouda and pork sandwiches, apples, and water. We ate quietly by the light of a single candle, still hearing the faint rumbles and booms of Hitler's "lightning war" coming from miles away. We would learn later that the bulk of Hitler's invasion of Holland was focused in the northern half of the country with attacks launched on urban-industrial areas such as the port city of Rotterdam, Amsterdam, and Utrecht.

The temperature in early May in Holland is usually a comfortable sixty to sixty-five degrees Fahrenheit during daylight hours but, at night temperatures can still dip to the low 40's. Hence, my parent's repeated instructions for us to bring warm sweaters and blankets. It was quite chilly and damp that night. Holland is typically rather humid anyway, but dampness outside at night in 40 degrees is what many would consider cold. We bundled up in our sweaters and blankets, huddled together, shivering amongst the foliage of our temporary sanctuary until the fatigue of the day finally overtook us, and one by one we all fell asleep. Annie fell asleep first, as usual. As soon as she was wrapped tightly in her blanket, snuggled next to my mother she was fast asleep, and soon after I heard both of my parents' familiar quiet snoring. I was the last to doze off. Lying on my back, staring up at the starry sky, my mind was occupied with racing thoughts, all of which were tainted with fear and anxiety. For the first time in my young life, I was terrified of the future, a horrible state at any age, much less an eight-year-old child. Had I not been so physically and emotionally drained, I may have lain there staring at the stars all night contemplating our future but, fatigue soon took over, my eyelids grew heavy, and I drifted off into the peace of sleep.

Just before sunrise, I awoke to the sight of my father peering over the tops of the shrubbery concealing us, scanning the road, and our surroundings for any sign of trouble. I quickly noticed the unpleasant, cold, wet morning dew that had moistened my hair, face, and blanket. I could see my breath as I exhaled into the frigid morning air. Although it was morning, the sky had become completely overcast during the night and the new day brought with it a damp, chilly, dreary, gloomy ambiance that only served to worsen our already somber moods.

Concerned that the day would bring rain and slow our progress, my father hurried us to roll up our blankets and provisions and get back on the road as quickly as possible. The cold of the morning had us awake and alert rather quickly and within moments, we were trudging along for what we all hoped would be the final half of the walk to Mia's house.

Shortly before noon, we began to hear a distinct and steady humming sound, from far off in the distance, steadily increasing in volume. For several moments we apprehensively looked about us in all directions, until finally, the source of the humming sound became visible.

Far above us and to the east, flying northwest were dozens and dozens of planes. When they were finally close enough, I was just barely able to identify the markings on the planes. I had seen pictures of them in newspapers and quickly recognized the German's infamous black iron cross on the plane's wings. It was Hitler's air force which he called his "Luftwaffe". It was the first time we had witnessed this many planes anywhere, ever. Nazi warplanes had a very unique and distinct sound and in years to come, the Dutch people would learn very quickly to discern the sounds of German planes from British, Canadian, and American planes, especially at night, when they couldn't be seen.

I looked at my mother and could see the fear in her eyes as she customarily put a hand to her mouth whenever she was shocked or scared. Looking up at the planes she whispered, "My God". Annie asked innocently, "What is that Mommy?" "Nothing dear, just some airplanes," my mother answered quickly. I glanced worriedly at my father as he gazed upward and saw a very stern and concerned look on his face. He looked down at me, no doubt seeing the fear in my face, put his hands on either side of my face, and with a small grin, winked and reassured me. "Don't be scared Toosje, we'll be ok, they're heading north, far away from us." Even with my father's assurances, the sight of so many Nazi planes flying above Holland chilled me to the bone. I'd read in my father's newspapers how Hitler used his Luftwaffe to bomb Poland into submission.

By mid-afternoon, the temperature had dropped, and a very light but steady rain fell for the rest of the day. As we crested a hill late in the afternoon, we were relieved by the sight of the many small cottages situated on the outskirts of Deurne. We had made it, thank goodness. We were all sopping wet, cold, tired, and hungry and as a bonus, Annie had become extremely cranky. Tante Mia was standing outside holding an umbrella as we approached. She'd been waiting and watching for us all afternoon from her window. My Father, not trusting Hitler for a second, had written to Mia months earlier. Mia already knew that if the Nazis invaded Holland, we would be coming to her home first. She came towards us, smiling broadly, but I could see in her eyes and her body language that she was a nervous wreck as she hurried us all into the house. Mia's home was bright, warm, and clean and for the first time in two days, I felt a slight feeling of security, a welcome relief to some of the anxiety I'd felt all day, if only for a short time.

We took turns washing some of the road dust off and changing out of our damp and dirty clothes. As my father put away the few belongings we had, my mother fed and put Annie down for a nap that lasted until morning. Mia's husband, my Uncle Gertt, came home from work, he was an electrician, and we sat down to a quiet evening meal of split pea and ham soup, cheese, fresh bread, and butter Tante Mia had already prepared for us.

Not long after dinner my father leaned towards me, whispered in my ear, and quietly suggested I try to go get a good night's sleep. I promptly thanked Tante Mia for a wonderful meal, excused myself, and went to the small guest room Tante Mia had prepared for Annie and me. I poured some water in the basin, washed my face, brushed my teeth, put on my nightgown, and got into bed. A short time later, as I lay in bed, looking through one of Tante Mia's picture books, my parents, Tante Mia and Uncle Gerrt were still seated at the dining table and I could hear them conversing loudly over glasses of beer and gin, speaking in ever-increasing anxious tones of voice, discussing the current situation of our little country. My parents had described to Mia and Gerrt, in great detail, the sheer magnitude and might of the Nazi war machine we'd seen on the ground and in the skies above. They predicted and drank and theorized and drank and conjectured back and forth on possible conclusions and outcomes and drank some more 'til the wee hours of the morning.

I laid in bed, clutching the covers and staring up at the ceiling, listening to the fear and anger in the voices of my parents, Aunt and Uncle as my eyes welled with tears until finally, fatigue overtook my fears and I fell into a deep sleep.

We stayed with Mia and Gerrt for a week or so, just long enough for my parents to figure out what, exactly, they were going to do and where we were going to go. Tante Mia's home was comfortable enough and we were welcome there, of course, but Deurne was just a tiny little village that one could walk through in about 15 minutes. My Father never had any intention of staying there permanently. Deurne had no potential source of income available for my parents. Aunt Mia kept a small sidewalk style cafe with a few tables in front of her house where she served light fares such as soups, sandwiches, coffee, and tea, but only during the warmer months and clear weather. Most of her customers were travelers that happened to be passing through Deurne. My Uncle Gerrt was a skilled electrician and the only one in town. There's only so much work available for an electrician in a small village like Deurne. Uncle Gerrt had spoken openly several times of the prospect of making good money from the Germans by doing electrical work for them. The fact that Gerrt would even consider the idea of working for the Nazi's concerned my parents and Mia a great deal. He didn't say it in front of Gerrt of course, but my Father viewed such thinking as treasonous. My Father would sooner die jumping off of a bridge than do any kind of work for Hitler and his Nazi's! I can tell you from personal experience in that war, anyone that worked for the enemy was considered the enemy! The Dutch had particular reasons to despise the Germans and many Dutch citizens that were caught collaborating with the Nazis in any way suffered severe consequences, up to and including their lives. Nevertheless, some of our fellow countrymen were of poor enough character that they attempted to profit financially through collaboration with the Nazi's.

For the next several days, my father spent most of his time poring over documents and maps, listening to news reports on the radio, talking with other men in town, and weighing our options in order to plan our best course of action.

Finally, one morning over breakfast, my father asked Mia and Gerrt if he and my mother could borrow their bicycles and ride them to Asten to look for jobs and a place to live. Asten was a much larger town about ten miles east of Duerne with much more potential of having available employment opportunities and small houses or apartments for rent.

Shortly after breakfast, my parents packed water and a few sandwiches, kissed Annie and me goodbye, and pedaled Mia's bicycles out of Duerne for the ten-mile ride to Asten. I stood in the street and watched my parents pedal away until they were out of sight. My heart was bursting with fear, hope, faith, skepticism, and dread . . . all at the same time. The exact level of the Nazi's resolve had become clear to us in recent days as they had demonstrated a willingness to exact death and destruction upon civilians. While staying at Aunt Mia's, we had received word of the now infamous German "bombing of Rotterdam", a day burned forever into Dutch memory much like the Japanese attack on Pearl Harbor is burned into the memories of Americans. The German command had issued an ultimatum to the Dutch forces in Rotterdam, surrender or be bombed. The Dutch army conceded right away but before even discussing terms of surrender, the German's mercilessly bombed Rotterdam anyway! Hundreds of innocent Dutch civilians were killed instantly, thousands were injured by shrapnel or horribly burned. Thousands more were left homeless. Many of the buildings had been hit with incendiary bombs and caught fire. With a change in the weather and shifting winds, the fires spread building to building and the center of Rotterdam became an inferno. Churning winds fanned the flames and the fire spread to other parts of the city. Rotterdam burned for several days. For many years to come, the Dutch would talk of the fires in Rotterdam that were so bad that the sky glowed red above it and could be seen for miles.

Learning of the horror that the Nazis unleashed on Rotterdam only intensified my fear of the Germans tenfold. Although I had not personally witnessed death and carnage at the hands of the Nazis . . . yet, I was now frightfully aware of how indiscriminately they killed. Now, my parents were gone all day bicycling to Asten, and it was by far, one of the longest days of my life. I was absolutely worried sick! I remember trying my best to occupy my mind by playing with Annie and helping Tante Mia with some chores around the house, but my thoughts were consumed with worry for my parents' safety. Where were they? What were they doing? Did the Germans catch them? You can imagine my emotional relief when finally, late in the afternoon, I heard the familiar ring of the bells coming from the handlebars of Mia's bicycles. My parents had returned! I had never felt such joy and relief in my life! I ran outside into my parent's open arms, big smiles, and my father's joyful announcement, "Good news!"

Good fortune had smiled upon our family in a huge way! My parents were very intelligent people and quite capable of being charming, personable, and shrewd individuals when they needed to be, especially when intuition told them they were in the right place at the right time, which they had been.

The trip to Asten had exceeded all expectations and my parents happily told us how they had succeeded in acquiring another two-story Inn in downtown Asten that had become available only the day before. It was complete with a working, furnished pub with a full-length bar, stools, and beer taps, a large kitchen on the ground floor, living quarters on the second floor, and a basement. It was everything we could have possibly hoped for, especially in a time of war. As my parents had experience in being Innkeepers the owner was more than happy to rent it to them right away.

We didn't waste any time and within a few hours after sunrise the next day we were ready to head out for the 9 km walk to Asten. We packed what little we had and through a lot of tears everyone hugged and said goodbye. Mia watched us go, handkerchief in hand and waving several times.

Fortunately, it was a nice, warm sunny day that lifted our spirits a bit given the circumstances. My Father expected at a steady pace we would reach Asten by early afternoon. We walked quietly for quite some time, each of us deep in our own thoughts I suspect. I know I was. I remember being hopeful and scared at the same time. That happened a lot in those days, experiencing more than one emotion at the same time. When your life is virtually torn out from under you and all that's left is chaos and living day by day fearing the future, not knowing what the next day will bring it often evokes multiple emotions at once. I had heard about Asten. It was supposed to be a much larger, busier town than I had ever seen with lots of shops and different businesses and a significantly larger population. I also wondered what the Germans were doing, where they were, and if and when we would see them. Just then our spirits that had been lifted by the sunny day were quickly darkened by the sound of many planes again, far off in the distance. I can close my eyes and still hear that menacing sound today. We arrived shortly after one in the afternoon and walked into Asten with a collective sigh of relief. The streets were busy enough with people going about their daily business albeit with slightly somber faces. Not many people were smiling, and it was rather quiet. The usual jovial smiles and cheerful chatter I had become accustomed to in Tegele had been replaced with hushed conversation coming from angry and worried-looking faces.

After walking several blocks, we arrived at our new residence, the local pub, as it were. Actually, it was more of a two-floor house with a pub. The pub was on the first floor in the front of the house. It was similar in appearance to the pub we had in Roermond except the building was a bit larger and the actual bar was much longer. There was a door on one end of the pub that led to a small room that my parents would use as a bedroom. The bar had a doorway with a pair of double doors that led through a large alcove of sorts and into the kitchen located in the back of the house. The large alcove would serve as mine and Annie's bedroom. A door in the back of the kitchen led outside to a flushing outhouse behind the building. The only other source of water was a large manual pump in the kitchen.

On the right side of the kitchen, another door led to a squeaky wooden stairway down to a dark and musty basement with one light bulb. The carbon dioxide tanks for the beer taps were kept down there.

There were three bedrooms upstairs, for guests, each sparsely furnished with a bed, a dresser, and a washstand with a basin and pitcher in each room. One of my jobs was making sure the rooms were always prepared with fresh linens on the beds, freshwater in the pitchers for the washbasins, and clean towels. There was no shower, no bathtub, or sinks with running water. Each room also had a chamber pot if they had to pee in the middle of the night. For #2 they had to hoof it to the outhouse behind the building. There was a large metal tub in the kitchen about 4 feet long and maybe 3 feet high that my parents and Annie and I used for bathing that we filled with water from the pump in the kitchen . . . cold water. Sometimes in the winter, we would heat up a couple of pots of hot water to pour into the cold tub water. For heat, there was a cast-iron potbelly stove in the pub that burned coal, wood or peat and a cooking stove in the kitchen that burned the same. The only things that used electricity in the house were a few lights and our one radio, that's about it.

Apparently, the previous tenant had been a very tidy person and since he had vacated just a few days before we arrived, the whole place was rather clean which, of course, allowed my parents to begin setting up shop right away.

There was a nice clean and well-stocked grocery store right next door where my mother could buy just about everything we needed. The only food she ever made available for her bar patrons was a soup of the day or some kind of stew which she kept warm on the stove in a big 5-gallon pot. Once the kitchen was set to her liking, my mother spent the next few days stocking the bar. She made a list and sent my father to the local beer, wine, and liquor distributor to place the order, which was delivered by horse-drawn wagon. At first, the bar had everything, liqueurs, whiskey, brandy, vodka, rum, Heineken or Amstel draft beer, wine, and Jenever gin. Jenever was a very popular Dutch gin and any Dutch pub had to have a good supply of Dutch gin! The bar was polished to a shine and the glasses sparkled. We were busy almost right away. My Mother was a charming Innkeeper, gregarious and chatty and within a few weeks, our pub was the meeting place for the who's who of Asten. My mother was very skilled at establishing a steady return clientele. The local dentist, veterinarian, doctor, attorneys, shop keepers, police officers, the local deacon, and even the town mayor all became regular patrons. Both of my parents were very good with people and were capable of rubbing elbows with customers from, as they say, all walks of life. Everyone liked and respected them, and my mother was more than happy to have fun drinking, smoking, and socializing with the patrons. Yes, she was definitely the life of the pub. We had a fairly steady flow of travelers renting the rooms upstairs as well.

Our family was doing quite well. For quite some time, maybe a year and a half, I can't recall exactly, life was actually normal. My parents even allowed me to adopt a puppy from a local farmer. I named her Tilly. The Inn was busy and making money, the streets of Asten were peaceful, Annie and I went to school every day and played with a few kids in the neighborhood, and everyone seemed somewhat content and comfortable. We were well aware, of course, that a war was taking place. The radio news, when it was on, spoke of nothing else, as did the newspapers but, other than having to evacuate Tegele, we hadn't really witnessed nor suffered any real terrible effects of the war . . . yet.

A few months or so after moving to Asten, Tante Mia showed up on our doorstep one day out of the blue. She was an absolute, sobbing, quivering wreck. She told us through a steady stream of tears how three Dutchmen had burst into their house in the middle of the night, charging her husband Gerhardt as a Nazi collaborator, bound his hands behind him, and took him away. Not wanting to be alone nor being able to support herself, Mia had gathered up her valuables and what money she had and paid a man she knew to bring her to Asten with his horse and buggy. We never did find out exactly how Gerrt had collaborated with the Germans but, after hearing him express interest in making money doing work for the Germans, we weren't all that surprised. This kind of thing actually happened quite a bit during the war. Throughout the entire war and for years after, the Dutch were very unforgiving with fellow Dutch citizens that had been caught collaborating with the Nazis in any way. Unfortunately, there were some Dutch that saw a possible profit to be made working with the Nazis. There were even some Dutch that worked as paid informants and would report on their Dutch neighbors for working with the Dutch resistance or sheltering Jews. When these Dutch working with the Nazi's were discovered, especially by the Dutch resistance, many of them simply disappeared in the middle of the night just as Gerrt had, never to be seen again. Some were shot in their beds as they slept. The problem was there wasn't always a foolproof way to identify a Nazi collaborator so, consequently, no one could be trusted. War does many different things to people. Some rise to the occasion enough to survive, some fall apart, some become heroes, and sadly, some become traitors. It's no wonder the phrase "war is hell" exists. Mia stayed with us for the rest of the war and Gerrt was never seen or heard from again, ever.

The war came to Asten very suddenly one day with a shocking blast of a siren that made all of our hearts skip a beat. I believe it was Autumn of 1941. Knowing it was just a matter of time until the German war machine came into the town, the Asten police had an evacuation plan in place. We'd been warned ahead of time by local authorities what that siren would mean. They had been monitoring the area around Asten day and night and the siren meant the German army and/or German planes were headed toward Asten. Minutes later the Asten police were in the streets doing their best to see that everyone in town evacuated their homes immediately. There were several different means of evacuation. Some families living on the edges of town retreated to various farms just outside of town while others had made dugout shelters to hide in. My Father had already dug out a crude but effective shelter with a few other men and we headed for it right away.

There were a few basic rules that always applied and one of them was to get out of the house or any building immediately whenever the evacuation siren went off. The absolute worst place to be when bombs start to fall is inside of a building! It was quite possible, even likely to survive a bombing in a dugout shelter or outside of town on a farm or in the coun-tryside. The chances of surviving a bombed building collapsing down on you were slim to none. If falling lumber, brick, and plaster didn't kill you, fire and smoke most certainly would. Another rule necessary to survive was to avoid shrapnel at all costs. When bombs explode, they throw off white-hot chunks of metal of all sizes called shrapnel. The only way to avoid this is to be either far enough away from the blast radius or be below ground level in a trench or bunker so the shrapnel passes over your head.

Having no idea what to expect, the first evacuation was, of course, quite simply the most terrifying. Fear of the unknown is the worst kind of fear. It allows the mind to imagine all sorts of things and we had no way of knowing how cruel the Germans would be to us. We had heard some pretty horrific things about them already. We huddled shivering in our shelter listening intently as the sounds of Nazi planes flying overhead and tanks and soldiers proceeding into our town got louder and louder. Within thirty minutes I'd say, the procession of man and machine coming into Asten came to a halt with the sound of a tank coming to a stop right on top of our bunker and then its engine turning off! I can't find the words to describe how scared I was . . . a Nazi tank parked right above us!? A tank! I was so terrified it was hard to breathe. Try to imagine a moment in which you are completely terrified but in that same moment your brain says, "Are you $%(*^$!# kidding me?" Of all places, a tank could stop?! I don't know exactly how long we hid in that bunker, but it was long enough to force every one of us to have to urinate in it and long enough for all of us to pass out from exhaustion, sooner or later. I figure we must have been in there at least thirty-six hours, maybe more. When you can't see anything but darkness you lose all concept of time. I recall vividly how cold, dark, and wet it was in the bunker. It had rained earlier in the day before we crawled into it and the floor of the dirt bunker was a few inches of cold mud. Finally, the Panzer engine roared to life again, the squeaking and rumbling commenced until finally, it faded away into the distance. Not long after the Panzer drove away, one of the young men in the bunker braved a peek outside, made eye contact with one of the Asten police officers nearby, and ascertained that it was safe for us to exit. During the short walk back to our street the Asten police informed us that the Nazi commanding officers had already set up a command post downtown in the Mayor's offices and had left more than enough soldiers and vehicles to patrol the streets of Asten. Stepping out of the alleyway that led to our bunker back onto our street, the harsh and grim reality of the war suddenly hit us as we stood motionless for several minutes silently witnessing an intimidating and hubristic spectacle taking place on the streets of Asten. Our town was officially occupied by the German Army. For the next several days we witnessed what struck me at the time as a kind of organized chaos as the German army took over every inch of Asten with methodi-cal precision. They inspected every building and home including our Inn right away.

An angry-looking SS officer and five soldiers walked right into our Inn demanding to see the owners and he ordered his soldiers to search the place top to bottom.

The SS officer stood in the middle of the pub room for several minutes, hands folded together behind his back, chin jutting out, as if he were Julius Caesar himself, slowly studying every inch of the interior. He was dressed in an all-black uniform except for the bright red armband on one arm with a white circle on it with a black swastika in the circle. He also wore a black cap and on the front of it was silver skull and crossbones, very similar to what you might see on a pirate flag. Having established my parents as the owners he approached them swiftly and began interrogating them in a loud and harsh tone. I could see the abject hatred and fury in my father's eyes, but he kept his cool and answered the SS officer's questions calmly. The soldiers came back and shook their heads indicating that there was nothing to be found. The SS officer barked another order and one of the soldiers unplugged our radio and then they left, taking the radio with them. The SS officer eyeballed my father suspiciously for another moment and then walked out. You might be wondering what the SS was. SS stands for "Schutzstaffel", which is German for 'protection squadron". They were a Nazi paramilitary group that, in a nutshell, was largely responsible for orchestrating and managing the majority of the numerous atrocities Hitler's Third Reich committed during World War II. The entire German government and military were responsible, of course, but the SS was particularly sadistic and evil. I would venture to say, those that were SS were chosen because they enjoyed inflicting pain, destruction, and death ... often with a smile.

The speed, efficiency, and organization with which the Nazis worked were absolutely mind-boggling and effectively intimidating. The first thing the Germans did was to cut off all of our electricity, and it stayed off for most of the war. For the next few years, the only light we would have at night would be from candles or oil lamps and the only news we would get would be by word of mouth. No electricity, of course, meant no radios. They were determined to keep us in the dark in more ways than one. They imposed a curfew. No one at all was allowed to be on the streets after sunset for several weeks. According to the announcement that came through their loud Nazi megaphones, anyone caught on the streets after curfew would be arrested, and they patrolled the streets diligently. At that time, we couldn't walk a half a block without running into a Nazi soldier and we were required to have identification on our persons at all times. They systematically went house to house for several days identifying every Jewish family, recording their names, ages, and addresses in a ledger and from then on, every Jewish person had to wear the infamous Jewish arm badge of the Gold Star of David with "Jood" printed in the center of it. If they refused, they would be arrested. Every Jewish household and business were also emblazoned with a similar marking. Within days the Nazis knew every inch of town and every inch of the town had Nazi eyes watching. In the days and weeks that followed, we acclimated as best we could to live our daily lives whilst Nazi soldiers observed our every move. All the daily activities like school, work, church, etc., continued, but as much as the Nazis watched our every move, we watched theirs, not that they noticed. We learned their habits, their language, and movements. Pretty soon it became clear that they felt very secure in their control over us.

They exhibited such hubris and arrogance I have never experienced from anyone ever, especially the officers! Little did they know of Dutch resilience. We also started to figure out which of our neighbors was likely collaborating with the Nazi's. One was directly across the street from our Inn. It was some type of lumber company and the owner seemed to have an awful lot to talk about with Nazi officers and often. Almost daily he would either be out on the sidewalk in front of his shop chatting it up with German officers and soldiers or we would see German officers entering his store and then leaving ten or so minutes later, just long enough for a short conversation. My Father pegged him as a Nazi collaborator right away, and he was usually right about such things. In fact, my father identified several Dutch that collaborated with the Nazis during the war. Understand, in the months leading up to the German invasion of Holland, there was a minority of Dutch citizens that were of a mind that we should cooperate with Hitler, show him allegiance, and allow Holland to be absorbed into Hitler's Third Reich so, for some time everyone in Asten was walking on eggshells, so to speak.

It's truly amazing the adaptability that most humans possess, especially when survival depends on it. Fortunately, I was one of them. I began to grow up very quickly at that point. I'm no genius, but I am certainly not stupid either. In fact, when it comes to survival instincts, I learn and adapt rather quickly and in that kind of situation . . . my childhood didn't stand a chance. Everything changed. Things that had brought me joy just a few months before like dolls, spinning tops, and pretty picture books completely lost their appeal. I've never been able to play ostrich, so to speak. I am too affected by my surroundings. Some people have the ability to block out or ignore whatever is going on around them. I'm not one of them. My immediate environment has a profound effect on me. It always has. My environment had become one of violence, oppression, fear, uncertainty, and survival tactics.

As my father and his like-minded compatriots quietly studied and became acclimated to the German's daily operations our Inn soon became a regular meeting place for men involved in the resistance and my father was all too eager to step into a leadership role in it. There were many women involved in the resistance too, but mostly it was men. At first, there were a lot of discussions and gathering of information, attention to detail of how the Germans operated. My Father was a skilled planner. He had a temper, but he was not a brash hothead. He knew for any type of resistance to be effective it must be well planned, or else all that would remain would be tortured, interrogated, and dead resistance fighters. As in a chess game, one must study his opponent's moves.

Occasionally and always without notice, large German cargo-style trucks would speed into town in the middle of the night, and we would hear Germans shouting, people pleading and crying, doors slamming, and occasional gunshots. Sometimes this went on for twenty minutes or more and then the trucks would zoom out of town. In the days that followed we would learn of which Jewish families had been taken. We hardly ever witnessed the Germans round up Jews and take them away in daylight. It was usually done at night after curfew. Once, on my walk home from school I witnessed a Jewish couple that I had seen about town arguing in the street with a few Nazi soldiers just as an SS car pulled up, tossed the Jewish couple into the back seat, and sped away.

I never saw them again. On another occasion, shortly after curfew when everyone in town was still wide awake, I heard a truck come speeding down our street and come to a screeching halt less than a block from our Inn. I was upstairs cleaning a room and opened the window to see what was going on. I watched in absolute horror as several German soldiers jumped out, ran into several different houses, pulled several Dutch men into the street, lined them up in the light from the truck headlights, and shot them in cold blood. My mind could not reconcile what my eyes had just seen. I saw men, some that I knew by name, in the glare of headlights, begging for their lives, muzzle flashes, men falling to the ground as they clutched at their chests and then writhing on the street in pain and bloody agony. Then the Germans just drove off, as quickly as they had come, leaving the men dead or dying in the street. I stood there at the window in total shock listening to agonizing moans coming from the now dark street. The next day, everyone looked in horror upon the pools of blood that had soaked into the brick and cobblestone street. I was never the same after that night. I only witnessed that kind of heartless cold-blooded murder that one time, but, together with our Jewish neighbors disappearing in the middle of the night and the abject, vulgar arrogance displayed by the Germans that seemed to increase daily, my hatred of them was etched in stone. Whatever was left of the child in me died that night. I didn't become withdrawn or wallow in depression, quite the contrary. I became angry. Looking back on it, I became driven. Even though I was only ten or eleven years old at the time, I developed a quiet fury and a courage that would mature quickly during the next few years, and for the rest of the war and many times later in life, it would serve me well. I don't know what exactly these men had done to deserve such a heartless and despicable fate. Most likely they were involved or suspected of involvement with some sort of resistance activity and some hateful SS officer decided to make an example of them and terrorize us with the gruesome spectacle while we were all still awake to see and hear it. The Germans had many different divisions and ranks of soldiers and officers, but we learned very quickly how truly evil and inhumane the SS could be. As far as I was concerned the SS was a separate class of evil, similar to Arnold Shwarzenegger's terminator . . . cold, deadly, and devoid of empathy. They were easy to spot in their jet-black uniforms with the SS markings on their lapels. Consequently, no one had any doubt as to the pure evil these Nazi SS bastards were capable of after that. Of course, we dared not defy them openly to their faces, but the steady increase of systematic cruelty they exhibited only served to turn our fear into pure fury and hatred which gave rise to calculated defiance.

One day, not long after that, many months into the German occupation of Asten, my Father approached me while my mother was busy in the kitchen and asked me to take a walk with him. We walked to a little park just a few blocks from our Inn and he sat me down for a heart to heart talk I've never forgotten. He held my hands in his and put his face close to mine and said, "Toosje, I am going to need your help now, more than ever. I don't have any sons and Annie is too young. Besides that, I can already tell she's not nearly as strong as you. To tell you the truth, I doubt she ever will be. Your Mother is strong, but she has to manage the Inn and quite honestly, she's not taking all of this very well at all, at least not yet anyway.

I need you to be the son I never had, just for a while, just until these fascist Nazi bastards lose this war and get the hell out of our country! You may not know it yet but, you have a toughness that your mother and Annie don't have. I need you to take care of things at home, watch over your mother and Annie when I need you to, be my eyes and ears for me when I have to be away, just until these Nazi bastards lose this war, and trust me, they will. Can you do that for me?"

I loved my father, very much, and much of what he was telling me I knew. I also knew he was asking this of me because of his increased involvement in the Dutch resistance. As was his way, he was planning ahead, again. What he was doing with the resistance was very dangerous and I'm sure he was preparing me for the possibility of his imprisonment or death at the hands of the Nazis. He'd been a vocal patriotic political activist all his life. It only made sense that he became an active leader in the Dutch resistance! History is replete with civilians that fought for their country without ever having worn a uniform and World War II was no different. I could see that my father was very passionate about this and sincere in what he was telling me. I remember feeling so honored that my father would consider me capable for such a responsibility and I looked back into my father's eyes and answered, "Of course, Papa, anything you need me to do I will." My Father was planning ahead like he always did. He was simply constitutionally incapable of sitting idly by and watching Adolph Hitler militarily and economically rape Holland at will with no resistance! He absolutely despised dictators and refused to accept this kind of tyranny quietly.

As the Asten faction of the Dutch resistance became more organized my Father got the brilliant idea of using me to collect information. The German commandant of our area had set up his offices in one of the government buildings just a few blocks away. I couldn't tell you which government building exactly but I do remember it had stone benches around it and when my father asked me too, I would take Tilly for a walk and go sit on the bench right outside the commandant's office window and eavesdrop on the conversations taking place inside. It didn't take me long to figure out which window was his, he was such a loud-mouth! He didn't speak, he barked, and he was always angry. The German soldiers, most of them, were typically boisterous and loud so those of us that didn't already know how to speak some German were able to learn enough of it pretty quickly just by listening to their conversations day in and day out. We gained a surprising amount of information just from listening to the regular enlisted soldiers. By the time my Father started sending me on my eavesdropping missions, I had learned quite a bit of German. Sitting on that bench I was able to find out a great deal of what they were planning, such as which houses they planned to raid next or who they suspected to be resistance fighters. For instance, if I heard the German words "Juden", (Jew) and "aufhalten", (arrest) and then an address in Asten, all in the same sentence, that was a pretty good indication that the Germans were about to raid the home at that address in Asten either for being Jewish or for hiding Jews. In the latter part of the war, the house raids were always to find Jews being hidden. The fate of Dutch families that were caught hiding Jews was no better than the fate of the Jews they hid. Most were never seen again.

The resistance was very busy with many different tasks such as smuggling Jews and downed British pilots out of Holland, acquiring forged papers, blowing up German ammunition supplies, bridges and train tracks, and more, so the more they knew about German army movements ahead of time the more successful they would be. It never occurred to any of the German soldiers walking by that the skinny little Dutch girl sitting on the bench with the fuzzy little dog was eavesdropping on their commandant and bringing valuable intel back to the Dutch resistance. I always made sure I had a doll and a picture book with me. The picture book was to jot notes to take back to my father. I would just innocently smile and wave whenever the German soldiers would walk past and look at me. They never approached me or made me leave. They just smiled and waved back. Rather a good idea my father had, huh? We saved more than a few lives that way. After my eavesdropping "missions", on several occasions, the Germans raided houses they thought were sheltering Jews only to find nothing. Eventually, they did begin to suspect my father's activities and would harass us from time to time, search our home, interrogate my parents, question the bar patrons in hopes of finding one willing to divulge information but always to no avail.

Several times in the months that followed the Germans increased the pressure, so to speak, and made a point to make their presence known both inside of our Inn and out in the street directly in front of it. Occasionally, the SS would burst into our Inn after hours in a display of intimidation, demanding to see my father and interrogate him harshly, hoping to scare him into making a mistake. It never worked. Sometimes it was a bit like what you might see in the movies, where the evil Nazi officer wearing a monocle is interrogating the prisoner and says, "Vee have vays of makink you talk!" Except of course this was reality, and the Nazis had a thousand ways of getting what they wanted, most of which were inhumane, in one way or another.

One night a pair of unusually tall nuns dressed in full habits came into the pub. They sat beside one of the small tables and ordered glasses of wine. As they reluctantly sipped their wine, they both seemed to be studying the room and the clientele. My parents spotted them right away. First of all, none of the Catholic nuns in Asten had ever come into my parents' pub. My Father whispered in my ear, telling me to go get Annie's bouncy ball, pick a nun, and throw the ball into her lap. When I tossed the ball into the nun's lap, she clapped her knees shut to catch it and my father, watching with a big grin on his face, waved at them and shouted from across the room, "Guten abend, wie gehts?" . . . which is German for "Good evening, how are you?" The "nuns" knew they were caught. You're wondering how my father knew right? In those days, Dutch women only wore dresses. To catch something tossed into her lap, a woman would almost always spread her knees apart in order to catch the item with her dress. A man used to wearing only pants would clap his knees together to catch something tossed into his lap. My father knew when they walked in, they weren't nuns at all but a pair of Germans, probably SS, dressed in full habits in hopes they could gather some information by eavesdropping on conversations among the clientele. With everyone in the pub looking on and trying not to laugh, the two German "nuns" stood up and very quickly exited the pub.

Humorous as this whole scene was, at least for a few minutes, it was obvious to me right away this worried my father quite a bit. I could see the lines of concern on his face as his gaze stayed on the door for several minutes after the two Nazi nuns had left. It was clear that the Germans still suspected my father was into some kind of resistance activity and even though the harassment and interrogations had been ineffective thus far, he knew they were still hell-bent on obtaining proof. That was another characteristic the German's had. They were unrelenting persistent bastards. Local members of the Dutch resistance in Asten had met to discuss plans and strategies in our kitchen in the wee hours of the morning numerous times at this point in the war and had accomplished quite a bit of successful resistance missions against the Germans.

Within a few days, my father and his resistance compatriots decided to cease operations for a while, and to make it seem even more legitimate my father left town for a few weeks. The Germans came, asking my mother where he was. She gave them some story like he was visiting a sick Uncle or something to that effect and the harassment stopped. My Father used this ploy more than once throughout the rest of the war effectively. I missed him terribly when he was gone but I knew it was necessary and I did my best to keep the promise I'd made to him to watch over things while he was gone. Several responsibilities fell to me while he was away, the most constant of which was taking care of Annie. I'd like to have a dollar for every time I heard "take care of Annie" in those days. I'd be a very wealthy lady! Most of the time I felt more like Annie's mother than her older sister. With my Father busy with the resistance, among other things, and my mother taking care of the Inn and clientele, the job of watching over Annie, naturally, fell to me. As the war dragged on and every aspect of daily life became more and more difficult for the citizens of Asten so did it become more difficult for me. Make no mistake dear reader, the lives of children are not exempt in any way from the horrors of war! I was called upon more times than I care to count to accomplish certain tasks and run very long errands. On one occasion when my father's ulcer was acting up quite badly and causing him a great deal of pain, my mother instructed me to get on my bicycle and ride out to one of the local farms to get milk to calm my father's ulcer. Normally, this would not have been an extraordinary task accept, when the Germans had initially occupied Asten, one of the things they had confiscated our Gazelle's. Gazelle is a Dutch-owned bicycle company that has manufactured high-quality bicycles in Holland since 1892. We had three of them until the Germans confiscated them from us. They confiscated a lot of people's bicycles and used them to patrol the streets. My Father did manage to find us one replacement bicycle, but it was a rusty, heavy hunk of junk of a bicycle that rattled and squeaked and had solid hard rubber wheels and an old, cracked hard leather saddle. During the war, soft rubber bicycle tires and tubes were impossible to find. Rubber was a valuable commodity that all armies needed very badly. It was late in the afternoon when I set off my junker bicycle. With its hard rubber wheels, I felt even the tiniest bumps in the dirt road that led out to farmland. I had to ride to three different farms just to find one quart of milk. By that time the sun had begun to set, and I still had to ride home.

Every inch of my body was either in pain or numb from the constant vibration coming through those horrible hard rubber wheels into the handlebars and that awful hard leather saddle! By the time I got back to Asten it was dark. As I approached the edge of town, out of the dark I heard, "Halt, oder wir werden sheissen!" That's German for "STOP or we'll shoot!" My body was so sore, and I was so exhausted, sweaty, hungry, and thirsty, something in my young mind simply snapped and yelled back at them, "Go ahead and shoot me then!" Even though I was only 11 or 12 years old at the time I was well on my way to developing the anger and defiance of an adult. Once the two Nazi dimwits saw that I was just a little Dutch girl on a bicycle they put their rifles down and chuckled. I remember instantly thinking of several profanities I'd heard my father use regularly that I wanted to scream at them. Unfortunately, that was only one of many times I had to ride that battle-ax of a butt breaking bicycle to obtain what we needed.

Another of my many tasks was pumping the beer kegs. Our bar had two beer taps for draught beer. We had kegs of beer for most of the war but there came a point when my father couldn't buy any tanks of CO2 to pressurize the kegs, so my ever-clever father rigged a bicycle tire pump to each keg. Many busy bar nights my mother would call for me to go into the cellar to man the bicycle pumps and pressurize the kegs. I know there were some nights that were so busy I must have made two dozen trips into that cellar to pump those damn kegs! Annie would help occasionally. Tanks of carbon dioxide and rubber weren't the only things that got scarce. As the war dragged on just about everything got scarce. Flour, sugar, coal, kerosene, lamp oil, clothing, eggs, meat, vegetables, gasoline . . . pretty much anything of any necessity became scarce and eventually ended up on the black market. The more needed it was the more it would cost! Once, late in the war, my mother needed shoes so badly she ended up having to pay $50 for a pair of shoes that sold for $2.00 before the war! Another time we needed to replace two of our kerosene lamps that had broken but they were far too expensive on the black market, so my father acquired two big red horse and buggy lanterns at a good price. In those days, some people still owned horses and buggies which for night travel would have two big clear lanterns in the front and two big red ones for the rear for night travel. From the outside, they gave the Inn a reddish glow.

Coal was crucial in the winter because we had coal-burning stoves to cook with and warm the house. The winters of 1943 and 1944 were brutally cold winters for us because we couldn't find any coal at all. We could replace coal with wood and occasionally did, but wood burned so much faster that it was difficult to acquire enough of it to keep two stoves going all winter. What we ended up using most of the time in place of coal were peat bricks.

Holland has many, many square miles of peat bogs. Peat is a brown deposit resembling soil, formed by partial decomposition of vegetable matter in wet and acidic conditions of bogs. One use is for gardening. The other use, for thousands of years, is fuel. When there was no coal to be found we burned peat bricks. Peat smolders very slowly and burns a long time like coal does but doesn't put off nearly as much heat. I rode that bicycle many times to go get peat bricks too. My father had put panyards on either side of the bicycle as well as a basket on the handlebars that I would fill with as many peat bricks as I could carry.

There was a particularly tragic story that swept through Holland during the war of a Canadian squadron of Sherman tanks that unknowingly drove into a peat bog and several of them sank to the bottom with the tank crews trapped inside. We were all heartbroken to hear of this. The Canadians fought the Germans bravely in Holland. We had much love and respect for them. To the untrained eye some peat bogs can look a lot like a grassy meadow but beneath the grassy surface are typically anywhere from 2 meters to 15 meters deep. In December of 2016, a WWII Canadian Sherman tank was discovered under 15 meters of peat during a construction project near a municipality named Groningen in northern Holland. To this day I still shudder to think of the horror those Canadian soldiers must have experienced in their final moments trapped in a tank at the bottom of a peat bog!

Food eventually became scarcer as well. Where we were located, in Asten, we were fortunate enough to be surrounded by countryside and many farms. Consequently, I made quite a few bicycle rides out to those farms as well, as you can already imagine, I'm sure. In Asten we never faced starvation, although much of Holland did, especially in 1944/45.

The winter of 1944/45 in Holland came to be known as the "Hongerwinter". The Allied landing in Normandy, aka. D-day was followed by a huge military operation called Operation Market Garden in September of 1944 which, very simply put, was designed to drop a massive force of allied men and machine into France that would move through France, into Belgium, through Holland, and into Germany. The Dutch government, from exile, in an attempt to cause chaos for the Germans and aid the Allies, ordered a railway strike in Holland. Operation Market Garden failed and in retaliation for the railway strike, Hitler ordered a blockade of Holland cutting off food and fuel shipments. Out of the 8.7 million people in Holland, 4.5 million almost all of whom were located in the western half of Holland, suffered from hunger and starvation. At its worst in early 1945, half of Holland's population was surviving on roughly 500 calories a day most of which was provided by a network of soup kitchens and a system of rations coupons. 22,000 Dutch, mostly elderly, did die of starvation and hundreds of children were born sickly, ill or with birth defects from malnutrition. In this respect, we were more fortunate. Asten is in the far southern part of Holland and in those days just a small town of no real military significance. In those days it was surrounded by countryside, forest, and farms and was much less affected by Hitler's blockade. We were still issued the ration coupons and the shelves in the grocery store were a bit sparse, but at least we had some alternatives that the western half of Holland did not. For instance, on one occasion my father made some kind of deal with a local farmer and he came rolling down the street one day with a borrowed horse-drawn wagon loaded with 500 pounds of horse meat. My Father was always thinking, always figuring out ways to survive and help his family and community. In addition to being a patriot he was a doer, never missing an opportunity to help his family and community. He fed hundreds of people that day.

It was at this point in the war, late in 1943 when I turned 12, that everything really started to get to me. Fear and insecurity diminished as anger began to set in. Between my father being away weeks at a time and my mother being either occupied with the running of the Inn or drinking with the patrons, I was always busy with something!

There was always something for Toosje to do! Unless I was at school, it was Toosje, take care of Annie! Toosje, ride your bike to the farmers and get your father some milk! Toosje, go eavesdrop the on Nazi's. Toosje, go clean rooms! Toosje, go pump air into the kegs! Toosje put peat in the stove! I almost looked forward to school, almost. At least I could sit down and rest there. I looked around at my immediate world and those within it. My little sister, Annie, even though she was 8 or 9 years old at this point was basically no help at all and was always given a pass anyway. My Aunt Mia was useless! Aside from being a bit of a slut, she drank and smoked all night and then slept until noon! My Mother and Father had their fun as well, at night also, drinking and smoking. Annie got tucked in at night with a kiss and sometimes even a story read to her. All the adults around me had their fun. What about ME?! I started to become resentful, a little bitter and felt taken for granted and that's not a natural place to be for a 12-year-old girl. What we experience during our adolescence can have a great deal with who and what we become as adults. It was about this time that I discovered my life long true love, a love that has endured from that moment and will until I draw my last breath . . . nature. One day, I took Tilly out for her walk, and for some reason, I just kept going until we were deep into the forest that surrounded most of Asten. I'm pretty sure it was late summer/early fall because it was a nice warm sunny day. I remember sitting down on a fallen tree for a few moments and then it hit me . . . peace! I closed my eyes and took it all in, the light breeze on my face, birds chirping, the smells of honeysuckle mixed with the musty aroma of the leaves on the forest floor. I opened my eyes and looked all around me at the green splendor around me, the height of the trees, birds chirping and darting here and there, squirrels running about, foliage waving slightly in the trees and for the first time in years, I felt safe and happy. There were no Nazi's, no yelling, no screaming, no shooting, no drunk and loud bar patrons, no one bothering me with chores, no nasty nuns, no sirens . . . just peace, tranquility and the life force of mother nature all around me. It flooded my senses and quieted my soul, allowing me tranquility that I'd never experienced until that day. I found my source of solace that day and it was life-changing, literally. For the rest of the war and the rest of my life, nature and the forest would bring a peace of mind that nothing else on Earth ever has. In retrospect, since I had already experienced living in fear and uncertainty and had witnessed first-hand the violent inhumanity as well as the devious selfishness that human beings were capable of, it's no wonder the peace and beauty of the forest had such a profound impact on me. To this day, nothing brings me quite the joy that being surrounded by forest does.

Several times from late 1943 well into 1944 we were evacuated several times. At that point in the war, there were Canadian troops and "Tommies", that's what everyone called the British soldiers, fighting the Germans in Holland. They fought back and forth for territory in Holland for months and months. The sirens would go off and the whole town would head a couple of miles outside of town for the countryside. Nowhere was safe but the countryside and the farms were a heck of a lot safer than being in town. We'd gather up blankets and a few necessities, my father would throw as much food as possible into his wheelbarrow and push it all the way to whichever safe spot we found outside of town. Farmers would let the townsfolk sleep in their barns and haylofts, but they filled up quickly. By this time there were several dugout trough shelters already dug from previous evacuations and on one occasion my family and I had to shelter in one for the night because the farmers' hayloft was too crowded. We huddled in that trough all night, listening to the sounds of war just a couple miles away. The next morning the farmer came out to us and told us two families had headed on to another farm and there was room for us in his hayloft. We were thrilled! Compared to a dugout trough shelter a hayloft was like first-class accommodations! At least it was warm and dry. The fighting was still going on. We could hear the gunfire, mortar, and artillery rounds exploding.

Later that night as we tried to sleep on our beds of straw in the hayloft, but still awake listening to the rifles and machine guns not far away, we suddenly heard the dreaded whistle of an incoming bomb or artillery shell as it got louder and louder. For a few brief seconds, all we could do was stare wide-eyed at each other in the candlelight, praying that it would miss us. Just outside the barn, there was a bright flash and a deafening explosion. We heard the soil thrown up from the explosion land on the roof above us and there were a few very loud thumps against the outside of the barn. A collective sigh swept through the hayloft. Albeit this was rather rare. Neither the Germans nor the Allies had any reason to bomb farms. The next morning when we all got up all was quiet. There was no gunfire, no shells. We went outside to wait for the Asten security force to come and give us the all-clear to return home. Outside we saw chunks of wood torn out of the outside of the barn and a large piece of shrapnel stuck in it. Not far from the barn was the still smoking crater left by the shell. My father started walking toward it and then when he was about halfway to it, he suddenly stopped. He stood there for the longest time motionless and then he turned slowly and looked at us with the most ghastly, blank horrible expression on his face I had ever seen. I ran to him to see what was wrong with him and when I got there and looked, I froze in shock, horror, and just plain disbelief. I can't begin to describe the chaos that was happening in my mind at that moment. The dugout shelter we had slept in just a night before was gone and replaced with a blast crater three times larger! Had the two families that left the day before not done so, we would have been sleeping in that very spot! How many times does one see their life flash before their eyes? Needless to say, my parents and I were preoccupied with the thought of that blast crater for the rest of the day.

Finally, we got word from the Asten security force that all was clear we all walked back into town. This was the way it was for many, many months. Sometimes when we got back into town it was full of Tommies, sometimes Canadians and then sometimes Germans.

After one particular evacuation, the walk back into town was quite gruesome. The road home was strewn here and there with the bodies of dead and dying German soldiers that their Nazi comrades hadn't picked up yet. It was a horrific sight and Annie and I tried to stare straight ahead and not look but that was very hard to do. One of them, covered in blood and barely alive pleaded with my father to help him and my father stopped and screamed at him, "Die and rot in hell you Nazi filth!" My father was not a hateful man by any means, but after years of tolerating German arrogance and brutality, he certainly had his reasons for his fury toward that soldier. Annie was about 9 or 10 at the time. Old enough to understand but still naive enough to not really be able to form an opinion about it. My parents and I had done a fair job of sheltering her from the worst of the war. Consequently, she doesn't remember very much of it at all, just the last year or so, mostly after the Tommies had forced the Germans out.

On one occasion, I think it might have been right after the last time we were evacuated, when we got back into town, we found our Inn was full of Tommies, dozens of them! They had occupied every room, upstairs and down. They were shaving, washing uniforms, playing cards, smoking, just making themselves at home! My parents were absolutely beside themselves! My father walked in and attempted to tell them they had to leave, that this was our business and home. More than likely due to the language barrier, they had no idea what he was saying through his very broken English! I don't think one of them spoke Dutch. Frustrated, my father told us to stay put and went looking for the commanding officer. He returned with an English Lieutenant about an hour later who promptly ordered his men to exit our establishment. Apparently, during the walk back with the English Lieutenant, my father had struck quite a conversation with him because the next day, two of his men showed up driving a large military truck full of food! This was a Godsend! It was well into 1944 and everything was scarce. The Allies were well aware of the starvation in Holland due to the German food blockade. Everyone clapped with joy as the Tommies unloaded the truck. For some reason, I remember what they brought us. It was a whole side of beef, 100-pound bags of rice, cases of corned beef, gallon jugs of cheddar cheese, 100-pound bags of flour, cases of cigarettes, hundreds of loaves of bread, and 50-pound bags of sugar. It was almost enough to feed the whole town! My Father had negotiated with the Tommies and obtained $1,000 worth of military rations for $150! I don't know how he pulled that off, but he did. So, for quite some time, our Inn was full of Tommies. The very first time they came into our Inn they looked around with big smiling faces and asked, "Where's all the girls Mum?" Puzzled, my mother asked them, "What girls?" One Tommy answered, "Oy, pardon Mum, we seen the red lanterns from across the way and figured this must be the place." With our gaudy red lanterns, they thought in addition to beer and gin we had prostitutes! Well, we didn't exactly have the type of girls they were looking for, but we had Mia. Aunt Mia was very pretty and became the main attraction, so to speak. She certainly had no reservations about "entertaining" the Tommies, if you know what I mean. My mother always said she was a bit of a tramp. I thought she was an amoral hussy! She disgusted me!

One time when Mia was in the back of an army truck with some Tommy, I whipped open the canvas flap and told her so. Four years of war had made me bold and a little mouthy.

I had screamed at my parents a few times at 3:00 in the morning when I was trying to sleep, and they were still up boozing and smoking and singing. "SHUT UP!", I screamed. "Stop drinking and go to bed!"

With the Tommies in town for a while, it wasn't long before my parents figured out that the bar was going to run out of beer and gin pretty quickly. The next day my father carried the 50-pound bag of sugar into the cellar. Then he was banging around in the kitchen and carried some of my mothers' biggest pots into the cellar. Then he went next door and came back with a paper sack full of something and took that to the cellar. I had no idea what he was doing but I assumed he had some brilliant plan as usual. For the whole next week, he must have gone down into that cellar a hundred times. Annie and I were forbidden from going down there, of course. Then, one day about ten days later, there were at least a dozen liquor bottles behind the bar and several different colors! My Father had made sugar liquor, flavored it with extracts that are used for baking, and colored it with different colors of food coloring! It was brilliant and the Tommies loved it! They never questioned it. They drank it up, got bombed, and had a ball!

The day finally came, late in 1944 that the Germans were forced out of southern Holland for good. We had gotten word of the Allied invasion in France and by September English, American, and Canadian troops and equipment were rolling into southern Holland by the thousands. The Allied war machine was on the move, and we heard the Germans were retreating east back toward Germany as fast as they could. Essentially, Asten was liberated long before the Germans actually surrendered in May of 1945, about eight months before. For the rest of the war, we would take in Allied soldiers whenever they passed through and stopped in Asten to rest for a bit or drop off shipments of food for the locals. I remember being so impressed with the American GI's. They were so kind and polite and gracious . . . and handsome! They would hand out chocolate bars to the kids, Dutch women would hug and kiss them out of sheer joy and gratitude, Dutch men shook their hands, and the GIs were perfect gentlemen every minute. We appreciated all the Allies, of course, but we knew it was the military might of the Americans that was the winning factor that defeated the Germans. It had begun as a European war in our part of the world. We knew that the USA could have continued to just supply the English and leave it at that. Instead, they mobilized in record time and came across the Atlantic Ocean to save our lives and our country. In the years that followed we learned of the selfless effort the citizens of the USA put forth to restore our freedoms, people they had never seen 5,000 miles away. For that, those of us that lived through it, were eternally grateful.

CHAPTER 3

AFTER THE WAR

······································

As abruptly as World War II had smashed into our lives and destroyed our peace, it suddenly ended. On May 7, 1945, the once mighty and evil Nazi war machine that had terrorized all of Europe for six years surrendered to the Allies. I was 13 years old. The official date of the Liberation of Holland is May 5, 1945. On that day the German commander or general in Holland signed a capitulation agreement surrendering to a Canadian general. As it turns out this was just a formality as the Allies had already entered Berlin in April and Hitler had shot himself in the head 5 days earlier on April 30. It was painfully ironic and pathetic that the once-mighty, boisterous, all-powerful little dictator turned out to be nothing more than a gutless little man that took the cowardly way out rather than take accountability for his actions. A true leader, a man of integrity would have gone down with his ship, as they say. Perhaps even as maniacal as Hitler was, he was aware of the evil he had unleashed upon the world.

As I'm sure you can imagine, everyone was bursting with joy to hear of Germany's epic defeat and surrender. In the end, Nazi fanaticism took Germany to utter destruction. We read news reports about how Hitler ordered his people in Berlin to fight down to the last man, some of which were adolescent boys, while he hid in an underground bunker and committed suicide.

There aren't words to describe the emotional exuberance that took place in the streets of Asten. The streets were filled with people crying, laughing, dancing, hugging, waving American, British, Canadian, and Dutch flags. The celebrations, however, soon gave way to the reality of what the war had done, the death and destruction it left behind. With the newspapers back in full circulation and the electricity back on, we heard and read about the aftermath for months. Jubilation gave way to shock, horror, and grief for millions as the extent of destruction across Europe and the world was revealed to all. The horrific truth of the Nazi concentration camps and what Hitler had done to millions of Jews became known around the world. In time we learned that in addition to the horrific Jewish death toll figures were also 7 million Russian civilians and 1.8 million Polish civilians. Of the nearly half-million Dutch forced into slave labor in Germany, thousands upon thousands of them never returned. In our little town of Asten, dozens of Dutch were arrested for collaboration with the Nazis during the war. Young women that had cavorted with Nazi officers were shaved bald and put on display in the town square. Some even had swastikas painted on their faces or had signs with "Nazi whore" hanging around their necks. Some Nazi collaborators were put on trial, and some were even executed. Even a lot of Nazi collaborators that managed to avoid arrest were blackballed by everyone in town so badly they had no recourse but to pack up and leave. Then there was the heartbreak of forever lost loved ones to deal with, largely family members that had been taken to concentration camps or German labor camps and factories and were never seen or heard from again. Some people searched for loved ones for years. Many members of the Dutch resistance had been captured, interrogated, tortured, and killed by the Nazi SS. The war had left indelible scars on all of us, one way or another.

Even though our town, Asten had been liberated in late 1944, our lives did not return to normal right away by any means. Many of the effects of war remained until it actually ended in May 1945, and then some even after that. Supply lines, communications, transportation, and many other aspects of modern daily life for that time were still in disarray. Getting back to "normal" took a long time and, for some people it never happened at all.

For myself and my family, thankfully we had all survived. My father was especially fortunate given his constant work with the Dutch resistance. Just about every country in Europe had a resistance. Thousands of members of the resistance in other countries as well, such as France, Poland and Belgium, were captured and killed by the Nazi SS.

I was able to be a kid again, albeit with a bit of a traumatized mindset. Today it is called PTSD and is normally associated with soldiers, but I have learned that it can be attributed to any number of different traumatic experiences, even with children. I continued with school and had some time to spend with the few friends I had. The days of endless chores and babysitting Annie 24/7 were over. Annie was 10 when the war ended, I was 13. She was much less affected by the war than I was. She was only 5 when it started. By the time she was old enough to really comprehend it, it was almost over. She remembers bits and pieces but to her, most of her memory of it is not much worse than a bad dream. I envied her for that for a long time. I tried to move on and join the world again as I had known it before the war but, it was different now. I felt different. I was different. Quite often I felt grouchy or depressed. I lost interest in a lot of things that used to make me happy. I didn't feel as affectionate toward my parents, Annie, or even my friends as I had before. I was still harboring a lot of emotions that had been prevalent during the war, some even necessary. I became more driven and competitive. One thing that aggravated me to no end at that time was a particular girl in school. She was very pretty and very smart. She always had her hand up, always had the right answer, and always got perfect marks. I developed a form of juvenile contempt for her and was determined to outshine her in class, but I never really did. Hard as I tried, she was still the better student, and still prettier. I became impatient and irritable quickly if something or someone wasn't moving fast enough for me. I still have limited patience for slowpokes and procrastinators. There's an old saying my father used to use, "Lead, follow or get the hell out of the way." I've remembered that one my whole life. During the war years, I had been under the stress of doing things immediately and efficiently, even in the presence of danger. During the war, hesitation could get you killed. I had learned out of necessity to bury my fears and act quickly, mentally dismissing the distractions of fear and apprehension.

However, life went on and I grew up and grew out of or into most of the behaviors and feelings that came from the horrendous experiences of the war, or at least I learned to manage them. I'm well aware of the fact that much of my attitude, personality, and how I have approached adult life were influenced in part by my childhood experiences, especially the war. Some of the personality traits I acquired in my childhood and the war years have served me well throughout my life, for the most part.

Within a year or two of the end of the war, I started to become quite irritated with my parents and often. My mother still ran the Inn, sort of, and my father went back to work, doing what I can't remember. I was busy with school and still helping my mother at home, of course. My mother's drinking was increasing until it was a daily routine. For a while, she kept it under control but eventually, it caused serious problems. My father was running around with other women and spending money on them that we didn't have. I don't know if my mother was aware of it, or perhaps that was the reason she drank so much. Things carried on in this tumultuous way for a few more years.

When I turned 16 in 1947, I went to finishing school for two years. That's what "good Dutch girls" did in those days. Finishing school was where Dutch girls would learn the fine points of being a refined woman, mother, and wife. Anything and everything associated with being a homemaker and a dutiful wife and mother was taught such as cooking, cleaning, sewing, childcare, and etiquette, etc. We were taught how to speak and move with poise and grace. We even had to walk down a long flight of stairs balancing a book on the top of our heads. It was certainly a much nicer atmosphere than the Catholic school and those strict nuns! The teachers were kind and patient. The school was very pleasant and comfortable inside.

One interest that developed in my early teens that lasted my whole life was history. I became simply fascinated with world history. I spent as much of my free time reading about history as possible. It didn't matter what period, the Roman Empire, the Egyptians, the history of the United States, Ancient Greece, all of it fascinated me. I went to the library every chance I could get and sat among the stacks just reading for hours on end, and for as long as I could. I think maybe it was the war that sparked my interest in history because I remember wondering how such a horribly destructive thing could be allowed to occur. That question, among many others, baffled me. So, I went in search of answers in the library, and in history books and I found them. Except, the more I read the more questions I had. To this day the more I learn, the more I realize how much I don't know! We're all capable of learning until we draw our last breath. I feel pity for anyone that has lost the enthusiasm to learn. Never lose the enthusiasm to learn new things. Education and knowledge are two of the few things that can never be taken away from you.

It was during my time at finishing school that my father went into business for himself.

Given his poor history of business and money management skills, I was skeptical but hoped for the best. He started a flooring business with a product that was called Magnesite. All I know is that it was used to cover concrete floors. It was applied as a thick liquid that was poured and spread out and then it dried into a hard surface. It hasn't been used since the fifties due to the asbestos in it. He had a small crew working for him and for a while, they were getting a lot of business. It seemed as if he was doing very well with it. Meanwhile, my mother was maintaining the Inn, while drinking every day, and smoking incessantly! I never saw her without a cigarette in her mouth. It wasn't uncommon. People smoked like crazy back then and drank too much. Cigarettes didn't have filters in those days either and had three to five times the tar and nicotine of the average cigarette today. It's no wonder so many people used to die in their fifties and sixties back then. By the time drinkers and smokers reached fifty-five, their lungs, heart, and liver were shot!

By the time I graduated from finishing school, everything my parents were doing was in complete shambles! My mother was drinking so heavily that she was losing money with the bar clientele by drinking with them, giving free rounds, and being unable to keep track of people's tabs, among other things. My father's Magnesite business was completely bankrupt. In fact, he lost money. He had to give some clients refunds because all too often instead of supervising his workers he was out philandering and spending money on other women and the men working for him botched several jobs.

Things were deteriorating rapidly. My father decided before we ended up living in the street that we had better move to Amsterdam. For those that don't know, Amsterdam is a bona fide big city and the capital of Holland. The population of Amsterdam in 1950 was over 800,000. My Father sent my mother, Annie, and me ahead to Amsterdam to look for an apartment with what money they had left, whilst he finalized all of the business and financial matters in Asten. I remember him saying to my mother, "You make damn sure Toosje really likes the apartment because if she doesn't, we're not living in it." In some ways, I was still Daddy's little girl. My father always made every effort to make sure my immediate home environment was as much to my liking as possible. He had noticed when I just was just a small child the negative effect my immediate surroundings could have on me. The interior appearance of my home has always had an intense effect on my psyche. I'm very sensitive to my environment. I've been that way my whole life.

With our luggage in tow, the three of us bid farewell to Asten and boarded the train for Amsterdam. One of my mother's sisters, my Aunt Ida lived in Amsterdam so we had arranged to stay with her until we had found our own place. My mother had been to Amsterdam many times, so she knew her way around the city quite well. Within a few days, we found a rather nice, clean apartment in the western part of the city, an area that was still well within city limits but not nearly as busy as downtown. We found a few good job prospects in the newspaper and boarded the tram, aka. streetcar, to go check them out. Between several tram rides and transfers and several applications for jobs we finally all found jobs in the same place as chambermaids at the Park Hotel in downtown Amsterdam. Annie and my mother would both end up working there for nearly ten years. Not me! I saw it as a starting point and nothing more. I had no intention of working there one minute more than I had to. I'd had my fill of cleaning rooms. Considering our current financial situation, it was important that I work, but I spent every one of my days off looking for another job. I was only 18 years old and being that I'd never had a real job, I had no idea of what to look for. My father joined us a week later and quickly went job hunting. My father abhorred manual labor, so naturally, he looked for a job where he could stay clean, warm and, not have to do any heaving lifting. I've no doubt my father interviewed very well. He could sell a ketchup popsicle to a woman in white gloves! He came home, the first day, with a job as an usher in one of the most prestigious opera houses in Holland. I thought that sounded fantastic. Not long after that, I was an usher as well at another one of the popular theaters downtown . . . much nicer indeed!

Then, in the spring of 1952, just a few months before I turned twenty-one, something wonderful happened.

CHAPTER 4

THE BALI YEARS

·······································

One day a coworker of mine told me that her boyfriend, who was a busboy at the Bali restaurant, overheard that they were looking for a hostess. Bali was an Indonesian restaurant downtown and the most popular and successful restaurant in Amsterdam. In fact, it was one of the most well-known restaurants in Europe. In 1955, when the famous Michelin guide added restaurants to their guide, Bali got three out of three stars year after year. Three stars meant the restaurant was worth a long trip, it was that good. Anyone who was anyone, the who's who of Holland was much of the regular clientele at Bali. It was strictly black tie, very classy, tasteful, and elegant. You didn't get in without a tie and jacket. Famous actors, singers, dancers, and even a few millionaires were regular guests. On many nights, especially in the warmer months, there was a line to get into Bali that extended out the door into the street. For several specific times of the year like holidays, reservations were made months in advance.

I was up before dawn the next morning, hell-bent on getting that job at Bali. I pulled out one of my finest dresses and shoes, made up my hair and make-up until I liked what I saw in the mirror, and then headed downtown. I was dressed to the nines, for an interview that is. I was dressed tastefully, makeup conservative but accentuating, feminine and elegant, not sexy. There is a big difference between elegant and sexy.

I intentionally got there long before they opened for business in hopes of getting an interview with the owner early before he was busy with a restaurant full of guests. I was in luck. Within minutes of arriving a man came walking towards me, pulling some keys from his pocket, and walked past me to a side door of the restaurant. Quickly before he could unlock the door and disappear inside, I asked him if he was the owner. He said that he was and introduced himself as Max. I introduced myself as Catharina Hazenberg, adding that all my friends call me Toosje. I told him politely that I had come in hopes of applying for the hostess position and he smiled and asked me inside. Inside I met the other owner, Max's sister Dini, and her son Sabo. Sabo had been the host and bar manager for many years but had found a different job. The minute I heard they needed a bar manager as well I blurted out, "I can do that too." I explained all about the two Inns my parents had run and how I had grown up in that business and promised them I knew everything about it, no problem. I was being sincere too, I did know. I'd watched my parents work in it for years. I was completely confident that I could do both jobs, and well. I had watched it and lived with it most of my life. To make a long story short, I was pretty much hired on the spot, as they say. After what couldn't have been more than fifteen minutes of conversation he said suddenly, "Well, Toosje, I've seen enough, you're perfect, you're exactly what I'm looking for, you're hired, when can you start?!" I was stunned but overjoyed! I thanked him and Max graciously allowed me time to give the theater proper notice. I started my new job in Bali two weeks later.

I left Bali, grinning ear to ear as I walked to the nearest tram to go home. I remember pulling my pocket mirror out of my little clutch purse to check my hair and makeup like women do and, as I was looking at my reflection, something clicked that day. It's hard to describe. I started to feel something, something wonderful. A warm rush of pure satisfaction mixed with excitement and realization flowed through me. I had come into my own. I wasn't the ugly duckling anymore with knobby knees that no one wanted to babysit. My hair and eyebrows had gotten very dark, my voice was deeper, and my gangly little girl body had become a young lady's body. I was feeling a new kind of confidence and a renewed optimism about life. I didn't avoid my reflection anymore. I was happy with what I saw in the mirror. I was also very aware and pleased about the fact that now I had some control over my life. My starting salary at Bali was 600 guilders a month. A guilder was the Dutch equivalent to the US dollar except worth half as much. Now they use euros. Adjusted for inflation that's roughly equivalent to $65,000 a year, albeit, $65,000 goes a lot further in the US than 65,000 euros does in Holland. Not bad at all for a 19-year-old hostess! Bali paid so well for two reasons. One, Bali was staffed with the best professional servers and bartenders in Holland. In those days being a server in a three-star restaurant required education. To serve at Bali, one had to know all about wine, food, all the proper etiquettes, etc. and, had to have years of experience. To keep the best staff, you'd have to pay them more than your competition can. The second reason is simply that they could. Bali made an absolute fortune. Hence the status of working there. My parents were thrilled that I had landed a job in Bali. They were well aware of Bali's golden reputation and prestige, and the income. The income made my family's life a lot easier.

Speaking of money, while we're kind of on the subject. I'd like to share what I think is some of the wisdom that I have acquired with age. First, money changes everything! Anyone that tells you it doesn't is either poor or a liar. At 90 years old, I can tell you from 70 years of adult life experience, aside from terminal illnesses, incurable diseases, and, apparently for some people, happiness, there aren't very many problems that cannot be solved or made a lot more manageable with money! Now, before you get the wrong idea, I'm not talking about greed. I abhor greed. I abhor the type of filthy rich that arrogantly look at the rest of us like peasants whilst they live in their dream world completely oblivious to reality on Earth. When I say "money", I'm referring to what used to be a part of the logical order to life . . . education, occupation, income, food, clothing, shelter, then . . . marriage and children. I don't know why so many young people today think that dropping out of school and making babies without an education, skills, employment or a place to live is acceptable.

Remember this golden rule. Never let your basic necessities exceed two-thirds of your income. Use a little for fun and save the rest. One more thing, try to earn and save as much money as you can in your younger years. No one is guaranteed to have perfect health until they retire, and most things in life become progressively more difficult the older we get. I'll give you a perfect example of that later in my story. We never know what problems may arise in the future. If you have some savings, many problems can be easily fixed, but if you're broke, a lot of minor problems can become major problems quickly! Food for thought. I promise, whatever wisdom I share with you, I only share because I lived it. Trust me, there were a few times in my life when I should have listened to the advice of the older and wiser and didn't.

For the younger readers here, please, believe me, most of the time older people don't give unsolicited advice because they want to control you. They usually do so because years before, they made the exact same mistake you are about to! A good friend of mine with four kids used to have a funny plaque on her kitchen wall that said, "Kids, if you ever get tired of living by our stupid rules, move out, get a job, and pay all your own bills now while you still know everything." Ain't it the truth?

Bali turned out to be a career for me for almost 13 years and truly one of the best times of my life. It was a wonderful place to work. The whole restaurant was absolutely gorgeous, quality from top to bottom. It was a big place. The entrance was a mahogany and glass revolving door that led into a large lobby where guests could wait for their table, check their coats, and have their first cocktail. There were several benches and end tables made of rattan and bamboo. Five steps led up to a large mahogany horseshoe-shaped bar, with thirty stools and surrounded by a dozen cocktail tables. It was a big bar, and even with the bar and the cocktail tables, there was quite a bit of standing room. That was intentional. Most guests spent at least an hour or more in the bar waiting for their table. Some spent the whole evening there drinking. The only food available at the bar was sauteed prawns and krupuk. Krupuk is an Indonesian deep-fried cracker made of starchy flour and prawns or fish. The walls throughout Bali were dark mahogany paneling. The floors were polished bamboo. The whole place was accented with rattan and bamboo and tall statues of Indonesian gods on either side of every entrance. There were three dining rooms, each of which had a large stone arch for an entrance. Each dining room could seat 100 guests. The tables were always set with white linen tablecloths, red linen napkins, and a solid copper candle holder in the center. There were three waiters dressed in all-white uniforms and twenty-five servers in black. This was a much different system than you usually see in American restaurants. A waiter and a server were two separate jobs. The waiters were the only ones that verbally interacted with the guests taking their orders, explaining menu items, and answering any questions guests may have, and waiters were required to have the answers, always. They never said, "I don't know." The waiters had to know everything there was to know about everything Bali served; the food, the entire wine list, the liqueurs, everything. Bali had an extensive menu and a wine list of at least fifty different wines that would change often. Waiters had to stay on top of that too. Every day they had to check the wine list for new or sold-out wines. Each waiter oversaw his dining room, his servers, and making sure guests were very, very happy, attending to their every wish. Being a waiter at Bali wasn't just a job, it was a profession. All the servers did was serve and clear, that's it, but being a server was a profession as well. They had a lot of responsibility, and they had to know the menu as well, so they knew what they were serving and to who. They had to have skill and grace as well to serve without ever spilling or dropping anything, know the correct serving order at the table, wine presentation, proper clearing, etc., and they had to do it all in an unhurried, relaxed manner and stay clean in the process. Not an easy task. Believe it or not, the whole affair was a completely relaxed and pleasant atmosphere, every night. No matter how many guests were there, the pace was always calm, mainly because Bali guests were never in a hurry. Dinner at Bali wasn't your average eat and run. It was a night out, a meeting place for wealthier locals and socialites, and took at least 3 or 4 hours. Typically, guests spent at least an hour at the bar drinking and socializing, then in the dining room more cocktails and another hour between ordering and serving, an hour for dining and dessert, then usually another hour for an after-dinner brandy or cognac. Some would head back to the bar after dinner and be there 'til closing time. The bar was usually still full at the last call.

As it turned out, I was a very quick study. I took to working in Bali like a fish to water. To Max and Dini's delight, within a few days, I was working there like I'd been working there my whole life. Before long I knew the names and life stories of all the regulars. It's amazing the personal information some people will share at a bar, especially regulars, and most of them were wealthy. I got to know a long list of doctors, lawyers, judges, bankers, singers, actors, and CEOs on a first-name basis, and they all loved me. It was exciting and actually fun. I loved my job, and I was very good at it. I remember once, a few years after I'd been working there, Max pulled me aside and told me if I ever thought about another job to tell him because he would pay whatever I wanted to stay. I giggled and said, "Anything?", thinking it was a joke. He looked at me seriously, with no smile, and said, "I'm absolutely serious." He was too. I got several nice raises while I worked there, without ever asking.

Despite my windfall in landing my job at Bali, I was still naive in many areas, one of which was men. I knew absolutely nothing about men. I hadn't even had a boyfriend yet! Catholic girls in Holland back then, to put it discreetly, had absolutely none of the "experience" that teenage girls do today. There was no intimacy of any kind ever with boys. That simply did not exist until adulthood! Dutch Catholic girls were still virgins when they got married. Once, when I was 18 years old, I went to a formal dance hosted by a local church. We were still living in Asten then. I was escorted by a nice young man named Paul that my friend Mimi knew. He was in his first year of university to become an architect. I guess it was what you would call a blind date. After the dance, Paul walked me home. At the door, we said goodnight, and thank you, and I walked into the house. My father was standing just inside the door waiting for me, fury in his eyes. I glanced at the wall clock and saw that it was a quarter after ten. I was 15 minutes late. Mind you, Paul and I had done absolutely nothing besides dance and walk home. Nevertheless, my father was livid! Never in my life had I seen him this angry with me, not even close. True, I was 15 minutes late but, I was in shock that he was this irate about it! He grabbed me by the chin, squeezing my cheeks, and screamed, "You've been kissing that boy! I can see it on your face!" Then he slapped me about the face and head several times and ordered me to get out of his sight. I ran to my room, slammed and locked the door, and sat on my bed in tears, pain, and shock. My lower lip was bleeding, and my left ear was ringing. I couldn't hear out of it for two days. Annie and my mother both knocked on my door to comfort me, but I yelled at both of them, "Go away!" I didn't want to be comforted. My shock turned to anger within minutes, and I wanted to hold onto that! I was furious with my father, and I had no intention of forgiving him any time soon!

Catholic or not, he went way overboard that night. I didn't speak to him for several days. He tried to apologize the next day, but I was not about to hear it! Before he could open his mouth, I shot him a hateful look and left the house and took a long walk in the woods. Now you have a clear picture of why I was so naive about the opposite sex at the age of 20.

On New Year's Eve, 1952, at a party my friend Mimi was having, I met a 26-year-old good-looking guy named Tony Zoet. He was short, five foot five, dark hair, hazel eyes, with a decent build, and dressed to the nines. We made the usual small talk. I told him I worked at Bali, and he told me he was working as a tour guide and spoke several languages: Dutch, English, Spanish, French, and German. Even with his looks and charm, there was something off about him. He was, I thought, overly impressed with the fact that I worked at Bali and made some remarks about having such a good income at my age. He told me what he made as a tour guide, no doubt hoping I would do the same. I said that I was doing alright and left it at that. Then he asked me out to dinner. After a few minutes of conversation, this guy was asking me out! I politely declined and shortly thereafter excused myself for the lady's room. After that night, I didn't see, hear or think about Tony Zoet for several days. Then, late one Saturday morning, there was a knock at the door. I had told Mimi days before that I would try to visit her Saturday afternoon. I thought maybe Mimi had decided to make the trip and come to me, as a surprise. I threw the door open and . . . it wasn't Mimi. It was Tony Zoet. We shared a couple of quick pleasantries and then he asked me if I would come and have lunch with him. I politely declined, made an excuse as to why I couldn't go, and bid him a good day. I closed the door, a bit flabbergasted, hoping that was the end of it. It wasn't. Several more times he came to our house looking for me. Every time he came, I had Annie answer the door and tell him I wasn't home. Then he took to standing on the sidewalk across the street, sometimes for hours, calling to me, and shouting things like how he couldn't sleep or eat because he couldn't stop thinking about me, I was the most beautiful girl in Holland, and so on, making a complete spectacle of himself! Finally, I walked across the street and told him to please shut up, and then reluctantly agreed to have lunch with him. In all my 90 years, that was probably the biggest mistake I ever made!

The following Saturday he took me to a very expensive cafe downtown. He was well dressed, still very charming, and very complimentary. To listen to him you would have thought he was on a date with Elizabeth Taylor! What I thought would be a one or two-hour lunch date turned into an all-afternoon affair. He did most of the talking. In short, I heard his life story that afternoon. Actually, I should say I heard his version of his life story. Without going into pages of detail, in a nutshell, it was tragic! His family was absolutely no good, drunks, and abusive.

They beat him as a child, and hardly fed him. He was bullied at school because of his size. His first wife cheated on him and took everything. He saved the best for last. He told me early in the war, a German soldier shot his dog, so he shot the soldier. He was arrested and sent to a concentration camp for the rest of the war. That struck a nerve with me. Shortly after the war, everyone found out how horrific and inhumane the concentration camps were. He told me a story about how he'd been caught smuggling, and the commandant of the concentration camp punished him with 70 lashes. He sat back proudly and told me that he refused to give the commandant the satisfaction and never once cried out while he was being whipped. The commandant was so impressed by his strength and courage, and being that Tony was not a Jew, made Tony one of his personal assistants, which came with much better food and lodging. I believed every word. By the time he was finished, I was almost in tears. I felt so sorry for him. After that, we dated regularly for a few months. He met my parents. My Mother believed every bit of his story as well and showered him with compassion.

My father, however, immediately disliked Tony immensely. My Father said, "Toosje, that guy is a no-good con artist! The only things safe around him are hot irons and wind-mill stones!"

That's a Dutch expression that means he's a thief and you can't trust him with anything. No one touches a hot iron, of course, and windmill stones are too big to lift. In English, it would be something like he'll steal anything not nailed down, hide the silverware or he'd sell his mother for a dollar. I was young and dumb. I should have listened to my father, but I didn't. I was just sure my father was misreading Tony and was just being protective of his little girl.

Tony proposed after we had been dating only a few months. It was rather sudden, and I didn't feel in my gut at all ready for marriage. I declined at first, but he persisted. He asked again several times over the next few months. I put it off as long as I could, but eventually, after less than a year of dating he wore me down, convincing me that he'd be a fine husband, and we got married. We got married a few weeks after my twenty-second birthday. It wasn't a big wedding mostly because Tony had no family to invite, or so he said. All I had was my parents, Annie, and my aunts, so we just had a small ceremony at the courthouse, a small reception at my parent's house and that was it. We lived with my parents for two years, which was not uncommon in those days. Living space has always been in short supply in Amsterdam, so much that there were waiting lists for apartments. It's still that way. You had to go to an office downtown with all your information, identification, employment record, and sign a waiting list for an apartment. I had already gotten on the list as soon as I got hired at Bali. I did not want to live with my parents any longer than I had to. I wanted my own place.

For the next two years, everything went fine. Tony was working at one of those European cafes that specialize in wine. That was one skill he did have. He knew everything there was to know about fine wine. My Mother and Annie were still working at the Hotel and my father had become director of admissions at a medical university. Tony was as pleasant and charming as could be. Even my father was tolerating him rather well. He still didn't trust him but at least they were capable of conversation together. For all intents and purposes, life was good, for the moment.

At this point working at Bali, I had developed a lot of regulars that I would see consistently, some daily. One of them that came in daily was Michel, (pronounced Mee-shell). Michel was one of those people you meet in life and never forget. One way or another they make a lasting impression on you. He was an unbelievably kind man, in his late 50's, short, a tad overweight, balding, and extremely wealthy! He owned high-end furniture company.

Anyone that has ever spent any considerable time bartending knows, if you work in a place long enough, you will come to know the life stories of many of your regulars, and boy . . . did I know Michel's! In one of his stories, I know every detail because we talked about it so many times. Michel was too kind, too giving, and too forgiving. He had to travel occasionally for his business. On one such occasion, his business was completed ahead of schedule, and he got home two days earlier. His wife wasn't prepared for that. Michel arrived home very late at night, after midnight. So as not to awake his wife that he was sure was asleep, he opened the door very gently and quietly and tip-toed toward his bedroom. When he got closer, he noticed a dim light shining from under the door and he could hear heavy breathing and someone quietly moaning. He threw the door open and there he saw his wife in bed with another woman!

Michel was devastated, absolutely and utterly devastated. He adored his wife, had given her everything, and then this? After that, all the days I knew that man, he was so sad, I thought he might be broken-hearted forever. I spent many late nights at Bali with Michel's head on my shoulder, so to speak. For at least two months I had to console Michel every night, usually after work. We would sit at a booth in Bali and talk. The man was an emotional wreck in every way. He couldn't sleep or eat. His business was beginning to fail. He confided in me, and I never even once considered not helping him. Apparently, our nightly talks eventually worked. After a few months, he began to come back to life as the Michel we all knew and loved. One night, very late, a month or so after Michel had returned to his old self, we were chatting at the bar and he reached into his jacket pocket, pulled out a small box, and placed it into my hand. He smiled and told me it was a gift for everything I had done for him. I opened it and it was a diamond ring with five diamonds, and not small ones either. I was stunned and immediately thought it was way too much of a gift! I'm pretty sure I said so as well. Michel said it wasn't and proceeded to tell me the thoughts that had come to his mind over and over about ending it all. He said simply, "Catharina, were it not for you I am certain I would not be sitting here, you saved my life." I left it at that. I would never have hurt his feelings by refusing it. So, I kissed him on the cheek and thanked him. As I said, you meet people in your life you remember forever.

An apartment became available for Tony and me in the Fall of 1953. I was 22 years old. We moved into it immediately, of course. It was actually a very nice apartment in a decent part of the city, and I would end up hanging onto it for a long time.

Tony's demeanor changed very quickly after moving into our own place. Suddenly he wasn't quite as charming and kind as he'd been for the past two years. Over the next several months he started drinking more and more. He was standoffish and not very interested in me unless he wanted sex. Before we reached our first anniversary, he was out at all hours quite often and I began to see less and less of his income. He was suspiciously absent whenever it was time to pay bills. My income covered them but, that wasn't the point. At first, I wasn't sure what to do about it. I confronted him quite a few times, calling him on his change of behavior but he shrugged me off, telling me to relax, or something along those lines. That pissed me off! I am not a woman to be dismissed. I was not about to be ignored, but the more I confronted him the worse his behavior got. I got fed up quickly. I was not about to allow any man to use me for sex and a place to live, no sir! The coup de gras came one Saturday morning. Tony was in the dining room with a cup of coffee, nursing another hangover when there was a knock at the door. I opened the door and there was a cute little blonde about my age standing there, and she asked, "Is Tony home?" I said yes and asked her who she was. She said cheerfully with a big grin, "I'm his fiancé!" At first, I was stunned for a few seconds, then I was furious for a few seconds, and then a wave of indifference washed over me. I told her to hold on and closed the door. I strolled into the dining room and said, "Hey, lover boy, your fiancé is at the door!" He looked shocked for a few seconds and then, to my disgust, his face morphed into a shit-eating grin, and he walked outside. That was that! We never slept together ever again. I never touched him again. We had separate bedrooms. We had different schedules.

By the time I got home from work at Bali, it was well after midnight, and he was either not home or passed out drunk. By the time I got up around ten am, he was gone. Of course, I wanted a divorce right away but that is much easier said than done in Holland. In Holland, both parties must agree to the divorce for it to happen in a timely manner. Otherwise, the spouse wanting the divorce must provide proof of why the other spouse is intolerable, and in those days, a husband staying out and drinking a lot, not paying bills, and having a mistress wasn't sufficient, even if you could prove it, which I couldn't. There were no smartphones in those days that could take a video of a drunk, cheating husband. Not to mention, my mother still felt sorry for him, what with all his sob stories of the concentration camp and his abusive, horrible family. Her attitude was that I should be understanding and forgive him. Of course, she loved her booze as much as Tony did and was used to having a husband that ran around on her. Not me! I've always hated falling down drunks and cheating men. I never bought into the mindset of men having wives and mistresses, even though that was common in Europe back then.

It was purely by accident, a year or two later, that I met Tony's sister. I was invited to a luncheon by a friend of a friend, some lady my friend Mimi knew, and was introduced to a pleasant woman named Sophie Zoet. I asked her if she was related to Tony Zoet, and she said with a smirk and eye roll that he was her brother. When I told her who I was she was absolutely floored. First of all, no one in her family even knew he was married or even where he was! We must have talked for two hours, and I found out what an enormous mistake I had made! In a nutshell, Sophie told me that her brother Tony was a pathological liar, cheat, thief, womanizer, embezzler, narcissist, sociopath, and then some. It was clear she hated her own brother. She literally said, "He's a monster with absolutely no conscience whatsoever!" She said Tony was never abused at home one iota, ever. Her parents had never laid a finger on him. She said her parents were gentle, wonderful people, and Tony had a comfortable upbringing. He was well clothed, well-fed, and loved throughout his whole childhood. Sophie told me she doubted the concentration camp story as well because their own father had been arrested as a Nazi sympathizer! She told me Tony stole from everyone he got close to. In fact, Tony only got close to people he could profit from, like a predator! He stole from his employers, his family, women, friends. To Tony, anyone that took him into their confidence was a mark. Once, Tony had conned a wealthy man into letting him house sit for him while the man was on vacation. When the man came home, he found that Tony had sold several pieces of his expensive artwork and sculptures and then blamed it on a burglary. Unfortunately, the man couldn't prove otherwise. Tony had removed the items, then called the police to report a burglary. He was a master at covering his tracks. He always had a ready alibi, Sophie said. Tony had even robbed a few of the tour boats he worked on. He came back in the dead of night and stole the whole damn cash register. He stole money from me too. I lived on a cash basis in those days, as a lot of people did. I paid all my bills with cash. I used to keep my cash in a metal locking box that I kept in the bottom of my closet, that is until Tony found it. I went to put some money in it one morning and found it empty, the lock all scratched up and the box lid twisted out of shape. Tony had apparently pried it open with a tool of some kind and judging by the damage to the box he had a hard time breaking it open.

Needless to say, I had a real sociopath on my hands, in every definition of the word. Not only was he a master at covering his tracks, but he was also adept at securing his position legally. We were legally married, and his name was on the lease so I couldn't kick him out. He had a marriage certificate and a copy of the lease. I let him know what I had learned and made it perfectly clear that he would never share my bed again, ever. We were through, period. I just had to bide my time, work in Bali, go on with my life, and tolerate having a part-time sociopathic roommate for a husband until I could figure out a way to get rid of him, which I eventually did.

Having made the conscious decision that Tony was for all intents and purposes dead to me, I focused on work, which wasn't hard to do. Psychologically, he was dead to me, so I had no problem excelling at work. Before long I was promoted to more than just a hostess. I oversaw seating and the bar operations, which was just fine with Dini and Max. They were quite happy to have someone that could supervise the bar operations as well as hostess.

Job security is a wonderful thing. Just an FYI, if you are in a position to make yourself somewhat indispensable at your place of employment, it is wise to do so. As difficult as it can be to find a job, it can be just as difficult to find good help. Everyone makes mistakes. Even the best of employees can make mistakes but, if you are somewhat indispensable in your position, most employers are quick to overlook the occasional mistake. Whereas, if you're a mediocre employee, that same mistake might be all that is required to replace you. By the time I'd been working in Bali for three years, I had done my best to become indispensable. I knew almost every guest that came into Bali by name. I knew what they drank, where they liked to sit, and what their favorite menu items were. I also learned the fine art of diplomacy and discretion. In those days many of our wealthy male guests had wives and mistresses and I had to be cool about it. I kept my mouth shut and I made darn sure to remember which one was which. When dealing with the public on a daily basis, the art of diplomacy is a must! You might be thinking, how could I, as a woman, keep that kind of secret from another woman, right? Well, I could for a few reasons. First of all, it was an entirely different world back then. It was the 1950's, and in Europe, no less. Even in the United States at that time women did not have anywhere near the power they have today. Secondly, many of the wives knew their husbands had a mistress. These men were wealthy, and their wives lived in the lap of luxury! To most of these wives, after decades of marriage, wealth was much more important than fidelity. To draw attention to the fact of a mistress in public would only cause embarrassment for everyone and would most likely cost me my job. Finally, I wasn't a marriage counselor, I was a restaurant hostess and bar manager. It was simply none of my business. My whole life I have had a policy of not injecting myself unsolicited into the personal business of strangers. That almost never ends well.

When I was 25 years old good fortune smiled upon me again. A man by the name of Max Heidemann, whom I had originally met at the bar in Bali, offered me an opportunity I simply couldn't pass up. He'd been in Bali a few times over the years, but I'd never really gotten the opportunity to speak with him at length, so I didn't know anything about him. It was late and he was one of a few customers left at the bar and we got into conversation. After a few minutes, he asked me if I'd ever done any modeling. Modeling?! I was a bit surprised at the question.

It had never occurred to me that I could be modeling material but, apparently to him I was. As it turned out, he was a very successful clothing designer and kept several models on his payroll to show his designs to prospective buyers four times a year, winter, spring, summer, and fall. It was spring, 1956 and he needed one more model to show his spring line. I jumped at the chance, of course. He smiled broadly, wrote down an address, a date, and time and said, "Great, I'll see you there!" The day came for my modeling debut, so to speak. I called a cab and after about a twenty-minute ride through the countryside outside of Amsterdam, the cab driver turned onto a very long driveway that led to a castle and stopped. "We're here", he said.

I got out of the cab a little dumbfounded as I looked up at an enormous castle. I was greeted by a very well-dressed gentleman who escorted me into the castle, down long hallways and up a few long flights of steps, and into an enormous, expensively furnished room. There were huge tapestries on the walls, fine artwork, and several chairs for the buyers set up all facing the same direction toward a huge flight of marble stairs that curved to the right and out of sight. Mr. Heidemann came in, greeted me cheerfully, and told me the other models were upstairs and would show me around. There were five other lady's upstairs that greeted me warmly. Each of us had a rack of clothing that we were to model for the buyers. For about four hours the other models and I donned some of the most beautiful women's clothing I'd ever seen and walked gracefully down marble stairs and modeled each outfit for the group of seated buyers. Much of the clothing we had modeled would later be sold by companies such as Dior, Chanel, and Givenchy. When it was all said and done that day, knowing that I had to be at work at Bali by 4:00 pm, Mr. Heidemann offered me a ride to work in his brand new 1955 Jaguar convertible. I must admit, I felt like the queen of Sheba that day. There I was, twenty-five years old, modeling expensive clothing in a castle and then getting a ride to work from the designer in his new Jaguar! Needless to say, I kept that gig as long as I could. For the next five years or so, four times a year for about two weeks each time, I modeled for Mr. Heidemann. I was loving life! Of course, it wasn't long before all of the staff as well as the clientele at Bali knew I was modeling for Mr. Heidemann. Some days at work I almost felt a little bit like a celebrity.

Well-to-do single gentlemen were asking me out on dates, and quite often I went. Why not? My marriage to Tony was completely kaput and he was out doing whatever he pleased. Why shouldn't I? I went out with doctors, wealthy businessmen, lawyers and always dressed to the nines! After modeling only a year I had earned the extra money to purchase a fine wardrobe of designer clothing, everything from coats to dresses to shoes. They took me out for dinner at nice restaurants, to operas, symphonies, and live theater. One gentleman even drove me to his summer home in Calais, France in his Mercedes convertible for a weekend. It was a four-hour drive through the Dutch, Belgian, and French countryside, and was simply beautiful. Mind you, every date I had was strictly platonic! I was a lady and I only dated gentlemen! I didn't sleep around, ever. Even though I was no longer a virgin and was married to a sociopath, I was determined to wait for Mr. Right! I'd made a naive mistake with Tony, sure, but I held onto the hope that someday I would meet the love of my life. A true gentleman knows how to treat a lady anyway, and that doesn't include coercing her into the sack right away. A true gentleman enjoys the company of a true lady.

There was one fellow that tried to manhandle me at my front door after a date, but I kneed him in the groin so hard he was still laying on the sidewalk ten minutes after I went inside, but he was the only one that ever tried that.

It was about this time I got a dog. I hadn't planned on it, but it happened. My friend Mimi had to go out of town for a month for some reason I can't remember and asked me to take care of her dog, Leksia, pronounced (Lek-sha). She was a sweet little black and white fuzzy mutt, and very affectionate. I took her for long walks every day and let her sleep on my bed with me. It was so nice having Leksia around I considered getting my own dog again. I hadn't had one since I was a child. Within a few days, after Mimi returned and Leksia was back home with her, Mimi called me, almost in tears. She said Leksia had been laying at the front door crying non-stop since the moment she had gotten home. Mimi said, "I think she misses you!" I didn't know about that but, I took a tram to Mimi's and when I got there, Leksia came unglued. That dog was so happy to see me, she jumped and ran in circles, jumped into my lap licking my face the whole time, I didn't know what to think. Well, long story short, I took Leksia home and Mimi got another dog. Leksia belonged to me, or rather, I belonged to her.

Even though I was doing quite well financially and socially, I made a point to not let any of it go to my head. I've always had a certain disdain for people that allow their looks or fame or fortune to go to their heads. Beauty is only skin deep, and fame and fortune so often come from a God-given talent or better yet, inheritance. Regardless of how one achieves any level of fame or fortune, it is never a justification for treating those that are less fortunate like dirt. Rudyard Kipling wrote a poem in 1895 that I've always loved titled "If". In the last paragraph of the poem is a line that reads, "If you can talk with crowds and keep your virtue or walk with kings ---- nor lose the common touch." I never understood the stories of stockbrokers that committed suicide by jumping out of skyscraper windows after the stock market crash of 1929 or actors and actresses that drank themselves to death or overdosed on drugs just because they aged and lost their youthful good looks. How sad is that, to kill yourself over money or looks? There are so many other things to live for on this beautiful planet. Maybe I was a tad old for my years. Living through a war can do that. I had seen with my own eyes how quickly life can turn into hell and how quickly everything can be taken away, and I had seen how suddenly life can improve, sometimes in a single day! Even though I was hobnobbing with some of the upper echelons of Amsterdam society I never forgot where I came from, and I never have. I knew that much of my good fortune came from being in the right place at the right time. I must say though, opportunity knocks only so often. It behooves oneself to be paying attention when it does! Just be prepared. Opportunity can also mean a great deal of work ahead. Don't be afraid of it, ever.

By the end of 1961, when I was 30 years old, I was at my wit's end with Tony. Oddly enough, it was at this time that Tony approached me with an idea that would ultimately result in me being rid of him forever, although that thought had never crossed his mind. He wanted to emigrate to the United States. I discovered later it was because he had accumulated a lot of enemies in Holland and had established a criminal record as well. He was running!

Tony had already established a sponsor in the United States in Baltimore, an older couple he had conned years before on one of the tour boats he had worked on. He had sweet-talked them into sponsoring him should he ever decide to emigrate to the United States. At first, I thought he'd lost his mind! I had a great job, money, friends, respect, and couldn't comprehend leaving my mother and sister, especially after what my father had asked of me.

My Father had just died the year before, in November 1960 of lung cancer. He was only fifty-five when he died, and it was quite a shock for me. He was diagnosed with lung cancer shortly after my birthday and died three months later. I put on a brave face at work, but I was sick with grief for many months. I visited him every chance I got before he died. He had always loved oranges, so I always brought a few with me when I visited him. The last day I saw my father, he must have known it was the last time because he pulled me close and said, "Toosje, take care of your mother and Annie, you're so much stronger than either of them will ever be, they need you." I never forgot that. Ultimately, I would change my life to protect them.

Some months later, Tony was harassing me again about emigrating to the United States. I must have told him a hundred times, "Give me a divorce and go, please!" No, he wasn't about to do that! Over the following year though, I plan started to hatch in my brain. In a nutshell, I started to mull over how I could go to the United States with Tony, then leave him there, and come back to Holland. I mentioned the idea to a few regulars at Bali and Max and Dini as well. Max and Dini openly hoped I'd never go, but promised me my job would be waiting for me until I got back, no matter how long it was. Michel begged me not to go to the US. He even offered to build me a house if I would stay, he loved me so much he said. Michel owned a furniture factory and was extremely wealthy, so I believed he would have. I could have never accepted that though. That would have been too much. No, I had to figure out a way to take my life back from this financial and emotional parasite of a man. I began weighing the pros and cons of all my options. It was clear that if I stayed in Holland, I would never get a divorce from Tony without one hell of a lot of money and a long court battle. I thought long and hard about how to make emigrating to the US with Tony work in my favor and get rid of him for good. After mulling it over for a long time, the obvious finally occurred to me. One thing I knew for sure, Tony was incapable of keeping his hands off other women and other people's money, two bad habits that would probably not go over very well in the US. So, I figured that I could emigrate to the US and when Tony got caught with his hand in someone's cookie jar and got arrested or got wrapped up with another woman, which I was sure he would, I could return to Holland and get my divorce with no contest. A spouse being arrested in another country is a slam dunk for a judge to grant a divorce.

The icing on the cake, so to speak, had come one day at work a few months earlier when I got into a conversation with a gentleman at the bar in Bali that turned out to be a criminal psychologist. When I introduced myself, he immediately asked me if I was related to Tony. When I told him I was married to Tony he got a very somber look on his face. Instead of telling me what he knew right then and there, he asked me if he could give me a ride home after work. The ride home was enlightening, to say the least. I remember wishing I'd met this psychologist when I was just dating Tony. It was bad enough though that this psychologist was willing to violate client confidentiality to tell me the potential danger I was in.

Of course, I assured him I would never divulge what he'd told me. It was he who taught me the true meaning of the term sociopath and why he had diagnosed Tony as such. He had seen Tony as a patient a few years after the war. In a nutshell, he told me he had diagnosed Tony as a sociopath, charming to the last but completely lacking in empathy or conscience and would steal everything not nailed down, including my sanity. He was much more explicit than that but, that was the gist of it. The most poignant comment the psychologist made to me was that I had to get away from Tony as quickly as possible. After that, my mind was made up. I would emigrate to the US with Tony, find a job, and bide my time until Tony got himself jammed up and in trouble, which I knew he would. Then I would return to Holland as soon as possible. I also knew we both had to go. There was no way I could leave Holland without him. I knew he would make my mother's life a living hell. It was a gamble, but a safe one in my opinion. I knew Tony couldn't help himself. All I had to do was sit back and give Tony enough rope to hang himself, so to speak. After all, a sociopath is a sociopath no matter where they live. Once I had made the conscious decision to do this, I knew that I had a great deal of work ahead of me.

I got busy . . . doing what I had to do.

CHAPTER 5

LEAVING HOLLAND

....

My decision to leave Holland required a great deal of thought and preparation. Emigrating to the United States from Holland is not a process that happens overnight. I knew my job would be waiting for me until I returned, so that was covered. Max and Dini made that promise to me and I believed them wholeheartedly. In the last months I was there I trained my replacement with the understanding that it wasn't a permanent position. Max and Dina told her that in all likelihood I was coming back. She was happy to have the job anyway. My residence was another matter. If I'd let it go, I would've had to get back on the waiting list for another apartment whenever I returned to Holland, and I certainly didn't want to do that. What I could do, legally, was sublet my apartment while I was away. After several interviews, I finally decided to rent it to a Chinese doctor. At least I knew he had ample income to cover the rent. Tony and I both made appointments at the US Consulate to begin the application process for visas to emigrate to the US. Tony contacted his potential sponsors in the U.S. in Baltimore to get that process rolling. There was a lot of paperwork back and forth for many months. The couple that Tony had conned into sponsoring him was a retired doctor, and his wife, Dr. and Mrs. Emmett. Apparently, Tony had struck quite a conversation with them because, according to him, they invited him to dinner that evening and liked him so much that they offered to sponsor him should he ever choose to emigrate to the US. Tony contacted them right away and got the ball rolling, so to speak. Once everything was in place and all the forms had been filled out by all parties, all I could do was wait. The immigration process takes months. If I remember correctly, it was almost a year. Eventually, in the early months of 1962, we got the news. It was good news for me but bad news for Tony. Tony could only qualify for a temporary visa. I qualified for a permanent/work visa, which would also enable me to pursue U.S. citizenship. This was when I found out that Tony had a criminal background, owed back taxes, owed thousands of dollars of child support for a child he had fathered AFTER he married me, and, he had debts all over town in my name, including an $800 tab at a liquor store! I thought my head was going to explode! The criminal background alone was grounds for divorce as was the illegitimate child, but now it was too late for that! I was committed. The Emmetts were committed. There was a Chinese doctor with a signed and dated lease for my apartment in hand, waiting for me to depart. There was no way I could back out of that, so I was stuck with my decision. Tony, being the successful manipulator that he was, was ready to go anyway. He assumed he would be able to change his immigration status in the US after he got there, one way or the other.

I bought two first-class tickets on a Seven Seas ocean liner from Amsterdam to New York, booked for May, and hid them in a coat pocket in my closet. I continued working at Bali right up until a few days before I was to leave.

For the next few months, most of my time off from work was occupied with parties and lunch dates with friends, coworkers, and several of our most regular customers that all wanted to give me a personal goodbye. Most of them encouraged me not to go but ultimately wished me success.

A month or so before I was set to depart, I went to my closet and reached into the coat pocket I had put the tickets into and pulled them out. I glanced at them and was about to put them back when I noticed they were for steerage, aka. second class! There was only one way this could have happened! TONY! I confronted him later and he arrogantly admitted to selling the first-class tickets and getting the much, MUCH cheaper second-class tickets, saying we didn't need to waste the money on first class. What? It was MY money! I threw them in his face! I screamed, "You might go to America second class . . . not me!"

A few nights later, very late at Bali, as most of the staff was cleaning up and I was about to shut down the bar and count the till Michel was still sitting at the bar and made me the same offer he'd done before that I'll never forget. He called me over to him, held my hands in his, and told me again that if I would stay in Holland, and not go to America, he would build me a house, whatever house I wanted wherever I wanted, and even get me a car to get to work. He really was a sweet man and loved me dearly but, even an offer this great would never get Tony out of my life. Divorce or not, he would never leave me or my family alone and I knew it. Tony had already told me if he couldn't have me no one could. I thanked Michel from the bottom of my heart but told him I had to go. I promised him I'd be back and, at the time I meant it. Be careful what promises you make. Life may change in such a way that it's impossible for you to keep that promise. I never intended to leave Holland forever. Then, he reached into his jacket and pulled out a first-class ticket for me. I had told him what Tony had done with my tickets and Michel said, "No way in hell am I going to let you travel any way but first class."

My last night at Bali was a night I'll never forget. I walked into work and was greeted with the place full of friends and regular guests and full applause! Everyone was in black tie, formally dressed to the nines! I was stunned! All these people were applauding me, smiling at me and it was one of the most memorable nights of my life, albeit very bitter-sweet. Bali was even closed that night. The only event taking place was a farewell party for me! I don't think I've ever been so humbled, excited, and saddened all at the same time. It's a wonderful thing to feel loved and needed and even more personally exalting when people show it. At that moment I was determined to accomplish my mission and return as soon as possible but . . .

. . . . you never know what life is going to bring the next day.

CHAPTER 6

STARTING OVER IN BALTIMORE

••

The day came to leave my native land for America. It was May 1962. I stood on the docks in Amsterdam with my mother, sister, and several of my friends from Bali for what felt like an eternity while my luggage was put aboard. Everyone was tearful as if they'd never see me ever again. Michel was there too, of course. I told them all several times to dry their eyes, assuring them I would return and probably very soon. Finally, the call came to board the ship and I said my last goodbyes to everyone, promising them all one last time that I would be back as soon as I could. In the meantime, I had spotted Tony getting aboard moments before without saying goodbye to anyone, steerage ticket in hand. I didn't see him again until we got to New York. I had no idea what he was doing the entire trip and quite frankly, I didn't want to! More than likely he was drunk, stealing or conning an innocent passenger out of money or seducing some innocent young woman still naive enough to fall for his slippery charms. The trip was better without his presence!

I actually had a very nice trip, especially traveling first class. The ship wasn't one of the enormous ocean liners with extravagances like swimming pools and tennis courts. It was one of the smaller ocean liners but was still a pretty big passenger ship. I don't care for the open ocean very much at all and I felt safe on it, put it that way. My stateroom was very spacious. There were special facilities for pets of first-class passengers too, a special potty area. Yes, I took my dog with me, of course! I wasn't about to leave my Leksia behind in Holland. How could I leave him behind? I met the captain. He was a very handsome well-spoken gentleman. I had some of my best Chanel dresses with me, so I could look my best. If I was going to travel first-class, I was going to look, first-class! First-class accommodations included dinner at the captain's table every night. The food was exquisite! There were a lot of cocktails and dancing. I danced with the ship's doctor quite a bit. He was a fantastic dancer. All in all, I had a nice time, considering the circumstances. The trip took about a week if I remember correctly so I was thankful to have such comfortable accommodations. I figured why not enjoy it? I may never be on an ocean liner first-class ever again. As it turns out, I wasn't.

Finally, I saw the famous Statue of Liberty as the ship steered into New York Bay. I had read as much as I could about the United States, its history mostly. History always fascinated me. Most of anything else I knew about it I had read in magazines over the years but, I would learn that didn't reveal as much as I would have liked. Tony finally showed up and shortly after we disembarked. We went through customs, and there, waiting for us were Dr. Paul Emmett and his wife Lila, our sponsors. Dr. Emmett was a professor of some sort at a university in Baltimore. Almost immediately after the greetings and handshakes, I became uncomfortable when Lila barked, "I didn't say you could bring a dog!" Dr. Emmett intervened quickly, quietly saying it would be fine. Dr. Emmett was kind and soft-spoken, Lila not so much!

It was a long drive from New York to Baltimore but not at all boring for me. I stared out the window in amazement. Everything was so . . . big. The buildings were big. The highways were big. The cars were big!

The Emmetts had a beautiful car with four doors and an enormous trunk that held all of our luggage with room to spare. About half an hour into the drive something suddenly occurred to me and, I became a bit concerned.

When the conversation in the car between Tony, Dr. Emmett, and Lila included me, with questions along the lines of what Tony and I hoped to accomplish together in America . . . it hit me. This whole thing, coming to America and starting out on a new life as a happily married couple in the Emmetts home was more or less a ruse. During the voyage to the US, it hadn't occurred to me that I was going to have to become an actress the minute I arrived. The only thing I planned on accomplishing was getting rid of my slimeball of a husband as quickly as possible! I wondered if I was going to be able to pull this off! Of course, Tony could lie to anyone at any time without a shred of guilt. Tony could charm a nun out of her habit if he had to! All of his life Tony had lied to, cheated, and stole from everyone he encountered, and he could still sleep like a baby. I, on the other hand, had a conscience and self-respect. My reputation was extremely important to me, and I had never had to pretend day after day after day to have affection for someone I loathed. All my life, with me, what you saw is what you got. I don't pretend or feign affection. I've always had a particular disdain for people that are all smiles to your face and then verbally cut you to pieces when you're not around. If you don't like me, just say so. I'm a big girl. Even as a child, I was aware that some people did not like me and vice versa. I have a habit of speaking my mind honestly without apology and some people don't like that. I hadn't practiced the art of such deception since I was a kid dealing with the Nazis! With the hatred I felt for Tony, it was challenging to even smile when I was in the same room with him. For all but the first year of our marriage, we had lived separate lives. Now, at least for the near future, I had to pretend that I actually liked him! I had to be cordial with him as a wife would be! So, this was going to be one of the biggest challenges of my life. Pretending to be the happily married wife wouldn't cause the Emmetts any harm but, doing so was completely contrary to my character and personality. I did it but, considering the abject disdain I felt for Tony Zoet, I should have won an Oscar!

Thankfully our room in the Emmett's home had two separate single beds. That was a blessing. They were old school. A lot of couples' bedrooms were set up that way back then. Have you ever seen "I Love Lucy"? For the younger readers, it was a TV show in the 1950s. Lucy and her husband Ricky had two separate beds. At any rate, the separate beds made the whole thing doable for me. The Emmetts had a huge, gorgeous home in a posh section of Baltimore. The house was filled with fine expensive furniture. The house was surrounded with gorgeous gardens and lush green lawns. They even employed a full-time housekeeper and a gardener. I won't bore you with more details. In short, they were wealthy.

The first order of business was finding jobs. I had a little income coming in monthly from the Chinese Dr. that was renting my apartment in Holland but that was not nearly enough to strike out on my own in the US.

The Emmetts showed us which newspapers were best to buy for employment ads. Tony had learned to speak English rather well from dealing with American tourists in Holland for so many years. My English wasn't as proficient as Tony's, but I had learned quite a bit from working in Bali.

Most educated Europeans can speak English as a second language anyway and I had learned quite a bit over the years from the customers. I spoke what you might call "broken English." I said a lot of things incorrectly but close enough that Americans knew what I meant.

Luckily, Tony found a job rather quickly. An upper-level manager at the Sears in downtown Baltimore lived directly next door to the Emmetts. About three weeks after we had arrived, Dr. Emmett found out from him that Sears had an opening in shipping and receiving at Sears. Tony applied right away and got the job, which was a blessing for me because that was eight hours a day I didn't have to see his face. We only lived with the Emmetts for a matter of months but, I hated every minute of it. I found out pretty quickly that Lila was a kind of a bitch, rather nasty most of the time, especially when her husband wasn't there to intervene. She was much more pleasant in his presence. She was constantly complaining about my dog, even though Leksia was very well behaved, and never made any mess in the house whatsoever. The house was dark and dismal because she always kept the curtains closed as if she was allergic to sunlight. It was obvious she didn't like me, at all. Once she berated me for ten minutes just because she caught me cleaning the bathroom Tony and I used. "Stop that!", she screamed. I wasn't used to anyone cleaning up after me. "We have a housekeeper for that!" It was very uncomfortable for me there and I was ready to jump at any chance to get out of there. I told you earlier in my story how important my immediate environment is to me and my psyche. I couldn't take Lila and her dark, dismal-looking home much longer! I spent almost every waking moment looking for a job but, finding work suited to me was a little more challenging than I thought it would be. My work experience was a bit limited. There was plenty of labor-oriented work available such as housekeeping but, I was trying to find something a little better than that. Just as I was about to apply for and accept a job I really didn't want, another miracle happened. At least it was a miracle to me, at the time. The Emmetts neighbor, the manager at Sears informed us of another position at Sears that had opened up in the women's clothing department. He wasn't sure what position it was exactly but, I was told to ask for Fran Hughes. The next day I was up at the crack of dawn. I did my hair, makeup, put on a pair of conservative earrings, and put on one of my best Chanel business dresses, with pair of my best shoes, and a matching clutch. I had to catch a bus and after that, a trolley to get to Sears. Between the bus and trolley, it took over an hour to get there. I remember thinking that if I got the job, the next thing I would be doing is looking for an apartment downtown as near to the Sears as possible. I walked into Sears and noticed rather quickly that a lot of people were looking at me as I walked by them, although at the time, I wasn't sure why. I found the women's clothing department and told a lady that was folding clothing on a display that I was there to see Fran Hughes. She flashed a bright smile and very politely said, "Oh, yes ma'am! I'll get him for you right away." Moments later a man walked up to me and introduced himself as Fran Hughes and said, "Good morning ma'am. How can I help you today?" "I'm here for the job.", I said. He looked at me very strangely for what seemed a long time and finally answered with, "The job?" I nodded.

Looking a bit perplexed, he studied me a bit, my dress, my earrings, and after a long pause said, "Oh! Yes . . . the job, we need a fashion coordinator. Are you experienced with women's fashion?" I explained in my broken English how I had modeled in Holland part-time, and I was very familiar with women's fashion, which I kind of was, with expensive European designer fashion, except . . . I was in a Sears, in the USA. I didn't have a clue. Worse than that, I didn't have a clue that I didn't have a clue! I remember Fran having the most confused look on his face. He asked me a few more questions and I think all I caught were words like a mannequin, windows, dress, seasonally, and maybe a few others. When he was finished, I simply nodded and said yes again. I wasn't entirely sure what he had asked me, but I wanted to get out of the Emmetts house so badly I probably would have said yes to cleaning the toilets in Sears at that point. I figured the worst that could happen was getting fired and I'd have to look for another job. After another long pause he smiled and said, "Ok then, we'll see you next Monday at 9:00 am." I shook his hand and thanked him and left, walking out in my Chanel dress and heels, gold earrings, and satin clutch with every employee watching me go every step of the way. I had about a week until my first day at Sears so when I got home, I immediately asked Dr. Emmett if he could show me apartments downtown, as close to Sears as possible. I had managed to save enough money from Bali and modeling in Holland to rent one in Baltimore. After looking only a day or two, I found a partially furnished apartment just a few blocks away from Sears that would also accept Leksia, in an apartment building called "The Hamiltonian". My only concern was that it was close to work and allowed me to have my dog. With those two needs met, I rented it immediately. Tony tried to give me an attitude about renting an apartment without him being there, but I quickly told him to shut his mouth, that I had already paid for it and

I was moving into it and, if he didn't like it he could go somewhere else. That shut him up. He wasn't about to do that.

A few days later, Dr. Emmett dropped us off at the Hamiltonian with our luggage a day or two before I was to start work at Sears. I gave him a big hug and thanked him for his kindness and all his help.

I was off and running!

CHAPTER 7

SEARS AND MEETING FRED

•••

On my first day of work at Sears, I was awake before dawn. I was so excited to have a good job and a decent apartment I could hardly sleep the night before my first day at work. I got up, started the coffee percolator, fed Leksia, and took him out for his walk. It was August and already at 7:00 am it was hot. This had been my first summer in the United States and the heat had taken some getting used to. Summers in Holland aren't nearly as hot. Tony was still asleep on the couch. The day we moved in I told him I was taking the bedroom. He didn't argue. When I got back, I started getting ready for work. Again, I got dressed to the nines, determined to look my best and make a stellar first impression. The walk to work was hot! Amsterdam was busy too but not quite like this. At 8:30 am the streets of Baltimore were already busy with bustling pedestrians, city busses and traffic, car horns, and people yelling, "taxi"! Compared to Amsterdam, this was bigger and faster, for lack of a better term. I arrived at Sears a few minutes before 9:00 am and went straight to the women's clothing department. Introductions were made and I met several employees and shook a lot of hands. One of the ladies that also worked in the women's department spent the rest of that morning showing me around. It occurred to me right away why the employees had stared at me the day I came in for the job. I was overdressed, way overdressed! None of the ladies were wearing Chanel dresses or heels. They were nicely dressed but in clothing more suited for working in display at Sears like pants, light tops, and flats. One of my co-workers was kind enough to pick out a few outfits for me that would be more suitable. For a few days, I worked closely with the other ladies that worked in the department, learning the ropes, so to speak. One day I was asked to dress a mannequin in one of the display windows. One of the ladies I was working with asked me if I knew how to do that. I said, "Sure, no problem." I'd never done it before, but I figured how hard can it be, right?

I was left on my own to dress this mannequin and a couple of hours later when I was finished, the department head, the gentleman who had hired me, Fran Hughes came to take a look at my work. He stood there for the longest time, looking at my mannequin, scratching his head, eyebrows up, looking confused. I asked him, "Is it not good?" He said, "Yeah, it's wonderful, for the cover of Vogue, but this ain't Saks Fifth Avenue Toosje, it's Sears." My mannequin had movie-star quality. I'd found the finest dress and heels, a string of pearls, an elegant scarf, a wide-brim hat, sunglasses, and bracelets. My mannequin was ready for the red carpet. Fran was a kind man and said I was a hard worker and believed I had the skills for the job, I just needed some tutoring. He said, "Come with me, I want you to meet someone." We walked through the store to another department, and he introduced me to a handsome young man named Fred. Fran said to Fred, "Take the afternoon please, and show Catharina everything she needs to know about doing windows." For the rest of the day, Fred explained to me everything there was to know about dressing mannequins and creating display windows.

For those too young to remember, once upon a time, all department stores had big display windows in the fronts of their stores facing the street so that people walking by on the sidewalk could stop and see whatever clothing was being showcased at that time. Windows were changed constantly to coincide with the seasons and advertise new styles. It was an art form, really. For department stores, having employees that were skilled at dressing windows was an absolute necessity. Most of the larger department stores had several large display windows, so keeping them all beautiful, eye-catching and up to date was a full-time job.

Fred was a fantastic teacher. He took me all around town showing me different windows of different department stores explaining in great detail all of the necessary aspects of a well-done display window. By the end of the day, I understood perfectly what my job was at Sears. I'd found myself distracted by his good looks several times throughout the day he was that good-looking! I was attracted to him immediately. He was tall, dark, and handsome, six feet tall, 165 pounds, with jet black hair, kind eyes and, very much a gentleman. He had a quiet but energetic nature about him that intrigued me. At first, I guessed him to be in his early 20's but I soon found out he was just two years younger than me.

With Fred's help, I settled into my role as women's fashion coordinator at Sears and during the next several months made a lot of nice friends in the process, one of which was Don Via. Don would turn out to be not only a lifelong friend but one of the best friends I would ever have. Don was very close friends with Fred. They had met at Sears and quickly became the best of friends. I could see why. Fred was very likable. I couldn't keep myself from looking at him at work and, I saw him often. I knew he was married but so was I, on paper anyway. Tony and I had been living separate lives for years, just living in the same apartment. I never knew what he was doing and, didn't care.

In December, I had Christmas a party at my apartment in the Hamiltonian for the friends I had made at Sears. Everyone I invited came including Fred and his wife. I couldn't help but notice that she was significantly older than he was. I also got the distinct impression they weren't very fond of each other, much less in love. The party went well, and everyone had a good time. When it ended and everyone was leaving something happened, as Fred and his wife were leaving. As she was entering the hallway, Fred turned to me and while he gently shook my hand, thanking me for a wonderful evening . . . our eyes met and froze there for a moment. For a few seconds, time stood still, and all my senses came alive. We'd had a moment. No doubt about it. I could feel it.

As the months passed, Fred and I talked together more and more. It wasn't long until we established a working relationship, finding new reasons and ways to work together in different departments. Soon Fred and I were in charge of all the display windows, so we got to work together almost every day. We were undeniably attracted to each other, and we knew it. We kept our feelings at work discrete and professional for many months.

One day Fred invited me to join him for a drink after work at a place called Leon's. We couldn't have been there for more than a half-hour when Fred began to pour his heart out to me as if he'd known me all his life. Hours later we had shared our life stories with each other including the intimate details about the miserable marriages we were both stuck in.

Fred's parents and grandmother were dead by the time he was nine years old. After that, he had lived in an orphanage until he turned 18. Upon leaving the orphanage, to put it simply, he married the first woman he met. When he was 19, he started dating a woman 10 years older than himself and she had a seven-year-old boy. One thing led to another, the boy got attached to Fred and he married a woman that he wasn't actually in love with for the sake of a child. That was in 1953. Ten years later he was stuck in the nightmare of a toxic marriage with three more kids. For discretionary reasons, I cannot go into much more detail than that. Suffice it to say, Fred's marriage had become ugly, vindictive, and completely unsalvageable. His kids were the only reason he went home at night after work. He truly loved his kids. Every day, at five o'clock sharp, Fred bolted out of Sears to get home to his kids. I told Fred all about my life, Holland, the war, and everything there was to know about Tony, our marriage, and more. Eventually, it started getting late, and reluctantly we both agreed we had to go home. We both had to work in the morning. Outside Fred held my hand for a moment and thanked me for listening, I did the same and walked to my apartment. I barely slept that night. Fred had bared his very soul to me personally and I'd gotten a glimpse into a character the likes of which I'd never known before.

In Fred, I had met an obviously fiercely intelligent man that was thoroughly honest and honorable, sincere and full of passion, and yet had never known peace and true love of his own. He was born during the Great Depression, poor all his childhood. His mother died giving birth to him and his father resented him for that. His two older brothers abandoned him. When he was young, he was an altar boy and a priest attempted to molest him, which crushed him because the church was the only real thing he could count on. He'd been bullied terribly in the orphanage, especially during the war because he had a German last name. In fact, his father had emigrated from Germany in the early 1920s. He had lived thirty years with very little if any happiness or love at all, and yet, he was the kindest, most sincere soul I'd ever encountered.

He was living proof that still waters do indeed run deep. Looking back, it was our meeting at Leon's where I truly began falling in love with Fred. Of course, our feelings for each other were never the same after our time at Leon's. Now we were attracted to each other in a whole new way. We'd shared parts of our souls with each other. At work, it became virtually impossible to hide. We smiled like fools every time we saw each other. Every time we got within a few feet of each other it was electric! Most of our friends that we worked with at Sears knew what was going on and kept it quiet. Tony knew nothing about it. He worked in shipping and receiving and never came into the store.

For Halloween that year, the Sears display crew we worked with decided to go barhopping and Fred and I went with them. From bar to bar we went with "the crew" and, we'd been together all night, talking and finally, at some point in the evening . . . it happened. We were sitting at some bar, talking, our eyes met and it just happened. We fell into each other's arms and shared the most passionate kiss I could have ever imagined. My heart was pounding. My body was almost trembling.

I lost all sense of time and reason at that point! I had no care for consequences no matter what they were. I was falling in love and there was nothing I could do about it. Fred and I both acknowledged that everything would change. Everything would have to change.

During the months that followed, I pressured Tony relentlessly to give me a divorce. He flatly refused. In fact, he told me he would see me dead first. Meanwhile, Fred was doing the same to no avail. He had already pleaded for a divorce many times and his wife adamantly refused. We met in secret as often as we could. Fred knew of an old bookstore that had a sort of cafe in the back that wasn't frequented much. For a long time, the bookstore worked as our secret meeting place. We talked and talked for hours and hours and kissed . . . A LOT. We necked like teenagers! At one point we both acknowledged we were in love with each other. It was undeniable. Problem was, neither of us knew what we were going to do about it.

Sometimes in life, you gotta push the envelope, ALL THE WAY!

To be honest with you, the next several months are a blur. So much happened and it was such a short, stressful tumultuous time, the exact sequence of events is almost impossible to recall. I don't know how our secret got out, but it did, in a huge way and, a sequence of events unfolded in rapid succession. One day, Don stopped Fred and me on the sidewalk outside of Sears to warn us that we both were going to be fired. Our secret was out! A guy that worked in the main office was friends with Don and warned him. In those days, the General manager of that particular Sears took great pleasure in bringing you into his office on the third floor, firing you, and marching you down the stairs, through each floor so all the employees could see who was taking the walk of shame all the way to the door. Someone had called Sears and dropped the bomb about us. It was the early 60s in predominantly Christian America and adultery was still considered a very bad thing. Sears was considered an all-American, family-oriented company, so, there you go. With one phone call, we were unemployed. Don said we could stay with him for a while. His parents lived with him in those days so, that was temporary. At some point that day I must have gone back to the Hamiltonian to get my dog. I would never have left Leksia with Tony. Sometime later I did go back to my apartment again but with Fred with me. Tony was home. Tony ranted and raved at me, saying he'd see me dead before he'd let another man have me. Fred stood there unflinchingly looking at him while I grabbed whatever it was I came for. I remember screaming, "So be it, but I'll never ever come back." With that, Fred and I left. We stayed with Don for a few days. A few days after we'd been found out, Fred decided to go home and try to reason with his wife. His only concern was for his kids. He was sick with guilt about his kids. His wife went absolutely ballistic. Dishes were thrown, furniture was broken, and every stitch of his clothing was thrown into the yard. At least he was able to return with some of his best clothing. That was the end. He never went back. We stayed with Don for a few days while Fred went looking for work. For weeks Fred looked for work. For some time, we stayed at a rooming house called Rochambeau Apartments. Once upon a time, it had been a nice place but by the 60s it was what was known as a flophouse. Don paid our first week's rent

at the Rochambeau. I can't remember how long we stayed at the Rochambeau. At some point, Fred got a job at a messenger service. We were so broke. Don came by often to pick us up for dinner. At the time, the Rochambeau was a nasty place full of drunks and drug addicts, so as soon as he could, Don rented a small efficiency with a small bathroom and kitchenette for us on St Paul St. Besides a Murphy bed it was unfurnished. He paid the first week plus the deposit for us. I honestly don't know what we would have done without Don Via! He helped us at every turn without question. Don and Fred had been close friends for several years so, Don knew every detail of his wife and marriage. Don had also gotten to know Tony a little bit at work, enough to know he did not like him at all. Don said he disliked Tony the moment he met him, especially after Tony opened his mouth! Don is a very smart guy and a quick study of character too. Needless to say, Don knew what we were up against. For a little while, we scraped by on St Paul St. More than once, Don gave me $10 to get groceries with. For a while, all I had to cook with was a coffee percolator and an aluminum pie plate. With $10 I could get a dozen eggs, bread, fatback, a lot of beans, and flour. We ate a lot of beans seasoned with fatback and biscuits.

During this time is when we discovered "The Cage". The Cage was a very popular gay bar owned by two women. The Cage had a very nice, mostly professional clientele and, better yet, every Wednesday they had all-you-can-eat spaghetti! So, every Wednesday we went to The Cage for dinner. We actually made quite a few friends there. The owners adored us and before long we were known by all the regulars as "The Lovebirds".

One day, in the midst of all the chaos, Fred and I went to go visit a friend of his named Viviane. She was the mother of an old high school chum of his that he'd kept in touch with over the years. Fred said he had to get out of the city for at least a few hours. We got into his silver 1960 Ford Fairlane and drove out of the city. Aside from the drive into Baltimore from New York when I arrived in the US, I hadn't seen anything outside of Baltimore yet. I was amazed at how beautiful Maryland was outside of Baltimore. We drove down MD Route 2 from Baltimore for about 30 minutes or so to an area called Arnold. Fred made a right turn onto a one-lane paved country road called Joyce Lane. I was enchanted! On either side of the road was rolling green pastures, lined with old split rail fencing. Beyond the pasture all around was a lush, dense green forest. Some of the trees were so big I knew they had to be hundreds of years old. Birds were singing in the trees, squirrels ran about, like something out of an old Disney movie. The little road wound through it all 'til we came to a dirt driveway on our right that went up a hill. Fred turned onto the driveway and at the top of the hill, nestled among the dense forest were three little wood cabins. Fred parked at the first one. We visited with Fred's friend, Viviane, for a few hours. She was a very nice lady, and we would see her again many times until she passed away in 1978. When we got in the car to head back to Baltimore, I looked at Fred and said, "We're going to live here someday." Fred looked at me, reached over, and placed the back of his hand gently on my forehead. I asked, "What are you doing?" He laughed and said, "Checking to see if you have a fever, you sound delirious." Given our present situation, I understood his incredulity but, I was quite serious. That little simple cabin in the forest was exactly where I wanted to live someday!

A few days later, one morning, Fred left for work at the messenger service only to come back an hour later. His employer had received another one of those anonymous phone calls like Sears had, trashing Fred's character in some way and he was fired. Fred had to look for work again. This is how it was for us! Never a dull moment. We were living in a cheap one-room efficiency, with no furniture. Cooking beans and fatback on an aluminum pie plate for dinner. We hardly ever had more than a dollar between us. For all intents and purposes, life kind of sucked, to put it bluntly. But . . . we were happy! It was a hard, hard time, but we were happy because we were crazy in love. When you're in love, you know can get through anything, and usually with a smile. Love can make you feel invincible with optimism. Hungry, broke, unemployed, it didn't matter, because we were crazy in love and, we knew that one day, everything we were going through would pass. Besides, we always had spaghetti Wednesday at The Cage. Occasionally when we had a dollar we could afford to spend for a cocktail, we'd get a bottle of Thunderbird wine and mix it with 7 Up, so we could stand the taste of it. Sometimes I would take Leksia for a walk and sit and talk with the hobos in the park.

After Fred lost his job at the messenger service, he decided to go see his oldest brother in Chicago and ask for help. He was gone for a month. While he was gone, I got especially lucky one day. I saw an ad in the paper for a live-in nanny. I went immediately, that to apply.

Five minutes into the interview, she hired me and agreed to pay me $100 a week to care for her two children, ages 5 and 7, day and night, five days a week. That was darn good money in those days. The truth was she had a hard time finding a nanny because of her profession. She was a stripper in one of the popular nightclubs downtown. No wonder she could afford $100 a week. I earned it though.

I kept her house and laundry spotless, made sure the kids had three nutritious meals a day. I would read to them at bedtime. They were somewhat undisciplined when I started the job. Right off I knew they were used to getting their way and talking back but that didn't work very long with me. In no time at all, I not only had them listening to me but, they were affectionate as well. Most kids just need firm, consistent direction, and love. Their mother worked five nights a week and usually didn't get home until 3:00 am. She usually slept until noon and spent a few hours with her kids until she had to get ready for work. That was when I got a lot of the housework done. I had Saturdays and Sundays off. Fred's trip to Chicago had been useless. He called me and told me that his brother turned out to be no help at all. He wouldn't even give Fred money for the bus ticket to get back to Baltimore. I was at work so I called Don and gave him $100 to send to Fred via Western Union so Fred could buy a bus ticket home. Not long after Fred got home, he found a decent paying job at Howard Uniform Company. With my nanny job and Fred at the uniform company, it wasn't very long until we could start thinking about looking for a decent apartment. I only had two days a week I could do that so when the time came, Fred did the apartment hunting and by December that year, Fred found us not only an apartment but, a place that would turn out to be home to one of the most memorable chapters in our lives.

Me, age 14

My Parents

My Parents

Me, Age 14

Me, age 14

Me, age 13

Me, age 13

Bali, Sabo the bartender (left), me (center)

Bali

Bali, from left, me, a friend named Jachen, Sabo the bartender,and a US Air Force pilot

Bali, from left, me, Michael, and Deenie (the owner)

Me, 1956, age 25

My sister and Mother, Amsterdam, 1963

Fred and me when we were dating, visiting his friend Vivianne when she lived at 244 Joyce Lane, the house we would rent 8 years later and then return once again to buy it in 1985

Me, circa 1965, shortly after Fred and I were married

Wedding picture, April 25 1965

Wedding picture, April 25 1965

Our wedding 'reception' at The Cage

Our wedding 'reception' at The Cage

Our wedding 'reception' at The Cage, our best most wonderful friend, Don Via on the right

Park Avenue (my Mother center)

Fred and Freddie, February 1968

Fred and me, Summer 1968, Loch Raven Park

Fred, Freddie, and me, Christmas 1969

Freddie, in our courtyard, Park Avenue, Summer 1968

Leksia II, Summer 1968

Fred and 'Princess', Christmas 1969

Me and 'Princess', Christmas 1969

Fun with my Mother and friends in our courtyard at Park Avenue

Fun with my Mother and friends in our courtyard at Park Avenue

Fun with my Mother and friends in our courtyard at Park Avenue

Fun with my Mother and friends in our courtyard at Park Avenue

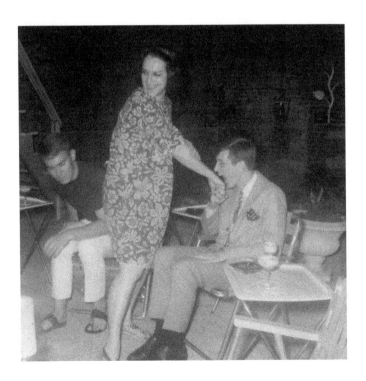

Fun with my Mother and friends in our courtyard at Park Avenue

Don, Fred and me partying one night at The Cage

Joyce Lane, Summer 1970 (note the old school 'antenna' on roof)

Freddie, me, and the dogs, Leksia II and Jason, Joyce Lane, Fall 1972

Freddie, me, and the dogs, Leksia II and Jason, Joyce Lane, Fall 1972

Fred, Freddie, Joyce Lane, Fall 1972

Don, Joyce Lane, Christmas 1974

Joyce Lane, Winter 1972

Joyce Lance, Christmas 1973

Joyce Lane, Summer 1973, Fred, Freddie, and Princess swimming in the Severn River

Fred and me, a birthday party at Gene Morton's house, 1971

Circle Rd, Thanksgiving 1975, Freddie Princess and me

Jason, Circle Rd, 1976

Fred, Freddie, Fort McHenry, 1976

Camping at Pedlar River, Summer 1979 (getting my tan on the rock at the 'swimming hole')

J.J. (Jason Junior), Summer 1979

Freddie and J.J., Winter 1979, Circle Rd

J.J., 'all growed up', Circle Rd, 1982

Camping at Otter Creek, Summer 1976, Fred and Freddie giving deer potato chips

Camping, Pedlar River, Summer 1982, Fred and Freddie crossing bridge over Pedlar River

Pedlar River, Summer 1982, Freddie and me on the trail

Jason and J.J., Pedlar River

Circle Rd., Summer 1983, my beloved 1977 Chevy Malibu Classic station wagon (350, V8, 4 barrel carburetor, ZOOM ZOOM!)

The 'patio', Circle Rd., Summer 1983

Circle Rd., Summer 1980, with friends on the patio

Circle Rd., Summer 1980, on the patio with my sister Anne

My sister Anne, on vacation in Palma De Mallorca, Spain, 1980

Joyce Lane, January 1986, as our 'dream house' looked when we returned to buy it!

Joyce Lane, Winter 1986-87

Joyce Lane, Summer 1988, after a lot of cleaning up, landscaping, and some remodeliing

Fred and me hiking Old Rag Mt., VA, 1985.

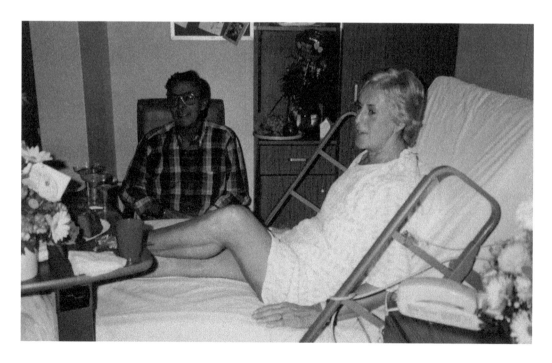

Fred visiting me in the hospital for breast cancer surgery,1989

Fred and me, Christmas, Joyce Lane, 1989

J.J. during his last Summer, 1990

J.J. during his last Summer, 1990

The new kid 'Sunny, aka Sonny', Spring 1991

Fred and Sunny, White Mountain National Forest, circa 1993

My birthday party at Gene's house, circa 1990

Fred and me paddling our canoe on the Severn, Summer of 1995

Fred and me, Christmas 1994

Our 'travel the country' GMC van and pop-up camper, 1997-1999

Cycling Photos, 1994, the CAM (cycle across Maryland). Thats me in the turquoise shorts, center

Cycling Photos, the CAM crossing Chesapeake Bay Bridge

Cycling Photos, Burlington VT

Cycling Photos, Burlington VT

Cycling Photos, 'Spring Fling', Eastern Shore, MD 2007

Cycling Photos, 'Spring Fling', Eastern Shore, MD 2007

Cycling Photos, Canada

Cycling Photos, Lancaster, PA

Cycling Photos, C & O Canal Trail

Cycling Photos, Great Allegheny Passage Trail, MD & PA

Cycling Photos, Great Allegheny Passage Trail, MD & PA

CHAPTER 8

PARK AVENUE

••••••••••••••••••••••••••

On a very cold day in December, Fred and I moved into apartment 17, at 716 Park Avenue. In those days 716 Park Avenue was located within a nice part of Baltimore. The famous Lexington Market, the Washington Monument, several reputable schools, nice hotels, and well-known, successful businesses were all located within a few blocks. Compared to the Rochambeau and our apartment on St Paul St, it was a huge improvement. The next year was challenging to say the least. To begin with, neither of us had succeeded in convincing our spouses to grant us divorces . . . yet. Not long after settling into our new apartment, I was hauled into immigration court. I wasn't in any trouble, but Tony had overstayed his visa and because we were still married, of course, I was summoned to court as well. My immigration status was fine, but Tony was facing deportation. This put me between a rock and a very hard place! I knew instantly that if, in fact, Tony was deported he would go back to Holland and make my mother's life a living hell in a hundred different ways. There was no way I could allow Tony to prey upon my mother, so . . . I lied. I had to. I told the immigration court that I couldn't make it financially without Tony's income. Of course, Tony kept his mouth shut about Fred and me in court! The last thing he wanted was to be deported back to Holland. Due to my plea, immigration changed Tony's visa status to a permanent work visa, allowing him to stay in the US. It wasn't long after that Tony came banging on the door of our apartment very late one evening a few days later. Fred opened the door and there stood Tony, very drunk and looking pathetic. I approached Tony at the door and asked him what he wanted. Speaking Dutch, Tony basically asked me if I was ever coming home, back to the Hamiltonian. Tony was such a narcissistic ass; you could say he literally could not see the forest for the trees. We had not functioned as husband and wife for close to ten years. Here I was, obviously in love with another man and still, he didn't get it? Tony stood there in our doorway, red in the face, still pathetically babbling about adultery, among other things. I calmly admitted to every bit of it and told him I would never come home to him ever, ever again, as long as he lived and that he may as well accept it and move on. Tony may have been a narcissistic sociopath, but he was anything but stupid. After ten years I knew Tony well. No doubt, what he finally conceded to was the fact that he'd gotten everything he was ever going to get out of me and figured it was time for him to move on to his next victim. He wasn't going to miss me for a minute! Tony never had any love for anyone but himself his whole life. He was just pissed off that he'd been rejected by someone before he'd been able to completely bleed them dry and kick them to the curb! It wasn't long after that, Tony finally granted me the divorce I had wanted for so long. I never saw Tony again. Many years later Don told me he just happened to spot Tony one afternoon in Baltimore, staggering out of a bar, balding, obese, with the tell-tale puffy red face of an alcoholic.

I always knew the day would come when Tony would be unable to prey upon anyone anymore. The only thing Tony ever had going for him was his good looks. Without his looks, I'm sure his insincere charms were useless.

Fred tried to reason with his wife one last time. He went to see her in hopes of getting an amicable divorce and establishing some visitation with his kids. Fred missed his kids terribly and hoped that she would be reasonable enough to allow him some contact with his kids. No such luck.

Instead, when Fred came home a few hours later he told me that she'd said that as far as his kids were concerned, he was dead and the only way he would ever see them again was over her dead body. To top it off she told him to go home to his Dutch whore. Had it not been for my experience with Tony, I might have found all of this hard to believe. Even still, I found it difficult to understand why a woman would be so venomous as to deny a father any contact with his children. I never understood that! A bad marriage is one thing. Intentionally and vindictively depriving children of their father is another thing entirely.

Nevertheless, when Fred was finally dragged into court over custody and child support, I heard the same tone from her that Fred had described to me after their last meeting. Fred's wife was visibly seething with contempt for both of us and extremely verbally combative. During the discourse with the judge, one of her demands was, "I want him locked up!" Of course, Fred hadn't done anything that would put him behind bars. During the proceedings, the charge of adultery was made, and Fred didn't dispute it. His wife demanded alimony as well as child support and refused to share any custody and continued to demand that the judge lock Fred up if he didn't comply. At one point the judge said, "Mrs. Brauer, do you want him locked up, or do you want child support because I can't do both?" At the time Fred's wife actually had a better income than he did so the judge didn't grant alimony but pending divorce proceedings, she was granted full custody and child support. When the judge asked Fred if he was satisfied with all that, Fred answered, "Your honor, she has been proving that she's a better man than me for ten years so . . . yes, your honor." With that, Fred's wife really had no choice but to grant him a divorce. Alimony was off the table, and she couldn't collect child support until they were divorced. In the end, unfortunately, it boiled down to a battle of wills, ego, and spite, none of which Fred was willing to be a part of. In other words, for Fred, it became an exercise in futility. Tony and I had no children which made divorce much simpler. Fred's divorce involved three kids, which made it all the more painful but, all Fred could do was hope for a relationship with them in the future. I've seen it happen many times in my life, divorces getting ugly and spiteful and children suffering for it. It shouldn't happen that way. Unless one or both parents are monsters, two mature adults should be able to part ways in an amicable manner that is beneficial for the kids.

We weren't in apartment 17 for very long. In the few months or so that we lived in #17, we became good friends with the building manager that had rented it to us, Betty Alban. Her husband owned 716 and 714 Park Avenue. Betty was managing both buildings, renting out rooms, collecting rent, and cleaning them for new tenants when they were vacated. Betty was a little older than Fred and me and was getting a little burned out on managing both buildings so, she offered me a pretty good deal. She offered me $25 a week plus free rent and utilities if I would take over managing 714. I jumped at the chance. It's a good thing I did too because child support was taking most of Fred's income at the time. I quit the nanny job right away. I gave her notice, of course, but she was still upset. She'd had such a hard time finding me in the first place and her kids loved me but, I had to make the change.

When the time came, Fred and I planned on having a child and I knew I wouldn't be able to be a nanny after that anyway. I'd have to be home. I found out very quickly why Betty was burning out managing both buildings. My management style was a little different than Betty's but, she didn't mind one bit. You could say I was a bit of a hardass. My childhood had instilled in me a very, very bad attitude about drunks. After watching my mother drink herself to eventual oblivion every day for years when I was young, not to mention many of her bar patrons that drank until they vomited or passed out on the bar or in the alley, I had no tolerance for habitual drunks. It was the 60s. I was in my early thirties. Alcoholism and addiction were not met with nearly the empathy or the medical and psychological support that they are today. Mostly it was met with public disdain and swept into the alley, so to speak. Unfortunately, I had to evict more than a few tenants for being daily drunks that had a habit of drinking their rent money and turning their apartments into cesspools. When I finally got the drunks and drug addicts evicted and out, and I entered the apartments, some of them were so disgusting, I had to cover my mouth and nose with a handkerchief! Two of them in particular not only had drunks in them, but they were also incontinent drunks! The odor of urine was so strong it burned my eyes. Urine was soaked into the hardwood floor. The mattresses and box springs were brownish yellow from months of being peed on. I honestly don't know how they slept on them. Other drunkard rooms were filthy in a variety of other ways. Bags of trash full of decomposing food waste and maggots piled in a corner, a refrigerator full of maggots because for some reason the drug addict tenant that had vacated the room a week before unplugged it with ground beef and raw chicken still in it, some of the rooms had cigarette burns everywhere, on the floor, counters, window sills, piles of filthy clothes, a toilet filled to the brim with feces because they had clogged it somehow and instead of getting a plunger they just kept pooping in it! The list goes on, but you get the picture. It took me almost two weeks to get all these rooms presentable. I had to throw away the mattresses and box springs in three units. I hauled them out to the street myself. Then I had to scrub all the units top to bottom with bleach, Pine-Sol, and Spic and Span. It was disgusting! There were other problem tenants as well. There was a couple in one unit that drank and fought constantly, violently, causing damage to the unit. I threw them out too. Another reason for my intolerance was that I had one tenant, an older gentleman, that was in A.A. and had been sober for twenty years. I spoke with him about it a few times and, according to him, there was help available for drunks in A.A. but, they had to want it and they had to want to get sober. That only strengthened my resolve about the matter. There were places in the city for drunks and bums. That's what places like "The Rochambeau" were for, not the apartments at 714 & 716 Park Avenue!

I inherited a housekeeper from Betty, a young black girl named "Goldie". She had given herself that nickname because she had a mouth full of gold teeth. She did a decent enough job but, eventually, I heard from one of the tenants that Goldie seemed to have a lot of "boyfriends". Boyfriends? I wasn't sure what that meant until one day I went to a unit she was supposed to be cleaning and when I got there, I could hear them from the hallway! I threw the door open and there she was, butt naked, supplementing her income with some guy off the street! Yeah, she had boyfriends alright! Needless to say, I fired her on the spot, and I chased her and her john out into the street. I couldn't have that going on! I must have gone through a dozen housekeepers the first year. Quite often I ended up doing the work myself. A few times I hired housekeepers and they disappeared the same day with my damn vacuum cleaner! I noticed a few things about this section of Baltimore early on. One, it was very gay friendly, and two, there were several schools within walking distance. I had several gay tenants already and I must say, they were all professionals, neat, clean, quiet, and always paid their rent on time. I made some inquiries and as I had suspected, a lot of students were looking for affordable rooms to rent. There was a law school a few blocks away that was full of students most of whom were between the ages of 18 and 25. I advertised there. In time I had a list of tenants that for the most part was low maintenance and trustworthy. Many of the students that rented from me relied on their parents for their tuition and rent. Sometimes parents asked me if I could keep an eye on their kids from time to time. A few even asked me to give their kids a curfew, which their kids readily obeyed if they wanted their rent and tuition paid. Every now and then I would catch one coming home past their curfew, and they would apologize profusely, "I'm sorry Ms. Catharina, I won't be late again, and please don't tell my dad." I didn't. They were all good kids, just trying to have a little fun now and then. Pretty soon it was common knowledge in that part of town that the apartments at 714 and 716 Park Avenue were gay friendly, available to students, and were under new management . . . some Dutch woman that kept the place clean, orderly, quiet, safe, and free from bums and drunks and any other undesirable "riff-raff"! Screening prospective tenants and only renting to gays and students and other sober professionals made my job a lot easier. The rent was on time, no one had to be evicted and when they moved out, the apartments were usually so clean, all I had to do was dust and vacuum and maybe mop the kitchen and bathroom floors.

Life on Park Avenue was tough for quite some time! Fred was still working for Howard Uniform and even though we had free rent and utilities, almost all of Fred's income was going to child support so, in a word, we were poor. Fred was always looking for a better opportunity but with only a high school education at the time, Fred's options were limited. Fred knew what his talents were and knew what he wanted to do. He just had to find the means and the time to do it. His flair was interior design. He learned that working at Sears. He had the talent and even a lot of the know-how, but he needed the degree, that piece of paper that says so.

His sights were set on the Maryland Institute College of Art, which was also just a few blocks away. With a degree from there, he knew he could get the job he really wanted so, we worked toward that. Fred left Howard Uniform to be a driving instructor. A friend of his had started his own driving school business and asked Fred to be an instructor for him. It paid more and was a little more suited to his character. Since Fred was friends with the owner, he managed his own schedule which gave him some flexibility. In addition to having a flair for interior design, Fred

was a natural-born teacher. He had infinite patience and compassion. The hours were better too. 1964 went by very quickly as I recall. So much happened and Fred and I were both so busy. The building management kept me busy almost every day and when Fred became a driving instructor, quite often I would double as a receptionist. The owner of the driving school offered Fred a little more money to manage his own client list and book his own appointments, so, sometimes I took the calls and booked the appointments. I remember once a lady asking me to please send my very best instructor for her daughter. Of course, I promised her I would send my best most experienced driving instructor! What was I going to say? There's only one?

Eventually, sometime in late '64, maybe early '65, Betty Alban made me an even better offer. She and her husband had been so impressed with how well I managed 714 that they offered us the best unit in 716, also rent and utilities free, plus $50 a week if I would manage 716 as well. The best unit in 716 was also the biggest, a two-bedroom ground floor unit with a separate living room, a nice size kitchen, a basement, and a big, beautiful courtyard. Well, the courtyard wasn't beautiful yet, but it would be! Again, we jumped at the chance. Not very long after we moved into 716, Don told us about a hotel a few blocks away that was going out of business and was going to be throwing away furniture. We hadn't brought anything from St Paul Street at all and over the past year had acquired a few pieces of cheap furniture from thrift stores but nothing like we retrieved from this hotel! Don helped us bring several very nice pieces of solid wood furniture from this hotel and soon we had a fully furnished apartment. We got a solid cherry dining table, a secretary, a couch, a trundle bed, a server, bookshelves, chairs, a chest, and a coffee table. Don borrowed some dollies from Sears and using the street sidewalks the three of us made several trips pushing furniture on dollies from the hotel to our apartment. It took us all day. I still have the trundle bed, the secretary, the chest and the coffee table! The trundle bed is in my loft bedroom. The secretary, coffee table and chest are in my living room. Don had the pulse of the city and he always seemed to know of cheap and creative ways we could get things done. I had big plans for the courtyard, but that would have to wait until Spring.

Toward the end of 1964, Fred's divorce was finalized . . . after more battling, of course. Fred had gone to see his old friend Elizabeth Mueller at the Family and Children's Society several times in an attempt to win some visitation, any visitation he could with his children, but his wife would never concede. Fred had met Elizabeth Mueller when he was a child in the orphanage run by the Family and Children's Society in Baltimore. She had been one of the counselors and a supervisor for the organization for decades. Out of all the hundreds of children Elizabeth had cared for over the years, Fred was the only one to go back after he left the orphanage and look her up. Fred had no parents or grandparents after he was nine years old, so he visited her quite often and they became very close. She was more or less the mother he'd never had, and he always said that she was like a princess to him, so much so, that's what he renamed her on his own, "Princess". It's a name that stuck for the rest of her life.

As a matter of fact, still caring for his life and well-being, and knowing in her heart it was a mistake for Fred to marry a woman ten years his senior, Princess had begged him not to marry his first wife, but he did anyway. We all learn the hard way. Years later she told me how upset she was the day he did that. When Fred introduced me to her, he introduced her as "Princess". She was born in 1898 so when I met her, she was already 67 years old. We watched over her for the rest of her life. She had never married so; we were the closest thing to children that she had. She told us once that she had fallen in love with a medical student in 1925 when she was 27 years old but that her mother did not approve of the young man so she could not marry him. After that, sad and despondent, she had thrown herself into a career with the Family and Children's Society and work with her alma mater, Goucher College, and never married. Her career and travel became her life. She invested her income into stocks such as Noxzema and General Electric back in the 1930s and ultimately became a very wealthy old lady. She'd seen much of the world traveling and her home in Towson was full of items that she had collected from many different countries.

With the Spring of 1965 came some wonderful things. Fred and I were married on April 30, 1965. We were so broke! The driving school Fred had been working for suddenly went out of business but, that actually turned out to be a blessing because Fred started driving a cab and because he could set his own hours doing so, he was finally able to take classes at the Maryland Institute at night. I hocked a gold ring I had to pay for the printing of the invitations. We invited our few closest friends. Don was Fred's best man. Betty Alban was my maid of honor. It was a small but elegant ceremony at the First and Franklin Presbyterian church right around the corner from our apartment. We had no money for any kind of reception so all of our friends at The Cage held a reception for us. We were so poor, we walked to the nearest church to get married and then walked to our reception party at The Cage and it was one of the happiest days of our entire lives! Oh, I'm sure a lot of people would have raised their eyebrows back then! Married in a church and then reception at a gay bar?! So what? I'll tell you this, take it from a 90-year-old woman, life is not a rehearsal! You only get one life to do what you want to do, your way! In the end, the only regrets you'll have are the chances you DIDN'T take. You'll never be happy doing things how other people want them done, trust me! Our reception was a blast, and everyone had a great time. We had some of our best times at The Cage! Incidentally, just an FYI . . . a champagne hangover is one of the worst there is.

Of course, there was no honeymoon. It's pretty hard to go on a honeymoon with fifty cents! So, we went home and got busy starting a family . . . often!

When summer came a couple of months later, Fred and I began eyeballing the court-yard. We both had all kinds of great ideas but, very little budget to accomplish them. Don, of course, was instrumental in this particular project as he was in many projects to come. What do you do with a cement courtyard and brick walls? You get creative, very creative. We knew we wanted some nature in the courtyard. We already had a few potted plants but, we had bigger ideas. We wanted A LOT of flowers, plants . . . flower beds? Yes, flower beds! With a ground made of concrete, how does one accomplish that? You build them. Don knew of a recently demolished building in town where we could harvest from an endless supply of red bricks. We made several trips from the demolition site to our apartment with the trunk of Don's 1963 Mercury Monterey loaded with bricks! Younger readers might not know it but . . . back in the '60s, a lot of full-sized, four-door cars had huge trunks, big enough for two people to sleep in! Once we had our bricks stacked and lined up as flower bed frames, we lined them with a heavy-duty plastic we got from Hechinger by the roll and filled them with soil. Hechinger was the equivalent of Lowe's and Home Depot back in the '60s. Some of the soil we dug from the demolition site and loaded into the trunk of Don's Mercury. The rest of the soil was 50-pound bags of potting soil we also bought at Hechinger. Don is the ultimate green thumb. Fred and I were pretty good gardeners as well. It took a few weekends and a lot of elbow grease but when we were finished, we had brick-front flower beds all around the perimeter of the courtyard filled with Ferns, Impatiens, Violets, and more. Don was always coming to visit with plants and flowers to add to our flower beds. Somewhere, I don't remember where from, we acquired some patio furniture and a few small outdoor tables, and we were able to have our friends over. We had a lot of great parties in that courtyard over the years. Good times.

My Leksia died that year. By 1965 he had become an old dog. He was already a few years old when I got him from Mimi in Holland. The vet told us he had terrible arthritis and was losing his sight, so we said goodbye to him and asked the vet to put him to sleep. It's such a hard thing to do but, if you love your dog, it is the kind thing to do. I cried for days, I missed him so much. Leksia had been with me for almost ten years. I'd woken up with him every day since 1956. Maybe a week after Leksia went over the rainbow bridge, Fred came home from work with a little fuzzy black and white puppy. It was always his opinion that the best way to get over losing a dog was to get a puppy. It was uncanny. This little puppy, which turned out to be a water spaniel mix, looked so much like my old Leksia that I named him Leksia too.

Something else happened in the summer of '65. In July, I discovered I was pregnant. We were ecstatic! I was going to be a mother! I called Holland and told my mother right away. She was overjoyed she was going to be a grandmother! My sister never had any children, so this child was to be her only grandchild. I quit smoking and drinking right away. I didn't smoke much, to begin with anyway, and only drank wine and even then, not until the evening.

I kept working right up until the day I delivered, no problem. I managed both buildings, collecting rent, cleaning the rooms, and rerenting them whenever they were vacated, which some months happened quite often! Both buildings were four floors, with six rooms on each floor. Sometimes I had several vacated rooms to clean, advertise and rent in one week. I was busy but I was 34 years old and healthy as a horse. Fred was driving a taxi all day and going to school every night. We were so busy, quite often the only time we got together was a few hours on the weekends. Occasionally, when we did get a whole Saturday or Sunday off, quite often we would pack a picnic basket and head out to Sugarloaf Mountain, MD, about 60 miles due west of Baltimore if you take Rt 95 west out of Baltimore. It's a small mountain, 800 feet, but it's part of the Blue Ridge Mountain range and a beautiful place! Sugarloaf Mountain was our little day trip getaway many times in those days.

Summer gave way to fall, fall gave way to winter. We had a quiet little Christmas together, just the two of us and Leksia. I was five months pregnant and beginning to show. Fred was working all the time and still going to school at night. I'm not sure how he did it. For about two years, between driving the cab all day, school at night, and homework, most nights he was lucky if he got six hours of sleep. I was amazed at his energy and drive. When that man made a decision and established a goal, he could just go and go and go and go. His mind was set on a specific plan, and he was hell-bent on achieving it as quickly and efficiently as possible. Neither of us ever complained. We were poor. We were tired. I remember days I was so tired from cleaning rooms, scrubbing floors and toilets, cleaning out refrigerators tenants had left filthy, dusting, vacuuming, hauling out garbage and belongings that tenants had left out to the dumpster, etc., my arms and legs felt like rubber! I knew Fred had endless, exhausting days too. Some nights he'd be busy with homework until 2:00 or 3:00 in the morning and then get up a few hours later to get into his cab for 12 hours, then go to school again until 10:00 pm. Sometimes that cycle repeated for days but, we did it. We were a team with a plan and a goal and that was it. It might sound corny to some but, we lived on love. We really did. We knew together, there was nothing we couldn't do that we set our minds to, and that made any hardships that came along easy to weather.

My pregnancy had zero complications. My doctor was happy as could be with me. The only serious food craving I had came around the eighth month . . . glazed donuts! I couldn't get enough of them! Fred started bringing them home a couple of times a week because he knew I was going to ask for them anyway. Donuts were cheap back then. I think Fred paid 40 cents for a dozen glazed. I never sat and ate a whole dozen glazed donuts in one sitting but, two or three, several times a week? Oh yeah!

That winter, Saturday, January 29, 1966, there came a decent snowfall, a little less than a foot fell. I'll never forget this weekend as long as I live. Fred was home, off for the day. I was six months pregnant. Don called around 11 o'clock in the morning and since none of us were doing anything, Don came over about an hour later with a gallon of white wine, a fifth of vodka, and a bottle of orange juice and he and Fred proceeded to get sloshed! Two hours later, after both of them were feeling fine, Fred made a brilliant announcement. With his finger in the air, he slurred, "I got, I got a great idea . . . Less go sledding, I know, I know the perfffikk place." I looked at my usually dignified, intelligent, articulate husband and his best friend who was now smashed on cheap wine and screwdrivers, and just shook my head. They deserved it. They worked hard. Don sat there grinning ear to ear and said, "Yeah, let's do it, let's do it!" I said, "What, go out in this? It's freezing out there!" Believe it or not, I never saw much snow in Holland. Holland doesn't get all that cold in the winter, and it doesn't get much snow either. Winter in Holland is typically damp, dreary and temperatures usually stay just warm enough for any snow to be wet, sloppy, and melt quickly. It was about 15 degrees outside, there were 9 inches of snow on the ground and these two inebriated 33-year-old fools wanted to go out and play in it!

Fred and Don jumped up, went into the basement, and came back up with three cardboard boxes. Then, they stood there looking at me like a couple of kids, waiting for me to say I'd go! We put on our coats and gloves and walked in the snow the few blocks to a huge hill that was behind Fred's school, and three grown adults in their early thirties went sledding down a big hill in cardboard boxes for at least two hours. Each of us slid down the hill a few times, to pack the snow down, and then when the bottoms of the boxes started to get icy, we were sliding down that hill so fast when we got to the bottom the momentum started shooting us across the field! It was hysterical! Eventually, all three of us were too tuckered out to climb the hill anymore so we went home. It was a simple bit of fun, but I'll remember it forever. The next day the whole city was snowed in because another few feet of snow fell. I believe it is little known as the blizzard of 66.

Spring came and along with it, my son. Freddy was born at 1:00 am April 8, 1966. Fred, Don and my mother were all present that day. I had borrowed the money to get my mother a plane ticket to come from Holland from a good friend. Fred was still in school and driving the cab so we really couldn't afford an airline ticket at the time. I knew when I got up on April 7 that day was the day. I had my first inkling of a labor pain at 9:00 am. My son took his time! I went through the whole day doing my daily things, made lunch for my mother and me, did a load of laundry, did the dishes, etc. Don arrived shortly after 5:00 pm with a gallon of Sherry and a couple of bottles of champagne. My Mother loved that, ever the party girl! Fred got home a few minutes after Don arrived. I was hungry, of course. I set out a platter of hor's d' oeuvres of smoked oysters, cheese, and crackers, and put a big pan of chicken drumsticks in the oven. Then, I started making champagne cocktails. I used to love champagne cocktails! I had not had a single drop of alcohol or a cigarette in nine months! I was hours away from giving birth and I must tell you; those champagne cocktails were delicious! Every half hour or so Don asked, "Shouldn't we start heading for the hospital?" I said every time, "Noooooo, not yet." We were having fun! I guess you could say we were having my son's very first "birthday" party. The doctor had told me not to eat or drink anything after I went into labor but, I guess I ignored that suggestion. I'm pretty sure he scolded me for it later too. Sometime after 10 o'clock, I was in the kitchen and my water broke. Don looked at me blankly and said sarcastically, "Gee, do you think maybe we can go to the hospital now?!" We did. I walked into labor and delivery at 11:00 pm and Freddy was born two hours later. I remember at one point during delivery the doctor said, "He doesn't want to come out." I said, "What? What do you mean he doesn't wanna come out?!" The doctor said, "I think he's sleeping!" I said, "Well, wake him up!" Of course, he did come, and it was the happiest day of our lives. Fred was just glowing with joy! I know every mother thinks that their baby is the most beautiful but, in our case the nurses thought so too! All-day long the nurses were taking turns holding Freddy and carrying him around. Freddy was such a pretty baby for the first few months of his life occasionally I would hear, "Ohhhhh, she's beautiful!" You should have seen my mother! Talk about a doting grandmother! She carried Freddy around all day cooing and talking to him as if he were a newborn prince!

My Mother went back to Holland a few weeks later and I got busy learning how to juggle being an apartment building manager and a mother at the same time. It was challenging at times to be sure. If I had to go clean a room and ready it for the next tenant, I just brought Freddy with me. We only had enough money for the basics. I didn't have a lot of lady friends so there was no baby shower. We received a few gifts from close friends. Right away, I bought two dozen cloth diapers, baby powder, pins, bottles, infant shirts, and the bare essentials. I bathed him in the kitchen sink, and I found a playpen that served as a crib as well. In time I found a highchair when I needed it. I had everything I needed to care for a baby, just not all the extras and conveniences some mothers are used to.

Still, money was tight but as I've said, we had a goal and stuck to it. Fred was still driving the cab and was doing well in school, although it would take some time because he couldn't take a full course load going only at night. The bills were paid, we had food on the table, and we found creative and economical ways to have fun and accomplish certain projects we had in mind, such as the courtyard. Fred had gotten lucky and acquired a used VW Beetle from a friend of his for something like $100, so we finally had a car. His friend had bought it for his wife, and she hated it. It was black and had a red interior. Before then, Fred had used the driver's school car or borrowed one from one of his friends when we need one. Fred had spent his whole life in Baltimore, and he had several old friends in town.

We began a bit of an animal collection. By the time Freddy was walking we had, 2 fantail pigeons, a dozen finches, two guinea pigs, two dogs, and a pair of mallard ducks. Don heard me say how badly I wanted a pair of ducks, so he made it happen. Some people weren't too happy about it. Ducks quack, a lot! Every now and then, usually at times like very early on a Saturday or Sunday morning, I would hear one of the neighbors screaming from a window, "SHUT THOSE DAMN DUCKS UP!" On another occasion, I'd accidentally left the gate open. There was a knock at the door, one of the neighbors telling me our ducks were walking down Howard St! I bolted out the door and found them, called to them, and believe it or not, they stopped. Looked at me and then followed me home.

For almost four years, every spring, summer, and fall Freddy had his own little playground/oasis in the courtyard with two dogs, two ducks, chirping birds, and squealing guinea pigs. He had a little wading pool that the ducks used more than he did, a few of the Fisher-Price toys, and his tricycle.

The second dog we got by accident, sort of. Fred had bought Princess a puppy for her birthday. It wasn't a very well thought out gift and within a matter of weeks, Princess called Fred in a tizzy and told Fred the puppy was peeing all over her Persian rugs and to come and get him. So, that's how we ended up with two dogs rather than just Leksia. Fred named the puppy Jason. All through Freddy's childhood, he had two dogs with him everywhere he went.

For a couple of years, we lived a very, very busy, frugal but comfortable life. We took great joy in watching Freddy grow. When you have a baby, everything else pales in comparison and you find that most of your fun and joy is in them. We still took our occasional trips to Sugarloaf

Mountain for our "R & R" out of the city. Fred introduced me to Maryland blue crabs. At first, I thought they were the ugliest creatures I'd ever seen and couldn't imagine eating one until Fred showed me how. After that, in the summer months, we had crabs and beer every chance we got. Crabs and beer were cheap in the late '60s!

Crabs were a few dollars a dozen and a six-pack of beer was about $1.50. We had quite a few crabs and beer parties in the courtyard with our friends and a few of our tenants as well we'd made friends with. The first time I actually sat down at a table full of crabs and beer I got very, very drunk! I wasn't accustomed to the Old Bay like Fred and Don were. Old Bay seasoning to me was so spicy and salty I was drinking beer like it was water! An hour after picking crabs I was hammered! So, I learned very quickly to keep a big glass of ice water next to the glass of beer!

Fred earned his Interior Design degree sometime in early 1968. He'd begun sending out his resume' several weeks earlier and had a few good offers by the time he graduated. One of the offers was from a well know display company called Baltimore Display but, it involved some traveling, so he passed. He ended up taking an in-store position with a department store called Hamburgers. He was hired to be the display manager for the entire store. Finally, Fred had the degree, the job title, and the income he'd been working towards! The years of 18-hour days driving all day and school at night were over.

The sixties were a glorious time. The music was wonderful. We were young. The country still had a strong sense of morality that is lacking today. In retrospect, things were affordable and life in America still allowed for people to accomplish literally anything they set their minds to. Life in the US in those days wasn't cluttered with inhibiting rules and regulations and priced out of reach. Being home all the time I had gotten to know every soul on our few blocks of Park Avenue. I knew all the shopkeepers. I knew all the stand owners at Lexington Market by their first name. I knew who was gay, who was straight. I even knew the names of the prostitutes, the gay ones, and the straight ones! As long as they kept it quiet, clean, and discrete, what did I care? The cops were always giving the gays a hard time back then. America wasn't as accepting in those days. Personally, I found all the gays I knew to be wonderful people. I'm a clean freak and anyone I caught littering I read them the riot act. After all, I managed two of the buildings on the block of the avenue so, I guess I kind of took some personal responsibility for the whole street. It wasn't long 'til everyone there knew better. I don't think I had a bad attitude at all. Some might see it as presumptuous or arrogant, but I think everyone should take a personal interest in where they live! How can you expect to live in a wonderful neighborhood without becoming involved and making sure it stays that way?!

The 60s were also a very tumultuous time. By 1968, people were very upset over Vietnam and civil rights was a heated topic and debate as well. In April of 1968, in response to the assassination of Martin Luther King, the city of Baltimore erupted into about a week of riots and civil unrest. Cops were fighting with protestors in the streets. Stores and businesses were burned and looted. By the end of it, six people had been killed, hundreds had been injured and thousands had been arrested.

The riots gave Fred and me pause. We'd read about the riots and civil unrest that were taking place in cities across the country, but we took notice of the fact that we never heard about such things happening in rural America. It was the first time we questioned the idea of raising a child in the city.

My Mother came back to visit us in 1968 except this time she stayed for nine months. She bought Freddy clothes, took him to the park every day, and showered him with unending affection. She saw everything there was to see in Baltimore, Ft McHenry, The USS Constellation, museums, parks and took Freddy with her every time. In the evening, she smoked and drank, sherry, port, chablis, whatever there was. For several weeks she came home all the time with bottles of Thunderbird because it was cheap and 20% alcohol util we talked her out of buying that stuff! She absolutely adored Fred and he loved her as well. The two of them would sit and drink and smoke and talk for hours sometimes.

She had endless stories. She was a bit of a bad influence on my husband for sure. I didn't like the excessive drinking and smoking but, I let it go. I knew she had to go home in a matter of months, so I let them have their fun.

My Mother went back to Holland shortly after Christmas of 1968. The following year would be one of great change for us personally. Fred was earning a comfortable income, comfortable enough that the free rent, utilities, and small income from me being building manager wasn't nearly as necessary as they had been. My mind was becoming more focused on taking care of my own home and raising my son, as well as being there for my husband when he came home from work each night. We began taking more trips out to parks in western Maryland and Virginia on the weekends. Each time we did, the drive home back into the city became less and less welcome. We loved our little home at 716 Park Avenue but, everything around it began to lose its appeal. Freddy turned three in April of 1969, and we had noticed his affinity for animals and nature. He'd spent two summers in a courtyard surrounded by plants and flowers and animals, but we knew that was a very limited environment. Outside of that courtyard was traffic and noise and smog. The first time he saw Sugarloaf Mountain his eyes lit up, or so it seemed to us. Maybe it's because we loved it too. By the end of 1969, Fred was a rock star of a display manager at Hamburgers, and word had gotten around. His work had been seen by important people he had no knowledge of. I don't know if I've said it yet but, opportunity usually amounts to success for those that are prepared. Trust me, that philosophy is almost always true! Never be afraid of change! When the opportunity comes along to do something different, bigger and better, don't hesitate!

Just a few weeks into 1970, Fred got an offer he simply could not refuse, and again, as it does so often in life . . . everything changed!

CHAPTER 9

CHARLESTON, WEST VIRGINIA

· ·

On a very unseasonably wintry, windy, and overcast morning in early March of 1970, Fred and I stood together on the sidewalk and took one last, long melancholy look at 714 Park Avenue, the three-floor brick row house that had been our first home together. "Park Avenue", as we would fondly refer to it for the rest of our lives, would forever hold a special place in our hearts. More than just a dwelling in which to live, we always looked back on "Park Avenue" as the most exciting, tumultuous, challenging, sometimes scary, and yet joyous time in our lives together. It had been our first home together, our beginning, where our son was born, and where the joy of our love for each other was etched in stone. It had been a time of putting an end to a few miseries and the beginning of many joys. Yes, "Park Avenue" has been and will always be a collection of indelible memories.

After many long discussions and weighing the pros and cons, Fred and I had decided not to raise our son, in Baltimore and send him to public school there. As I mentioned earlier, there had been quite a bit of racial and civil "unrest" in Baltimore in the late '60s, undeniable rumors of political corruption in the city council, and several unfavorable reports about the public city schools, all of which concerned us quite a bit, especially regarding raising a small child. The Baltimore riots in April of 1968 following the assassination of Martin Luther King had given us pause about raising a child in the inner-city. Neither of us was too keen on the idea of raising a small child within the concrete hustle and bustle of any inner-city anyway. Fred had spent his whole life in Baltimore, and I had lived in Amsterdam for fifteen years. Needless to say, we had both had more than our fill of city life. Both of us were nature lovers and had made the three-hour drive to the Skyline Drive in Virginia as often as possible for weekend getaways from the noisy, smoggy city and had fallen absolutely in love with the green splendor of the Appalachian Mountains. We had been in some discussion with a local priest we knew personally about sending our son to a private Christian K - 12 school called "Friends School" in Baltimore. Unfortunately, neither Fred nor I participated in the Church in any way anymore and neither of us was willing to be hypocritical, especially religiously. In those days, for children to attend Friends School, the whole family had to be members of the Church. After that particular discussion, we began making plans to get out of the city of Baltimore, and Fred began looking for jobs in his line of work in other more rural areas outside of Baltimore.

So, on that cold, cloudy morning in March 1970, my husband's black '62 Volkswagen Beetle sputtered out of Baltimore headed for our new rental home in Charleston, WV . . . loaded to the roof with dogs, bird cages, turtles, and an almost 4-year-old boy. I was already a little sad that I couldn't relocate all of our backyard "zoo" and garden, but I was determined to bring some of it! Somehow, we loaded two dogs, a cage with two fantail pigeons, another cage with half a dozen goldfinches, and Freddy with his two miniature turtles into the rear seat of that Beetle. Fred had been offered a very well-paying job at a large, upscale department store in downtown Charleston, West Virginia, and had rented a small 2-bedroom bungalow in a small, privately owned community called North Park just a few miles outside of the city. See, by 1969, my husband had become quite the hot commodity in Baltimore as commercial interior decorators and designers go. In those days, the decorating and designing of department stores was an art form and required a lot of talent and skill, both of which Fred had in spades. The news of Fred's talent and work at Hamburgers had made its way around the display world in Baltimore. The owner of the department store in Charleston had been to Baltimore and had seen Fred's work in several storefront windows in Baltimore and quickly took steps to acquire him. He even paid the airfare and sent a limo to the airport when we went to Charleston for the final interview. The offer was simply too good to pass up.

We spent a month saying goodbyes to all of the friends we had made on Park Avenue, the tenants, the local shopkeepers, our friends at the cage. I had established myself as a bit of a neighborhood watchdog over the years. People had told me that by cleaning up 714 and 716 and filling the buildings with decent renters, I had improved the neighborhood and the local shopkeepers and business wonders were thankful for that. Several of them said so before we left. The owner of the little drug store on the corner near us even asked me who was going to watch over the neighborhood now? I felt very honored by that. It's very gratifying to know that you've improved someone else's life, even in a small way. I handed off the management position to a good friend of ours who was ready to get out of the display business and do something else so, that worked out well.

We drove out of Baltimore expecting a 6-hour trip, give or take, but after about two hours the road began to go up, and up, and up . . . and up into the Appalachian Mountains. Fred's little, black, VW Beetle, loaded to the roof with 3 humans and a dozen animals, slowed a little, but chugged and sputtered along, birdcages swinging back and forth in the back seat with every winding twisting turn through the mountains, with Freddy swaying slightly side to side in the back seat while holding on to his little bowl of miniature turtles with both hands. I kept glancing into the back seat, sure that the water and maybe even the turtles would slosh right out of the turtle bowl, but, Freddy insisted that it wouldn't. Freddy looked at me very seriously and said confidently, "Don't worry Mommy, I won't let the water spill out, my turtles need the water." I was worried he would get tired of holding the turtle bowl but, he insisted he could handle it, and he did.

I must say IF you've never done it, driving through the Appalachians is an absolutely breathtaking experience! I highly recommend it for any nature lover's bucket list. From the first time Fred took me to Sugarloaf Mountain near Frederick, MD, I was in absolute awe of the beauty of the forests in America, and I hadn't even been west of Virginia . . . yet.

I've always been a forest lover. Even as a child during the war, the only solitude, happiness, and comfort I could find was in the forest near our home in Holland. When I was younger, I liked the beach occasionally for tanning purposes. I saw the French Riviera in my twenties. I can't say it exactly blew my hair back. It was a beautiful beach, and I got a great tan, but I am no water baby, not at all! I've never been an ocean lover, recreationally anyway. I'm very aware of its vital importance to all life on Earth, of course, I just don't enjoy swimming in it.

Finally, after what turned out to be about 8 hours, Fred turned our dusty tired Beetle into the parking space of bungalow #7, on Jonquil Lane in North Park, Charleston, WV. It was a cute little rancher-style house on a bit of a hillside overlooking North Park. In the center of North Park was the owner's "mansion". It wasn't actually a mansion per se, but it was a very large, three-story, 10-bedroom home, beautifully landscaped with enormous green lawns, a variety of shrubbery, dozens of large gardens, and several different sized lily ponds. North, east, and south of North Park was nothing but miles and miles of forest . . . to this day. To the west was the Kanawha River. Between North Park and the Kanawha was a mixture of mobile home trailers and a few very, very . . . very old houses. Our moving van arrived about an hour after we did, and we spent the next few days setting up the house.

At first, we were quite happy in North Park. From our little bungalow, the view all around us was a visual splendor of the green beauty of the Appalachian Forest. Fred was earning a fantastic income that exceeded our needs. The bungalow was in very nice condition, and we had a fun time decorating and making it cozy and comfortable. We felt very safe there and having just come from the constant noise and exhaust fumes of the inner city we were still in awe of the consistent calm and quiet of Mother Nature that surrounded our home . . . no horns, no sirens, no doors slamming, just the wind in the trees, bird songs, and by late April, crickets and tree frogs at night.

Within a month, Freddy had toured the neighborhood of six other bungalows rented there, making a point to introduce himself to everyone he met and make friends with the tenants of each bungalow. That's my son. He has always been a friendly and confident extrovert, even at the age of 4. He still is. For the icing on the cake, so to speak, we became immediate and very good friends with the owner, our landlord, Anne North. Anne was an attractive, pleasant, intelligent, and friendly lady in her late 50's and she adored Freddy immediately. In addition to making his regular rounds visiting the neighbors, Freddy spent quite a bit of time playing around Anne's home and she was often quite happy to invite him in for the all-time kid's favorite, peanut butter and jelly sandwich or milk and cookies.

Freddy loved Thomas's English muffins too, so Anne always kept a package of them on hand as well. I imagine with all of Anne's beautiful gardens, shrubs and lily ponds full of colorful fish and frogs, Anne's property looked like a natural playground to him. We had Anne up to our bungalow for dinner many times and enjoyed more than a few sunny Saturday afternoons on her plush lawn sipping wine and chatting under her big, beautiful shade trees.

It was in late May 1970, about the same time my sister Annie made the long flight from Holland to visit with us for a few weeks, that we began to look into our surroundings a little more and made a few unpleasant discoveries in the process. Prior to moving there, we'd known almost nothing about Charleston, or West Virginia for that matter. Unfortunately, we had made the uninformed assumption that being nestled within the green splendor of the Appalachian Mountains, North Park simply must be an idyllic, natural place to live and raise a small child, right? How could it not be? Well, we were mistaken, not so much about North Park, per se, but a few very unpleasant things that weren't far from it.

The first thing we noticed shortly after moving in was a frequent, strange hue to the sky. Even on cloudless, sunny days, that brilliant bright blue sky we all know so well was more of a dull, grayish blue in Charleston, West Virginia. There seemed to be an unusual, odd smogginess to the air above that seemed to come and go with no discernible pattern. We were also puzzled quite often when outdoors in the yard we smelled a number of different, unfamiliar, unpleasant odors, quite pungent at times, that would sometimes linger for hours or waft by on a stiff breeze and then be gone.

Fred managed to get some time off during the second week of Annie's visit, so we decided to take that opportunity to spend a day or two exploring our new surroundings. Bright and early one Saturday morning, I packed a big picnic basket and the four of us got into Fred's VW Beetle for a day of exploring in and around Charleston, WV., with the intention of finding one of the parks we had read about in the western portion of Charleston. Charleston is situated on the banks of the Kanawha River, in Kanawha County, West Virginia with the actual town part of it with the town center, shopping, businesses, as well as Fred's new job, situated on the east side of the river. We had only just moved in 6 weeks prior to my sister's visit and had spent most of that time setting up the house and getting acclimated to the immediate area. We had seen a little of Charleston on the east side, the grocery store, a five and dime and the department store Fred was working in, but that's about it. We hadn't seen the Kanawha River or the portion of Charleston that was on the west side of it.

The first thing we noticed while crossing Rt 64 bridge into west Charleston, was the ugly reddish-brown color of the Kanawha River and the ghastly plethora of trash along the banks of it. Strewn along the banks was a hideous conglomeration of tires, clothing, cans, bottles, plastic bags, old plastic toys . . . as if the contents of a fully loaded garbage barge headed for a landfill had simply been shoveled off onto the banks of the river as it floated downstream! In fact, there was quite a bit of garbage strewn along the roadsides as well. Mile after mile as we drove, cans, bottles, and fast-food bags littered the shoulders on both sides. That wasn't the worst of it though. It was later in the afternoon that we discovered the real environmental horror and the source of the strange odors, odd hue to the sky, and the weird smogginess in the air. It was not more than ten miles or so from North Park that we spotted the big, rusting, dingy factories and chemical plants situated one after the other on the banks of the Kanawha River. Fred stopped the car at a turn out along the side of the road and we all got out. We all stood there, mouths agape, staring in shock, disbelief, and disgust at several tall smokestacks towering out of several different plants, all belching out steady plumes of toxic smog and soot of various putrid colors! One stack belched out greenish-yellow smoke, another a mix of pink, orange, and brown, one was a sick-looking greenish-gray, and yet another was pure, dense black! After a long moment while still staring at these multicolored, gaseous plumes of who knows what, slowly shaking his head, my husband muttered, "This is not good, not good at all."

Sure, we both had seen factories and industrial plants before, in cities like Baltimore.

I had even seen a few in Holland. Perhaps we had been a little naive, but it had never occurred to us that there would be so many operating here, tucked away within the Appalachian Mountains! My immediate thought was WHY on Earth would anyone put such an ugly and toxic thing in such a beautiful place?! Needless to say, this was cause for great concern.

We made the best of the rest of my sister's visit however, the knowledge of the factories weighed heavily on our minds. After a little research over the next few days, Fred found out that the ugly smokestacks we had seen belonged to chemical plants. Fred and I shared our thoughts on the matter with one another a couple of times in the following weeks and being like-minded as we were, rather quickly reached an agreed conclusion. What good was a comfy bungalow nestled within picturesque, forested mountains if there were dozens of smokestacks of chemical plants only ten miles away spewing poison into the air? Grudgingly, we began to seriously entertain the idea of packing it up, again and moving.

A couple of months after our chemical plant discovery, summer arrived, and the heat was upon us. The summer of 1970 was a hot one, at least it was in Charleston, WV. Most days were in the mid to upper 90's and very humid. The high heat and humidity brought millions of flies . . . and the unmistakable stench of excrement! POOP! Even our little 4-year-old son, Freddy, looked at me very seriously one day while we were outside and asked, "Mommy, why does it smell like poop out here?" It was unbearable. Most days it was nearly impossible for us to enjoy a single moment outside without almost gagging!

After a week or so of the epic foulness in the air, Fred decided one Saturday morning that the odor must be investigated and ventured into the woods behind our bungalow in search of the source of the stench. He returned about a half-hour later, walked into the kitchen, picked up the phone, called Anne North, and asked her if she could watch Freddy for an hour or so. We stood in our driveway watching Freddy run down the hill to Anne's house, then Fred turned to me and said, "Let's take a little walk, you gotta see this", and headed towards the woods behind our house. I followed Fred through the brush, and we zigzagged through foliage and trees until we came upon a small path he had found. We stepped onto the path and proceeded . . . and the further we walked, the stronger the stench got. After we'd followed the path for about a half-mile, we came upon a shallow valley with a dingy stream at the bottom of it. On the other side of this little valley were dozens of shacks, at least, that was my first impression. Clearly, it was a neighborhood of some kind and appeared to be suffering from abject poverty. Some of these tin-roofed beat-up, run-down shacks had cars just as beat up and run-down parked next to them.

It was quite a depressing scene complete with chickens running about, a few skinny, mangy-looking dogs, crooked clotheslines, cars without wheels balanced atop cinder blocks, beer cans and bottles strewn everywhere, stacks of used tires, broken windows held together with duct tape and miscellaneous garbage. More cans and bottles and more old tires decorated the hillside down into the valley and then, as my line of sight followed the slope of the hill downward, I saw it, just as Fred was asking me, "You see that?" Lo and behold, poking out of the hillside behind these shacks, a little more than halfway down to the dingy creek below was the source of the stench and the flies . . . several open sewage pipes! Beneath the opening of each pipe was a long, slimy, brown, disgusting sludge of toilet paper and human waste stuck to the hillside oozing into the creek on the valley floor below. I stood and stared at the scene before me in disbelief until my husband and I looked at each other and he said sarcastically, "Well . . . isn't that just lovely?" I was speechless. We turned away and silently walked home.

The following Monday, late in the afternoon as I was preparing dinner, I heard the familiar sound of my husband's little VW coming up the driveway. Nothing else in the world sounds quite like a VW Beetle. Moments later he came into the house, red-faced, his shirt soaked in sweat. That day had been sunny, 98 degrees, horribly humid and VW Beetles didn't come with air conditioning. To make matters worse, Fred's Beetle was black which basically turned it into a black, bubble-shaped oven. As he entered, I greeted him with an ice-cold gin and tonic I had already made while he was walking from his car to the house and he said in a huff, "Well . . . I found out another wonderful thing about West Virginia today!" I told him to go change out of his sweaty clothes, rinse off, cool off, and then tell me about it over a drink. We always had a cocktail or three when he got home from work and talked about the day before having dinner, and in the summer, gin and tonic was the ticket! Moments later, we sat down with fresh gin and tonics and Fred explained to me what else he had learned about West Virginia. When Fred had gotten to work that morning, he had contacted a childhood friend of his that had become a public-school teacher in Maryland and asked him if he had any information about West Virginia public schools, specifically Kanawha County, WV. The answer was not good, not good at all. For obvious reasons, generally speaking, I'll just say that what Fred found out was that nationally, out of all 50 states, West Virginia public schools, at that time, ranked considerably below average, much worse than Baltimore City public schools. That was the last straw. We knew we couldn't stay in Charleston, West Virginia.

So . . . there we were, in a comfy little bungalow, with a wonderful landlord, beautiful mountain scenery, peace and quiet, Fred in a good job making great money, our son delighted with his room, his new neighborhood friends, and the natural playground all around him, except, there was raw human waste dumping into a creek a half-mile away producing excrementitious air and swarms of black flies, chemical plants ten miles away spewing toxic gasses into the air we were breathing and way below average public schools. The cons way overshadowed the pros.

We were experiencing firsthand what is known as a "life lesson". Those age-old sayings like "Look before you leap" or "All that glitters is not gold" exist for a very good reason. In our naivete', happiness in Fred's new job, and the pretty picture we had painted in our minds of a bungalow in the mountains, we had failed to do any kind of extensive research of the area whatsoever. Trust me when I say it is prudent to learn absolutely as much as possible about any area before you commit to living there.

Nevertheless, Fred and I were always inclined to believe that fortune favors the bold, the prepared, the willing, and that one should search for the silver lining even in the darkest of clouds. Dreams can and do come true, and just when you least expect it, opportunity may come knocking, provided you are listening and are willing to take immediate action.

Having unequivocally made the decision that we were moving out of Charleston, Fred and I got busy immediately. I began organizing all of our belongings for packing right away. We didn't know where we were going yet or where Fred was going to work, but I knew we were leaving. Why wait? I learned when I was very young to get things done when I had the chance. Life has a way of interrupting the best-laid plans and more often than not, you can find yourself wishing you'd done things when you had the chance! My husband, ever the skilled problem solver with a tentative plan already forming in his mind, went into action the very next day with a series of phone calls. His first call was to Baltimore Display, the commercial, interior decorating and design company in downtown Baltimore that had offered him a job just a year before. The owner of Baltimore Display was absolutely thrilled that Fred called and asked him when he could start. Being very good at your job is definitely an asset! Problem #1 solved. Now, all we had to do was find a house to rent within commuting distance to Fred's new job in Baltimore and close to a good elementary school.

The following Saturday, as Freddy and I were enjoying the afternoon with Anne North, Fred was sitting at our kitchen table making phone calls to real estate agencies for information about rentals near Baltimore. Anne was absolutely crushed that we were moving, so we made every effort to spend as much time as possible with her while we could. We had made such good friends with her. In a short time, we had grown rather close. We'd had a lot of good times together and she adored Freddy immensely. She even asked us, kidding, of course, if we could leave Freddy with her. That was definitely the most difficult part of leaving Charleston, leaving Anne. Her husband had died many years before and she had been rather lonely. She had told us many times that having us as neighbors in North Park was one of the happiest times of her life. You would have thought we were the kids and grandson she never had. Anne was one of the most wonderful people we ever met as well, and we missed her for a very long time afterward. She was always one of our fondest memories.

When Freddy and I returned from visiting with Anne, we walked in and Fred was still seated at the kitchen table. I closed the door behind me, and Fred looked at me, his elbow on the table, head cocked to one side, cheek resting on the palm of his hand, eyes twinkling, grinning at me like a cat that ate the canary!

Remember the quaint little cabin in the woods that I spoke of earlier in my story? The cabin Fred's friend Vivian Smith rented that I immediately fell in love with? On a whim, really, not expecting it to be so lucky, Fred had called Mr. Mylander while Freddy and I had been visiting with Anne North that afternoon to see if the cabin that Vivian had rented was by some miracle vacant, and it was! Being the kind man that he was, Mr. Mylander agreed to rent it to Fred over the phone and told him we could move in at our earliest convenience. Miracles DO happen!

My husband was a smart, practical man that planned ahead, always leaving his options open and always tried to lay the groundwork for potential opportunities in the future.

Even though I had been sort of dreaming out loud that day back in '64 and Fred had looked at me with raised eyebrows and asked me if I had a fever, he knew that I had fallen completely in love with the place that very day and to actually live in it would be a dream come true for me. The seed of that dream was planted in Fred's mind that day and he never forgot it. I never knew until many years later but because I had been so enchanted with Joyce Lane that day years ago when we had visited Vivian that Fred had asked her for the phone number of the owner, Mr. Mylander, and had called him shortly after to introduce himself and explain to him how much I had adored the cabin and to express his interest in renting it in the future. Fred had contacted Mr. Mylander several times over the years to inquire about that little cabin. My husband was a practical man that always planned ahead, leaving as many options open as possible to lay the groundwork for taking advantage of potential opportunities in the future.

The joy in our new good fortune would run into an ugly obstacle on the following Monday morning when Fred went to work and attempted to give his boss two weeks' notice. To make a long story short, his boss went ballistic. His boss screamed at him, literally, "Are you trying to kill me? "He had hired Fred to manage all of the display-related operations in the entire store. Looking back on it, Fred and I both understood why his boss was so upset after paying his airfare, picking him up at the airport in a limo, and giving him a great salary only to have him give notice four months later. Nevertheless, such is life, and it can turn on a dime. Unfortunately, his boss took it a lot worse than we thought and we soon found out he had quite a bit of influence in town. When we started trying to schedule a moving van, we thought it was a very strange coincidence that every moving company in town was booked for the rest of the month. Come to find out, Fred's employer owned half of the businesses in town, including some of the moving companies. Fred found out from a coworker that out of spite, the big boss had called every moving company in town and told them to refuse Fred's business. Luckily, the very same coworker knew of another moving company just outside of town and outside of his employer's sphere of influence.

We had drinks and dinner with Anne North one last time and said our goodbyes. There was a lot of hugging and some tears, but she wished us well and thanked us for our friendship.

The next morning as we drove out of North Park with the moving van right behind us, it was a very bittersweet moment. I looked over at Anne's big, beautiful house surrounded by her lovely lawns and beautiful gardens and I thought of all the people, places, and things in my life I had loved that I had to leave behind out of necessity in order to move on with my own life.

So often in life is joy accompanied by sorrow.

CHAPTER 10

JOYCE LANE

．．．．．．．．．．．．．．．．．．．．．．

Late in the afternoon, almost eight hours after leaving Charleston, Fred turned his VW Beetle onto Joyce Lane. I can only think of one way to describe how I felt at that very moment. It was like coming home. I just knew it; this is where I was meant to live. Even though I had not seen it for almost seven years I remembered Joyce Lane as if I had seen it only days before. I had a permanent vision in my mind. My heart swelled at the sight! To me, it was simply paradise and I reveled in the splendor of it all. On either side of the lane were several beautiful horses in big green pastures behind old, weathered split rail fences. Beyond the pastures all around us was a dense forest. The smells of sweet honeysuckle and green grass filled the air. Songbirds and butterflies flew about, and a constant chorus emanated from the cicadas in the trees. For a moment I was afraid that it might all be just a beautiful dream. I was more excited than a child on a roller coaster for the first time as we turned onto the dirt driveway that led up a hill to the little cabin of my dreams that was now ours. As we reached the top of the drive the cabin came into view and my dreamlike state became a wonderful, palpable reality.

Freddy had been a little sad about leaving Charleston but, after he climbed out of the backseat of the VW and looked around for a few moments at his new surroundings, he turned to Fred and me, a big smile lighting up his little face. That was an immediate relief for Fred and me, I can tell you. We had expected to have a sad little boy on our hands for a time. Fred and I were thrilled at the good fortune of acquiring a rental home in such a gorgeous, wooded area but, four-year olds don't always adapt so quickly or understand the benefits of such a move. Freddy has always been a country boy at heart anyway, just like his parents. He still is. He has never lived in a city, to this day. He still says, "I gotta live near woods or beach, one or the other."

Ours was the first of three small wood cabins, built side by side, a couple of hundred feet apart, along a dirt driveway. Mr. Mylander had purchased three "cabin kits" sometime in the late 1940s and had them assembled on top of this hill to use as rentals. It's my understanding that each of these kit cabins was designed to last about 50 years. I think the fact that mine is still standing in 2020 is a testament to the quality and craftsmanship that must have been put into them. Aside from the cinder block and cement basements, these were honest to goodness genuine wood cabins with interlocking, tongue and groove, pre-cut solid hardwood planks, inside and out.

Within a few days, we had the place set up to our liking, for the time being anyway, and began exploring our surroundings. The neighborhood of Joyce Lane is situated right on the east shore of the Severn River, just a few miles north of Annapolis as the crow flies.

Knowing that a beach was just a short walk from the house, the three of us, with both dogs in tow, set off down the driveway to find it. The only paved road was Joyce Lane itself. All the others in the neighborhood were dirt, gravel, and/or oyster shells, with decades of tire marks worn into them.

Along the sides of the dirt road leading to the river were lush green meadows and a few old but well-kept, brightly painted cottages with real wooden shutters, quaint gardens, oyster shell driveways. It truly was a country scene from bygone days. Were it not for the sixties and seventies model cars in the driveways, one could imagine it was decades earlier.

To me, the beach was glorious! Fred had seen beaches in Maryland, of course, but Freddy and I had not. Freddy surveyed the whole scene with cheerful curiosity. I was absolutely dazzled! The Severn River sparkled like a big wavy diamond-studded blanket under the morning sun and was alive with sailboats, water skiers, and seagulls. A hundred yards or so from the beach was an old man and a young boy in a rowboat fishing. It was picturesque as a postcard. After smoggy, smelly Charleston, and noisy, concrete downtown Baltimore, this was just Heaven on Earth. To the right of us about a hundred yards down the beach was a long wooden pier with a rather large boathouse on the end of it where Mr. Mylander kept his big, 60-foot-long cabin cruiser. He had already told us when we rented the cabin that we were more than welcome to use the pier whenever we liked. Fred and Freddy would catch their share of fish and crabs from that pier in the years that followed. We had our own fresh-caught Perch and steamed blue crabs for dinner many times in the summers there. Fred had come prepared wearing swim trunks and carried Freddy out into the water to introduce him to his first swimming lesson. It amazed me how fearless Freddy was! Within an hour Fred had him dogpaddling in place. Before the water got too cold as the summer ended, Fred had him swimming underwater! The kid took to water like a fish! Not me. I am no water baby, never have been. I had never been swimming in my life. I'm a pretty tough broad but I get a little girly when it comes to water with living creatures in it. The only water I'd ever seen as a child were the canals in Holland and no one swam in them, ever! I'd been to the French Riviera once in my twenties but the only thing I used the beach for there was tanning. Aside from our beautiful beach, we were surrounded by 350 acres of privately owned untouched forest with miles and miles of horse paths that we had permission to hike on. That forest still looks exactly the way it did in 1970. I'll tell you why later on. When the weather got too cold for the beach, we spent much of our free time walking in the woods. It wasn't long at all until Freddy and the dogs saw it as their own private kingdom, and just like he did in Charleston, in time, Freddy made a point to introduce himself to every one of the neighbors. He would just knock on the door and introduce himself! The neatest thing about Joyce Lane to this day is that no one knew it was there! It was like a really well-kept secret.

The property on either side of Joyce Lane stopped right up to the 50-foot-high embankment the railroad had been built on. It wasn't visible from the road on the other side, B & A Boulevard. It still isn't.

We met the neighbors a couple of days after we arrived. Next door in the second cabin was a woman named Anne and her teenage daughter, also named Anne, and in the third cabin was a retired couple, Ernie and Martha Bruegger. Anne and her daughter moved a few weeks later so we never got to know them very well.

The couple that moved in after Anne left, we did get to know very well, Gene and Letty. We were good friends with them for many, many years. Gene was a biologist and ornithologist working with the Smithsonian in Washington DC and Letty was a child psychologist working for the Maryland public school system. We became very close and spent a great deal of time together over the years. It wasn't long before we were celebrating birthdays and holidays together, either in our cabin or their cabin. We took turns. They liked Freddy right away. They didn't have any children of their own, but they had a lot of fun with Freddy over the years. Gene's knowledge of biology meant Freddy could satisfy his curiosities about all the wonders of nature that now surrounded him with questions like, why are leaves green? Why do birds sing? How long do trees live and "Mr. Gene", as Freddy called him, would kindly do his best to explain the answers to Freddy's many questions about nature in a way that he would understand. Letty, being employed in the school system, told us that our son had a considerably above-average vocabulary and was unusually articulate for a five-year-old.

Fred didn't have much time to relax in our new home. He had taken a week off to move so, after the actual move and set up I think he was left with two days to actually relax a bit. His new job at Baltimore Display was waiting for him eagerly. I remember wishing he could have taken a month off to stay home with me and decorate our new place, landscape it, go shopping for plants, you know . . . fun stuff! Alas, reality hardly ever works that way. The blare of the alarm clock at six am Monday morning came way too quickly. Fred rolled out of bed, stopped at the bathroom on his way to the kitchen to turn on the already prepared coffee pot. The drive to Baltimore Display was only 30 minutes in those days. With the doubling in population, it's easily twice that now. Fred was up for work at 6:00 am every morning for a good reason. He needed time to get ready for work. My husband was always mindful of his appearance and always left the house looking like a million bucks. He always said that you only get one chance to make a good first impression. Every day of his life he went to work clean-shaven, smelling of Vetiver, shoes shined, cufflinks, tie pin, pants pressed, shirt ironed. I was very proud of my husband and always made sure his clothes were ready in his closet, cleaned, ironed, and pressed. He was a handsome man, a real head-turner. Women took notice of him, that's for sure. It never bothered me that other women noticed my husband. I always took it as a compliment.

The next fifteen months were rather pleasant, for the most part. Life at Joyce Lane was, if I may steal a quote from Dickens, the best of times and the worst of times. Although it was the kind of home both Fred and I had always dreamed of, it would be yet another time in our lives and place where we would experience great joy as well as great sorrow and tribulation. Then again, I've never known a home that didn't.

We became very close friends with Gene and Letty next door, spending a great deal of time with them especially for birthdays and holidays. It was a friendship that lasted for many years. We took care of each other in many ways over the years. We had a lot of fun in the spring and summer of 1971 landscaping and putting in flower beds all around the house. Fred was at work Monday through Friday of course but he made every effort to make every minute of Saturday and Sunday count.

Also in 1971, I discovered that I was pregnant with my second child. We soon found out that it was a girl and we decided to name her Catherine when she was born. My pregnancy went very well, and Catherine and I were perfectly healthy every day of it. Christmas came and I was big as a house. Still, I decorated the house and made my Christmas cookies. I still cooked Christmas dinner for us and Princess. Fred did the turkey, as usual. I never changed my daily routine or limited my activity one bit during my pregnancy. I did turn forty that year, but my doctor insisted that I was healthy as a horse and the baby was fit as a fiddle! The day came in March of 1972 that the labor pains began, and Fred rushed me to the hospital. When I got to the hospital I sat in a room in labor and delivery by myself for the longest time, which I thought was odd. I remember thinking, "Where are the nurses?" Then I began to feel an odd warm wetness down there and reached my hand down to investigate. I pulled my hand back and it was covered with blood! I knew that wasn't good. I yelled for someone to come but for the longest time, no one did. Finally, after sitting in my own blood for, I don't know how long a nurse and doctor showed up and of course, became immediately alarmed. I was rushed into a delivery room but . . . it was too late. My baby girl was dead. Fred and I were told that Catherine had kicked the umbilical cord loose and it had wrapped around her neck. We never contacted a lawyer or demanded an investigation. We were too grief-stricken to think straight at the time. More than likely we could have had one hell of a lawsuit on our hands given the amount of time I was left unattended, but we never pursued it. No amount of money can ever replace a lost baby anyway. Possibly with the proper care and attention to me, the attending OB/GYN could have saved my Catherine but, who knows? One of our neighbors was pregnant with a little girl at the same time as I was. She and her husband decided to name their daughter Catherine in my honor. Freddy played with their two boys, and we had gotten to know the family very well. The next few months were somber, to say the least, but eventually, we came to terms with our loss. Life goes on no matter what the tragedy. We still had each other and a wonderful son to care for, so we took comfort in that and moved on. Unfortunately, tragedy is a part of life. It's necessary to move on. There really isn't a choice.

Sometime later that year, I finally had the time to get my American citizenship. Even though I had married an American and had permanent status, it was important to me personally to become a full-fledged American citizen. I love this country. Ever since I was a little girl and saw the American GI's that came to Europe to defeat Hitler, I thought the USA was the greatest country on Earth and I still feel that way. I always will. I studied all the material I had to diligently with Fred's help and passed the first time. I've always been from that day forward very proud to be an American citizen.

Baltimore Display was keeping Fred very busy. Fred was their top-selling Commercial Interior Decorator as well as a designer and draftsman. He had a very expensive draft board with which he would draw perfectly the floor plan of a whole store, with every measurement to scale. You could say he was a genius at what he did. Fred could walk into a store, any store, walk around in it for maybe an hour or two and he knew what was wrong with it. He was able to create and redesign the whole store, draft it and implement his design with their crew. Better yet Baltimore Display sold absolutely everything that was used in retail and department stores display in those days, I mean everything, from mannequins to fixtures, paint, wallpapers, Christmas trees, felt reindeer, silk flowers . . . anything! So not only did he sell a design, but he also sold everything to do it with. Every, and I mean every store Fred designed during his career increased their sales dramatically, every single one. Never did a store decrease in sales after Fred designed it, not one. There was a shoe store in Cumberland, MD that doubled their sales after Fred designed their store. They called him back every time they needed anything, such as wanting to make a seasonal change. Most stores did that in those days, change the design and decor to match the season. By the second year, Fred worked for Baltimore Display their income skyrocketed! Through the '70s and '80s, Baltimore Display was one of the top display companies in the country. They went out of business shortly after he retired.

His job routinely required that he travel out of town with each season throughout the year, sometimes for a week at a time. He had clients scattered all over Maryland, Pennsylvania, West Virginia, and Virginia.

For my younger readers, try to imagine doing Fred's job with no internet, no cell phones, no smartphones, no email, no GPS devices. If he had to make a phone call, he pulled off the interstate and looked for a phone booth. If he needed directions, he used a state road map. In order to be successful, he had to travel to and work with his clients in person several times a year. With no internet, he couldn't email photos or instructions, or designs. He had to physically be there. For that very reason, Baltimore Display gave him a company car of his choosing, and it was always a Chevy station wagon, preferably an Impala. He had to carry all different kinds of display samples with him when he traveled, big cases filled with all kinds of different things used to decorate the interiors of all different kinds of stores. Fred always said he was a Chevy man. Our friend Don called himself a Ford man. I didn't get it at the time. I figured it was just an American guy thing. My vehicle was a black with gold trim, 1965, Raleigh three-speed touring bicycle and, that was good enough for me for many years, although I did always like the look of Volkswagen Karmen Ghia's. I had never driven a car and was in no hurry to do so.

One of the best things from the time we left Charleston until September of 1971 was that Freddy wasn't in school yet. I had four whole seasons to spend with my son in the wooded splendor of Joyce Lane, and we had a ball! It was one of the happiest times of my life. Freddy and I and our two dogs, Leksia II and Jason, explored as much of the forest and the miles of trails as we could, even going off-trail. In the summer we spent many days at the beach, especially on the weekends when Fred was off. Fred always loved that beach, especially catching crabs. We had many crab feasts with Gene and Letty with the crabs Fred caught in the Severn River. It was a glorious time, and we were all so happy. Freddy was instinctively an outdoor kid. He never showed any fear and with Gene next door he learned so much about the world around him.

He'd learned that black snakes weren't poisonous so one day he came home with one! I was in the kitchen, and I heard him come in and say, "Mommy look!" I was speechless. There was my five-year-old son, standing in my dining room, holding a 4-foot-long black snake. I guess he saw the shock on my face because he comforted me and said, "Don't worry Mommy, these snakes are nice." I managed to ask him to take it back outside and let it go, which he did. Frogs, toads, beetles, millipedes, caterpillars, butterflies . . . Freddy was always bringing critters home but, he never ever harmed any of them. Gene had taught him how to handle them and had explained to him why it was so important not to harm them. Freddy had an affinity for living things anyway. He'd been surrounded by them when he was still in diapers. He learned a lot from Gene in the years we lived there, and in the years that followed.

I was definitely in my element, where I had wanted to be for many years. I had a wonderful home, the ideal husband, a beautiful child and, I was head over heels in love with all three. I was perfectly happy to be a wife, a mother, and a homemaker. I took pride in my home, my cooking, and my gardens. When the holidays came, I made sure my house looked like a Christmas wonderland. I cooked every bit of Thanksgiving dinner from scratch myself every year in my little kitchen. In fact, I have always cooked everything from scratch, I still do. I've never eaten or served processed garbage. My husband and my son had a home-cooked meal every night. Their clothes were clean, and my home was spotless.

The women's lib movement was a big deal in the 1970s. Sometimes when Fred and I attended a party or were out with friends somewhere, I would get confronted by women that heard I was a housewife. They would want to know why I didn't work for a living the way my husband was or did my husband not allow me to work? I had no problem setting these ladies straight. I told them that I didn't get married and have a son to go out and work full time and then chuck a couple of TV dinners on the table when I got home. I told them; I'd been a working girl making damn good money too. I told them I'd been a restaurant manager, bartender, and model for ten years and personally, I felt it was overrated, which was true. "Been there, done that", I said. I wanted to be a wife, mother, and homemaker. I told them that if I had wanted a career, I would not have had a child. I wanted to be home to greet my child when he came home from school. I wanted to take care of my wonderful husband when he came home after a hard day at work because I appreciated what he was doing all day. I had no interest in that rat race. I wanted my home to be comfortable and clean for my husband and son. A lot of women may get annoyed with me over this but, if a woman does an exemplary job of being a wife, mother, and homemaker it really is a full-time job!

Understand, I'm not trying to insult working women, not at all, but I have never met a working wife and Mom that did what I did. I didn't just cook and clean and do laundry. Just those three things aren't that hard to keep up with. No, I did A LOT more than that. In the spring and summer, I was busy with gardening. I had beautiful gardens all around the house. I still do. Someone came from Annapolis Magazine one year to photograph them! I rode my bike to the grocery store. It was only two miles away. Our house became the meeting place for all of our friends several times a year for birthdays and the Christmas season and I made everything for our guests from scratch, from appetizers to dinner to dessert!

I have cooked for ten, twenty, even thirty people many times. I used to spend several days getting ready for Thanksgiving. I spent several days decorating for Christmas, inside and out. Every year ALL of our friends got homemade gifts. It became a tradition. I baked ten different kinds of Christmas cookies. I baked a total of at least 400 cookies, 2 dozen for each of about fifteen friends. I also gave them homemade fruit cake and homemade cranberry sauce. I volunteered at Freddy's school many times to be a chaperone on field trips. Spring cleaning, the leaves in the fall, etc., etc. I had something to do pretty much every day. There was NO WAY I could have done all the things I wanted to do at home if I had a 9 to 5 job. Impossible.

I figured when my son graduated high school and went off to college or whatever, Fred and I would probably make a life change of some kind. Maybe we'd travel or start our own business, who knows? Fred had told me many of his dreams and ideas for us after Freddy would leave home and go out on his own. Life is a series of choices. For the next 15 years or so this was one of mine. Throughout the 70s and 80s, I knew a lot of married women that had kids and worked full time and, (unless they had a maid), and some did, usually, their homes were a mess, their kids were alone or with a sitter all afternoon after school. When the weekends came, more often than not they were simply tired or more interested in relaxing or doing something they enjoyed rather than spending quality time with their husbands and kids. If there is a way to make that scenario work, more power to you but, personally, I've seen very few situations where it did. Call me "old school", that's fine.

I've ruffled feathers many times in my life just by simply speaking my mind. Don't EVER be afraid to speak your mind if it's good and true! You'll meet people in life that will feel the need to demean you just because you do or think something different than they do, especially if it is against the status quo. I just wanted to put that little tip in while I was thinking about it. I've seen too many people afraid to speak.

One thing I think many parents would agree on is that parents have maybe 10 or 12 years to spend with their children before they become teenagers. When kids become teenagers, they become a lot more interested in their friends and spend more and more time with them instead of Mom and Dad. Life is a series of snapshots, small windows of time, and short periods of joy that come and go. Many of them, when they're gone, they're gone forever. You cannot relive your youth. You can't relive your children's childhoods. You never know when you may be experiencing a wonderful moment that will never show itself again, so I think it's imperative that we live in the moment and cherish it. This is not a rehearsal. These moments come but some of them, a lot of them actually, when they go, they go forever. We only get one shot at life, that's it. If you look at life in those terms, every day is important.

Freddy's first day of school came and it broke my heart . . . for a few minutes anyway. I walked him down the driveway to wait for the school bus. He was so excited he was about to burst. When the bus stopped and the doors opened, Freddy ran up the steps into the bus and went directly to a seat grinning ear to ear, without so much as a "Bye Mommy" or even a wave! The doors closed, the bus drove off and I started to cry! My baby boy wasn't even the least bit sad to be leaving me all day! I turned and walked back to the house, sniffling the whole way.

It was silly of me, of course. He was simply a very excited five-year-old boy. Six hours later he came into the house, "Mommmmyyyyyy! I'm hoooome," followed by "Guess what?" For the next hour, Freddy was an unstoppable chatterbox about school. He just loved school. He always did, all the way through high school. He didn't love every class, but he loved school. Even in his senior year in high school when he only needed a few more classes to graduate and could have gone a half-day, he took a full course load, including a psychology class that gave him college credit.

Yes, I was living the dream, my dream. I was living in a bright, sunny part of my life with the family and home, and surroundings I had always dreamed of. We even had wonderful neighbors! Unfortunately, for every bright and sunny time of life, there are inevitably storm clouds of some kind looming on the horizon, sooner or later. That's just life.

One day, late in 1971, I was in the kitchen and heard Fred's car pull into the driveway. I heard the car door close but, several moments later he still hadn't come into the house, so I looked from the kitchen window to see what he was doing. He was standing by the driver's side door of his car, head bent down, eyes closed, one hand on the top of the car, and his other hand clenched in a fist at his chest. I walked outside and asked him what was wrong. He looked up at me right away, shook his head, and said it was just indigestion, some heartburn from lunch, he guessed. I knew Fred liked his occasional cheeseburger with raw onions or Polish sausage with raw onions and spicy mustard, spicy fried chicken, or pizza with crushed red peppers all over it. I cooked good healthy food at home but, I'll admit we didn't always eat perfectly when we were out and Fred had a propensity for junk food for lunch in those days, so I didn't think anything of him having heartburn from lunch. He was only 38 years old, in great shape, and a perfect weight. The possibility of a heart condition never occurred to me, or him! Looking back, I recall Fred complaining of heartburn or indigestion a little more than usual over the next several months.

The next summer my younger sister, Anne, came to visit from Holland for several weeks. She was simply astounded. She thought Joyce Lane, our home, and the forest surrounding it were the most beautiful she'd ever seen. She looked around wide-eyed and asked me if we had become rich?! In Holland, a house like ours out in the Dutch countryside would cost a fortune and the owner would almost certainly be wealthy. She had a great time. We took her to the beach, partied with Letty and Gene next door, went shopping, went to DC, etc. Then, one afternoon while Anne was there and Fred was out of town for a few days on business at the navy base exchange in Norfolk, Virginia the phone rang. Fred had suffered a heart attack in his motel room and was in the ICU in Williamsburg, VA. A heart attack?! I was simply dumbfounded! At the time I wasn't exactly sure what that meant but, I knew it was damn serious, and all I knew at that moment was I had to get to Williamsburg right away! I didn't drive. Letty and Gene were not home yet, so I ran over to our other neighbors, the Brueggers, and told them where Fred was. Martha offered to take me to Williamsburg right away. I went home, began packing an overnight bag, and told Anne she'd have to watch Freddy for a few days 'til I got back.

She panicked and in Dutch screamed, "Wat? Ik weet niet wat ik moet doen!", which basically means "WHAT? I don't know how to do that!" My sister Anne never had any children, never cooked, never drove, she couldn't boil water. She spoke almost no English. Anne was good at having boyfriends and then husbands and being taken out to dinner . . . getting flowers, stuff like that. I told her, in Dutch, "Anne, give him a bowl of cereal in the morning, make him a sandwich and put it in his lunch box with a piece of fruit to take to school for lunch, make him something for dinner, make sure he brushes his teeth and put him to bed at 9:00 o'clock . . . that's it, it's that simple, OK?!"

I went to Freddy's room, kissed him goodbye, and told him I'd be back in a day or two, and to please take care of his Tante Annie. He was only six then. He knew something was up. I could tell by the look on his face that he sensed the stress and fear in me no matter how much I tried to hide it. I told him to be a good boy, take care of Tante Annie, show her what to do and I'll be back soon, something like that. Martha told me when she got back home, she would tell Letty and Gene next door what happened. My son was in good hands. Annie might have given him Oreos for dinner for all I know but I knew no harm would come to him. I knew Letty would take over as soon as she got home anyway and, she did. Actually, it was more like Letty and Freddy watched over Anne.

It seemed to take forever to get to Williamsburg! For three hours I sat in the passenger seat of Martha's pastel green '69 Mercury Marquis with a lump in my throat so painful I could barely swallow. It was 1972. There were no cell phones! I couldn't call from the car and find out how my husband was doing. It was the longest three hours of my life. Upon arrival, Martha waited while I ran inside to the reception desk and frantically gave them my husband's name and asked where he was. A kind nurse approached me, and gently putting her hands on my shoulders, and said, "Mrs. Brauer . . . he is alive and in the ICU." He was alive! Every muscle in my body relaxed a little and the lump in my throat went away. I was so happy he was alive I started to tear up. For three hours my mind had tortured me with the possibility that I might get there, and he'd be gone. What would I do without Fred?! So, when that nurse told me he was alive a rush of intense joy engulfed me for maybe a minute. Then reality seeped back in. Reality has a way of doing that. He was in the Intensive Care Unit. I'd been in the USA long enough to know that meant they were trying to keep him alive. He wasn't going anywhere, and neither was I. I went back out to Martha and told her the news and she knew right away she was driving home alone. No way was I going anywhere. I stood outside the hospital for a moment and tried to collect myself. I had calls to make. I looked at my watch. Letty and Gene were most likely home. I walked over to the phone booths outside, dropped some change on the shelf, and dialed. Letty answered. This is what true friends are. The second she heard Fred had a heart attack and was in ICU in Williamsburg, she said "Say no more, Toosje we got this here, don't give it another thought!" I had a six-year-old, two dogs, and a not-so-capable sister at home. This was not a small favor I was asking. I went back inside to the ICU, spoke to the doctor, got all the information I could. By this time, it was late. I think it was getting close to midnight. There was no way I could see Fred tonight. I went back to the phone booths.

Fred had a client that had also become a close friend of ours. Fred met her on the base in Norfolk working with her. Her name was Lizabeth Larson. She was a salty old southern gal that still swore that the North may have won the war, but the South won all the battles! Lizabeth lived in Seaford, not far from Williamsburg. I called and she came and got me right away. I stayed with her the whole time I was there, and she took me back and forth to the hospital for every visit I could make.

Fred did finally leave the ICU many days later. I can't remember how many days but I'm pretty sure it was more than a week. Fred was not allowed to drive, work or go anywhere near stairs for three months. His station wagon was still at the motel, but he couldn't drive it. Meanwhile, while Letty was taking care of things at our home, Gene took a bus from Annapolis to Williamsburg to get Fred's car keys. Lizabeth drove Gene to the motel in Norfolk. He got Fred's station wagon and drove us all home.

Think about this.

Four of our friends dropped whatever they were doing . . . instantly, without question or hesitation to help us. Letty called out of work for over a week, told her boss she had an emergency and would be back as soon as possible. Martha, who was in her early 70's at the time, drove 400 miles in one night. Lizabeth put me up, fed me and, drove me sixty miles every day I could visit Fred. Gene called out of work for three days, bought a bus ticket, rode a bus 200 miles, and then drove us all 200 miles home.

Do you have friends like that? Because if you do, cherish them. Be good to them. Believe me, friends like that don't enter your life that often. And when they are in trouble, you'd better drop what you're doing to help them as well. That's the true meaning of friendship. That's love.

My sister went home two weeks after Fred got home. Fred's discharge instructions were no work for three months, no driving, no stairs, no sex, no salt, no alcohol, no smoking, no anything. NO STRESS. No anger. He had several medications he had to take every day. I pulled out my trusty Raleigh three-speed bicycle. I had panniers for it, so I went to the pharmacy, the grocery store, the bank, wherever I had to go.

All went well for a few weeks or so, and he started feeling better, much better. He was looking and moving around like his old self again. He was still smoking though.

Over the next couple of weeks, he made a lot of business calls. His body language and manner began to resemble that of a man who'd never been sick a day in his life. I knew what was coming . . . and it did. He decided to go back to work several weeks before he was supposed to and without a word to me in advance told me had a trip to Norfolk in a few days. I couldn't argue with him. I didn't want him to get stressed or angry, so I decided to go with him. I insisted on that, and he agreed right away. He had heavy sample cases and several big heavy binders in the station wagon he wasn't supposed to lift. So, I did all the lifting. This lasted for a while. He spent a little more time working from home and making fewer trips. Still, every time he had a trip, I went with him, without question. I was learning his business a little bit in the process too.

Fred's oldest daughter came to watch Freddy quite often, sometimes Letty did. During one of our business trips, Letty even decided to take Freddy with her to Sarasota, Florida to visit her parents. I have to say, Letty and Gene really were indispensable at this time in our lives. They even agreed to become Freddy's godparents should anything happen to Fred and me while we were on the road handling Fred's business trips. It was the 70's and car crashes were more apt to be deadly back then than they are today. Speed limits were higher and safety features in cars were few compared to the vehicles of today.

The next year or so was rather uneventful. We enjoyed time with our friends, the holidays, in fact, 1973 was a nice year. It felt as if Fred had recovered. Fred's cardiac medication regimen and limited physical exertion seemed to be working until the spring of 1974 when Fred suffered his second heart attack, in a hotel outside of Norfolk while we were there again on Baltimore Display business. I dialed 911, the paramedics were there within minutes and Fred was taken to the ICU in Williamsburg, again. Hours later while doctors had stabilized Fred in the ICU and were deciding what course of action to take next, I was pacing the lobby, trying to figure out what to do next. I couldn't go into the ICU and see Fred, of course. I knew that Fred's client was due to meet him at our hotel at 10:00 am the next morning to finalize designs and fill out orders for a very large job to be done and it was already very late in the evening. A kind police officer approached me and told me had heard the 911 call over his scanner and asked me if I was the wife of the heart attack patient at the hotel. I said I was and introduced myself. He asked if there was any way he could help, and I told him I needed to get back to our motel. He offered me a ride and I graciously accepted! I was so tired and overwrought at that point any help was a blessing. Once again, my husband's life was in the balance and the fear of uncertainty haunted my every thought! The kind officer dropped me off at our motel and walked me to our room. I hugged him and thanked him, and he wished me the best of luck with Fred. I didn't sleep that night at all. Finally, around 7:00 am I stopped staring at the ceiling, and I got up showered, and dressed. I had absolutely no appetite, so breakfast was three cups of strong coffee and then I got ready for Fred's client. The client was there at 10:00 am sharp and after I explained what had happened to Fred and where he was I assured him that I was more than capable of concluding Fred's order for him. By this time, I had learned a great deal about Fred's business and was able to fill in for him for this particular meeting. Fred's client and I worked well into the afternoon on his order until we stopped for dinner. I had pizza delivered. We had dinner and a few drinks, after which we finalized the order and contract and the client left, but not before offering me a ride back to the hospital first thing in the morning. I accepted and thanked him and then called the hospital. Fred was stable but still critical and his doctors had certain procedures scheduled for him the very next day.

What they were I honestly cannot remember. It's difficult to recall all of the procedures Fred went through over so many years. I didn't sleep hardly at all that night either.

The next day Fred's client was there to pick me up bright and early and I spent the whole next day at the hospital. I was able to see him for a very short time later that afternoon, but he was so drugged he wasn't even really aware that I was there. I'll never forget the sight. It was like something out of a science fiction movie to me. My husband was covered with a conglomeration of tubes and wires and medical tape. Machines were beeping and buzzing all around him. His skin was ghostly pale and as I stood there it was almost impossible to control my emotional feeling of dread. Were it not for the slight movement of his chest and the constant blip of the monitor behind him I could not have been certain he was alive.

Finally, Fred was allowed to go home . . . again, albeit with a long list of instructions. He was not to lift more than ten pounds, no stairs, no sex, no alcohol, no more smoking, etc. This time his two daughters came to get us and drive us home in Fred's station wagon. Fred was on a new regimen of medications and again, in the months that followed seemed to be doing well as long as he took it easy, and I traveled with him when necessary. This had been the second go around in the ICU, so I wasn't nearly as confident in the future as before. I hoped for the best but was preparing myself mentally for the worst. Fred's oldest daughter, Deborah watched Freddy whenever we had to go out of town on business, which Fred did his best to make less and less.

All went pretty well until the late summer of 1974 when I got that dreaded phone call from Holland that my mother was on death's door. She had been diagnosed with colon cancer months before and, I had hoped for the best but knew better. I took the next flight to Holland and was there for nine weeks watching my mother slowly wither away. Cancer is a horrific fate. I hardly recognized her when I walked into her hospital room. She was so grateful that I was there that I couldn't even consider going home while she was still conscious and alert. I saw her every day that I was allowed to. Watching your parents die in such a horrible way is one of those things in life there is no way to prepare for. The sight of my once strong, vibrant, and gregarious Mother reduced to gray skin draped over bones was difficult to bear. Harder still was seeing her in such excruciating pain. There isn't enough morphine for that kind of pain. The last several days were the worst. The cancer advanced so rapidly and she moaned in agony most of the time. Finally, during a rare moment of calm, she looked at me, holding my hand, and told me to go home to Fred and Freddy. Medicine in Holland is a bit different than it is in the US. I got her doctor alone and begged him to do something for her to put an end to her misery. He looked into my eyes and knew exactly what I was asking. Since she was already on so much morphine, no one would ever question it. As I sat next to her bed holding her hand, her doctor put enough morphine in her IV to stop her heart. She smiled at me one last time as the morphine surged in her system and she slipped away quietly as I told her I loved her.

The next day as I was packing, my worthless Uncle showed up at my mother's house, flowers in hand. My Mother had not seen or heard from him in over a decade and he had the nerve to ask me where I was going and how I could leave before her funeral. Several times in my mother's life she could have used his help and he was never around. I snapped! I said, "She's dead, she doesn't need your sympathy now! You weren't there for her when she was alive so don't bother trying to be there now that she's dead!" I told him to take his flowers and get the hell out. I've never had any tolerance for phony sympathies and insincerity!

I called Fred and told him all of my flight information so he would know what time to pick me up at the airport. When the time came for Fred to pick me up at the airport, however, I wasn't there to be picked up. Of course, Fred was worried sick instantly. For hours and hours, Fred tried to find out what had happened to my flight. I can't imagine what was going through his mind. He was frantic I'm sure. I know I would have been. My flight from Amsterdam to Baltimore had been canceled and I had to board a puddle jumper from Amsterdam to London instead, then transfer immediately to a plane from London to New York. BWI had no record of my flight from Amsterdam to Baltimore being canceled. For half a day my husband had to contemplate what could have happened and hope for the best all the while wondering if my plane was at the bottom of the Atlantic Ocean. Finally, during my layover in New York, I had a chance to call him and tell him what had happened to my original flight, and he picked me up at BWI later that evening. When Fred finally saw me, he stared at me mouth agape. I was completely unaware until I looked at myself in the rearview mirror in his car. I looked haggard! My hair was unkempt and a dirty mess. I had huge black circles under my eyes and had forgotten all about putting on any makeup. When I got home the scale in the bathroom revealed that I had lost twenty-five pounds! I guess with all the stress of my mother's agony and dealing with family in Holland, I forgot to eat and take care of myself. The anguish of my mother's death was alleviated by the sight of my dear husband and my son! I was so glad to be home!

The rest of 1974 was nice. By this time, we had managed to make a few home improvements. Thanksgiving and Christmas were wonderful, and we hosted and went to several parties. Freddy was Zoro for Halloween and had a ball trick or treating. We had quite a bit of snow that winter and the three of us had fun playing in it when the county closed the schools for snow days. With Spring came the blooming of all the gardens I had worked so hard on. Azaleas, Impatiens, and Marigolds, butterflies, and honeybees brightened the air around our little house. It felt as if all was right in the world until 1975.

1975 was not a good year! Fred heart was struggling, and he collapsed a few times and was rushed to the hospital by ambulance. Each time he was stabilized and came home, sometimes with some new medication but, his doctors had begun talking about different options and the one they mentioned most was open-heart surgery.

An unscrupulous building contractor had spotted and targeted the property of Joyce Lane and made the Mylander family a lucrative offer for several acres of their property so he could build houses on it. When they flatly refused to sell him any, he vindictively reported them to the IRS. At the time, the Mylander family had dozens of acres of pastureland not really being used. This was subject to a pricey luxury tax that thus far they had avoided paying.

Not only were the Mylanders forced to sell a few acres they were also forced to raise the rent on every rental property they owned, including ours. By the end of that summer, our rent was going to double! Mr. Mylander was sick about it and apologized profusely but we understood he had no choice. In reporting him to the IRS, that greedy prick of a building contractor had increased Mr. Mylander's property tax by tens of thousands of dollars each year!

Unfortunately, we got this news well into the summer, the middle of July.

There was no way we could afford a doubling of the rent in those days. We had to move. Letty and Gene as well as the Brueggers decided to move as well. A mortgage at that time was much cheaper than the rent we would have had to pay. Letty and Gene found a home in Arnold. The Brueggers went to West Virginia, and we began searching. Letty and Gene moved before we did so one day before they left, we all had a party to say goodbye to Joyce Lane together. We all sat out in the driveway between our houses and got stinking drunk, starting with gin and tonics and then polishing off a whole case of champagne, drinking well into the night.

To us, it was the end of a small but memorable era. We would miss it for a very long time!

CHAPTER 11

CIRCLE RD

....

Once we had reluctantly accepted the heartbreaking fact that we had to vacate our little dream cabin in the forest that had been our home for four years, one look at the calendar and we quickly acknowledged the urgency of our situation. It was late summer, almost August if I remember correctly. Besides the fact that the substantial increase in rent was way more than we could afford in 1975, even for a month, Freddy was supposed to be starting the fourth grade in a matter of weeks, which meant we had to either find a comparable rental close to Freddy's current school within a month or, find a school that was acceptable with an affordable rental close to it. Over the next week, the search for comparable rentals nearby was completely unsuccessful. Every rental we looked at in the area far exceeded our budget at the time. Mr. Mylander had never been very concerned about the rent for the cabins. He saw them as nothing more than a little residual income, so he not only charged much less rent than most, but he also never bothered to raise it either. The $250 a month rent that we had been paying for four years was cheap, way below the average rent for that area. Arnold is a desirable location being that it is only a few miles from downtown Annapolis. It was clear that we were going to have to expand our search further and cheaper than Arnold. Since Fred was secure in his job, had impeccable credit and Freddy would be in school for another ten years, we decided to buy, so I called a realtor. Fred and I had one primary concern that outweighed all others, good schools. I simply asked the realtor if she could find us a house, we could afford monthly that was close to the best school she could find and I left it at that. She got back to me quickly in just a few days and told me she thought she had a winner for us. Just 12 miles north of us, there was a new, 3 bedroom, 1 bath rancher for sale, located only one mile and a half from the newest public-school complex in Maryland on Mountain Rd in Pasadena. All three schools were within a few minutes' walking distance of each other, Bodkin Elementary, Windmill Middle, and Chesapeake High school. All three schools had been constructed between 1970 and 1976, very new indeed. Fred had to go to work the next day, so I was tasked with going with the realtor to check out the schools and houses and then make a decision if need be. I asked the realtor to see the schools first. I was absolutely stunned! I had never seen such gorgeous schools in my life! Freddy's first school, Jones Elementary, had pretty much the same institutional look as the Catholic schools I had attended with the polished concrete floors, concrete block walls, uncomfortable hardwood desks and chairs, no air conditioning, ceiling fans, old school steam radiators, and very sparse landscaping. These new schools were bright and colorful with wall-to-wall carpet, central air, cushioned chairs in the classrooms, bean bag chairs in the libraries, huge gymnasiums, cold water fountains, plush green ball fields surrounded by lush shrubbery and benches, sound dampening walls, science labs, big auditoriums, cafeterias with big, shiny kitchens, art studios, wood shops and the high school even had a full garage where students could work on cars!

You're probably laughing at me but, compared to the dismal and cold Catholic school I went to as a child, these schools were like . . . resorts! It was just another small example of what I guess one might refer to as a bit of culture shock. There had been numerous things in the US that had astounded me since I had arrived in '62.

Having seen all I needed of the schools, the realtor and I got back into her car and proceeded to the house that was for sale. This was less impressive, MUCH LESS! We pulled into the driveway of 211 Circle Rd. and got out. Standing before me was the ugliest little box of a house on the ugliest little piece of property I think I've ever seen. It was a basic one-floor rancher with bright yellow aluminum siding and faux white shutters built on a dirt lot! The house was surrounded by clumps of crabgrass and rocky, clumpy reddish-brown dirt! The house had been built five years before but quite obviously had never been landscaped . . . at all! I stood there for a few moments, staring blankly at this ugly little rancher sticking out of the dirt trying to somehow get a grip on the moment and wrap my head around the concept of actually living there. I closed my eyes, took a deep breath, and channeled my practical, survival mode. I recalled how with patience, creativity, and a lot of elbow grease, Fred and I had transformed that dingy apartment and empty concrete courtyard on Park Avenue, how we had landscaped Joyce Lane and built the rock garden, and I had my answer. I turned to the realtor and said, "OK, I'll take it," and started walking back to her car. Incredulous, the realtor asked, "Don't you want to see inside?" I opened the passenger side door and said, "Nope, don't need to", and got in. The look on the realtor's face was priceless. I'll bet no client had ever done that before! Location, location, location, right? Besides, I didn't want to see inside for fear it might weaken my resolve. It was a one mile walk to the schools, a shorter commute for Fred, and the house was most comfortably within our price range. That was all I needed to know. Appearance can be changed, the location can't.

Later that afternoon after Fred got home from work, I recounted the day to him over a few gin and tonics. I asked him if he wanted to go see it and his reply mirrored mine, nope. Before we actually moved into it, we did go look at it one time for about an hour just to plan on what furniture would go where and what, if anything, would have to be gotten rid of. Fred's opinion of the place matched my own. Other than that, we spent our last month on Joyce Lane enjoying it as much as possible before we had to relocate to what I called the plastic yellow box on dirt. One Saturday afternoon before we left, we sat outside with Gene and Letty and had a kind of moving party well into the night, polishing off a case of champagne and then some in the process. I think the champagne was more of an emotional pain killer for all of us than anything else. We were all so depressed about having to move. We had become such very close friends with Gene and Letty over the years and they were just as depressed about the move as we were. With the rent being doubled, they bought a house shortly after that as well.

The day of the move was horribly hot and humid! It was 98 degrees in the shade and the humidity was almost sticky 80%! Of course, it was August, the worst month of the year to move or do anything strenuous unless you absolutely had to. Fred was still under doctor's orders to avoid heavy physical exertion, such as loading heavy furniture onto a moving truck in 98-degree heat, so Gene and Don were both there to help me with the heavy lifting. They loaded all the furniture on the truck and unloaded it when we got to Circle Rd. After two heart attacks in two years, there was no way any of us were going to allow Fred to move heavy furniture in that kind of excessive heat and humidity.

After all the furniture was on the truck, I was outside looking sadly at my beautiful rock garden. Don, Fred, and I had worked so hard to make that garden. We had collected big rocks from our trips to Skyline Drive, VA. Don had dug big, beautiful ferns out of the woods and transplanted them in the garden with the Azaleas, Impatiens, and the ivy that was now growing up the side of the house. Completely thinking out loud blurted, "I want to take my rock garden with me!" Gene looked at me kind of blank-faced and said, "You're kidding, right?" Don flashed a grin at Gene, shook his head a little, and said quietly, "She's not kidding." It was another one of those moments that define who your true friends are. Don and Gene both knew how heartbroken I was to be leaving Joyce Lane. For no other reason than for my happiness in being able to take a piece of Joyce Lane with me, Gene and Don hauled about two dozen heavy rocks, most of which were about the size of a basketball or a bit larger. I took some of my home with me!

Fred never actually said so but, I could tell he felt somehow responsible for us having to move from our cozy little wooden cabin tucked in the quiet privacy of a forest to a yellow aluminum-sided rancher on a dirt lot in the suburbs. Not that there is anything wrong with the suburbs, not at all. For me though, nothing compared to having a home surrounded by forest. I had gained a love for the forest and nature when I was a child, during the war. I have always felt the most comfortable and at peace surrounded by forest. During the war, my afternoon trips into the forest with my dog were the only peace, the only comfort available to me. The sounds of birds singing and the breeze flowing through the trees, the beauty of it all rescued me from the state of constant anxiety that comes from living in a war, if only for an hour or two. Sometimes, as I gazed at the beauty of the forest, I could almost forget the ugliness, fear, and death that was taking place around me day after day. Fred fell in love with nature at a very young age too. Occasionally as a child, he visited his Uncle

George's farm, somewhere in northern Baltimore County. Fred was a Baltimore city kid, born in 1933 and raised in the city, during the Great Depression, no less. He had a rather trying childhood as well. He'd been awestruck by how beautiful the countryside was outside of the city and for the rest of his life was drawn to the splendor of nature. As soon as he was old enough and had a car, he would make the two-hour drive out of Baltimore to the Skyline Drive in Virginia every chance he got.

I did my best to put on my brave face as always and accept the reality of it all with no complaint, but my husband knew me too well. He always knew what emotions I was trying to hide by how I hid them. I stood in the doorway for a long moment, looking at the now empty interior of my beautiful little cabin as tears began to well up in my eyes. I swallowed hard, closed the door to 244 Joyce Lane for the last time, placed the key under the doormat as Mr. Mylander had requested, and got into Fred's Chevy wagon. Apparently, Fred saw right through my attempt at a brave face because as I sat there in his car looking at my beloved little dream cabin one last time he reached over and took my hand, looked me right in the eyes, and said "I promise you, no matter what, one way or another, one day I'm going to come back and buy this place for you."

I spent the next couple of weeks setting up our new home in Pasadena as best as I could. Fred had to work, of course, so I did most of the moving, storing, and rearranging on my own. No big deal, I was only 44 years old then. I was strong as a horse. Compared to our cabin on Joyce Lane, this place was tiny. I didn't have my big basement anymore, so storage was a nightmare. For the longest time, the third bedroom served as a storage room. The place had minimal closet space, the laundry room was tiny and had the hot water heater in it, so it was fairly useless as storage too. The house had a dirt crawl space under it that was about three feet high, so I was able to slide a few boxes of stuff in there. Basically, I worked out temporary solutions until we could set up the house the way we really wanted to. Freddie started school shortly after we moved in, which gave me all day to organize the house without interruption while he was at school.

Within a few days, I discovered that Freddy was experiencing the pains of being the new kid in the neighborhood. In fact, he was being bullied physically too. This was something else I had zero experience with but, I learned quickly. It hadn't occurred to Fred and me just how drastically we had changed our son's world. We had moved Freddy from Jones elementary, an older, smaller school in Severna Park, MD to Bodkin Elementary, a new and much larger school in Pasadena, MD. Even though the addresses were only thirteen miles apart, the social and economic differences were significant. In 1975, Severna Park and Pasadena were different in a few ways. Severna Park was smaller, older, and more upper income than Pasadena. Most of Pasadena was much larger, newer, more populated, with a lot of new homes and more blue-collar. Freddy's third grade class in Severna Park had twenty-five kids in it. His fourth-grade class in Pasadena was divided into four "quads" with about thirty kids in each. On Joyce Lane, there were a few kids in the neighborhood. In Pasadena, there were hundreds within a couple of square miles. Consequently, Freddy had never experienced bullying of any kind from other kids his age. He'd never experienced the typical teasing and harassment that the "new kid" quite often does. Fred and I were never "helicopter parents" at all. We figured the kids would have their fun and, in a few days, it would pass. Unfortunately, that didn't happen . . . not that Freddy didn't try to get along, he did, but after several weeks it seemed clear that a few boys were still at it. Every day Freddy came home from school, as soon as he got off the bus, the same few boys would shove him around, and throw his books and lunch box over a fence into one of our neighbor's yards. Freddy had made friends with a girl next door in his class and her mother informed us that these boys were harassing Freddy during recess every day as well. Finally, Freddy came home with a good-sized black eye one afternoon and it was clear, he was going to have to do something. I had never experienced this ever in my life but, my husband certainly had. My husband grew up on the streets of Baltimore, the son of a German immigrant father. During World War II, that wasn't a good thing. Consequently, from the age of seven until the age of ten, he had to defend himself from time to time. At the dinner table that night, my husband gave Freddy simple instructions on how to handle his situation. He said, "Freddy, the next time these boys come at you, walk right up to the toughest one and punch him square in the mouth as hard as you can, and they'll never bother you again." Fred even showed him how to make a fist properly. Except, Fred forgot the part about not doing it IN school.

My immediate thought was that this advice was not such a good idea, but my husband promised me it was the perfect solution, that it was typical boyhood stuff and not to worry about it.

Two days later, the phone rang about an hour after Freddy had gone to school. It was Freddy's principal and Freddy was in his office. Freddy followed his father's advice to the letter and punched the toughest square in the mouth, splitting his lip wide open in the process. Apparently, the kid bled like a stuck pig. This principal annoyed me immediately. In a most condescending voice, he began lecturing me on his zero-tolerance policy for fighting, until I interrupted him. I said, "Well Sir, I've been informed by a few of my son's friends and their parents that the kid with the busted lip and several of his buddies have been bullying my son in school for almost a month, where was your 'zero tolerance' then?" There was silence on the other end of the line for almost a full minute. He didn't have an answer for that! Finally, he stammered, "Well, uhm, errr he should have come to me first." I snapped back," Oh, that's a great idea, so he can be pegged as the sissy tattletale that runs to the principal?!" Then this jerk of a principal had the audacity to say that it sounded like I was teaching my kid to solve his problems with his fists. That pissed me off! I said, "NO, we are teaching our son to defend himself when other kids try to beat him up!" . . . and I hung up. Idiot. I never heard another word about it and the bullying stopped immediately so, my husband was right. It was 1975. It was a different world then. From what I recall, helicopter parents were much rarer in those days than they are now but, they were more prevalent than when had been kids. My husband and I had both come of age in hard times, learning how to overcome and adapt to adversity, quite often on our own at a young age.

Naturally, we taught our son to solve problems on his own rather than hide from them or bother someone else to do it for him. Children that learn to assess and solve their own problems at a young age grow up to be confident, self-sufficient adults. After all, as adults, we encounter all kinds of bullies throughout our lives, whether it be on the job, in society, the government, and then some.

About three months after moving into 211 Circle Rd., in the first week of December, the worst of times fell upon us and the inevitable happened. Fred had his third heart attack, again while out of town on business in Tappahannock, VA. Again, he ended up in the ICU for several days, until they were able to stabilize him. Again, I made arrangements with friends to watch Freddy while I traveled to Virginia to get Fred and have someone drive us back in Fred's car. As long as I live, I'll never forget the look on the ICU doctor's face or what he said to me. I asked him how Fred was doing and without any hesitation, he said, "Mrs. Brauer, your husband needs to go into surgery yesterday!"

When we got home Fred saw our doctor, Dr. Goodman, right away who immediately referred him to a wonderful cardiologist. The ICU doctor in Tappahannock had determined that Fred was in immediate need of a triple bypass and reviewing the report and a few tests, Fred's cardiologist quickly concurred. Fred conceded to surgery but insisted on doing it after Christmas. He adamantly refused to miss Christmas! The cardiologist protested this, but Fred wouldn't budge. He updated Fred's medications to include nitroglycerin and Valium and acquiesced to Fred's insistence on being home for Christmas.

Dr. Goodman spoke to me alone and told me not to let Fred exert himself at all, in any way and to do whatever I knew would keep him in as good spirits as possible. He told me it was of utmost importance that Fred not get angry or upset at all or worry too much. Fred's heart condition had scared me many, many times over the years but, after the necessity for a triple bypass and the risks involved were explained to me in great detail, I carried around a nagging gut fear with me most of the time until the surgery and recovery were behind us. In a nutshell, coronary artery bypass graft surgery (CABG), in 1975 wasn't nearly as perfected or successful as it is today. Some surgeries only lasted a few years for different reasons. Some bypass surgery patients suffered blood clots or post-operative infections. Today blockages in arteries are much more easily treated, especially with the invention of stents in the mid-eighties, among other treatments and medications.

Throughout Christmas, I had to make a constant conscious effort of hiding my anxiety, which wasn't always easy! I am not very good at hiding my emotions. I'm good at controlling them. I can count on one hand the times in my life that I've fallen apart but, it was never for more than a matter of moments, a survival skill I developed as a child during the war. Normally, Fred was able to see right through whatever facade I created to mask my emotions but, Fred's cardiologist had prescribed him Valium which kept him calm and a bit sedated. He napped a lot and luckily for me, was much less observant than usual. Our closest friends made it a point to come and visit. We got a beautiful, live Christmas tree all three of us decorated. Freddy and I went into the woods and cut fresh Holly to decorate the house with. With the house was filled with Fred's favorite Christmas music, the smells of cookies baking, the fresh-cut tree, and the constant crackle of the fireplace Fred stayed in very good spirits, even though he was very weak and spent most of his time on the couch with a blanket over his legs. Sometimes it's the little things that can bring just the right amount of joy to get us through the worst times.

The New Year came and while we waited for the surgery to be scheduled, the inevitable happened. One night shortly after midnight, I was awakened by an odd sound and I got up to find Fred laying on the couch, taking nitro, clutching at his chest, and gasping for breath! I turned the lights on and saw the terror in Fred's face. His skin was so gray it looked almost blue. He was dying. I could see it! He gasped, "Call Mickey, call Mickey!" "Mickey" was Dr. Goodman's nickname. He had told us in an emergency to call him first. Doctor Goodman, planning ahead, had already consulted with a cardiac surgeon he knew well. I called Dr. Goodman in a panic, and I remember telling him, "Fred is dying! He's here on the couch dying, what do I do?!" He told me to get Fred to the University of Maryland Hospital immediately. He said, "Don't call an ambulance, they'll take him to North Arundel, and he'll die." North Arundel hospital had a rather poor reputation back then. He then said, "I've already spoken with the best cardiac surgeon I know at the University of Maryland that is prepared to operate on Fred at a moment's notice, just get him there, now." I told him I would and hung up. Somehow, I got Fred into his Chevy station wagon and I drove, with no license, through six inches of snow and still falling snow all the way to University of Maryland hospital.

To this day I don't know how I did this. I'm not sure how I got Fred to the car, he could barely walk. It was snowing and there were several inches of snow already on the ground. I had only driven Fred's car in parking lots a few times when he was trying to teach me to drive. I had been to Baltimore a thousand times, but I had never driven it myself, but I got him there in about forty-five minutes. I pulled up to the Emergency entrance, honked the horn several times, and before I knew it Fred was taken inside and headed for surgery. I waited in the ER lobby for hours until finally, a doctor came down to talk to me. By then it was about 4:00 am. He explained to me that Fred would be in surgery for several more hours and then moved to the CCU and I should go home. I wouldn't be able to see him for at least 48 hours. I got a cup of coffee from a vending machine and decided to wait for a few hours until the buses started running. I had used the Baltimore MTA many times and was familiar with their schedules and routes. I knew one would stop right at the hospital. I didn't want to press my luck and drive Fred's car home, so I parked it in the hospital parking lot and caught the first bus to Mountain Rd. in Pasadena around 8:00 am. I got off the bus at the bus stop on Mountain Rd about a mile from our house and walked the rest of the way home. I was absolutely exhausted. I'd had one hour of sleep in the past 48 hours. Freddy was staying with Letty and Gene. They had come right away to pick him up shortly after I had left to drive Fred to the hospital. Freddy had woken up as well with all the commotion and had seen his father lying on the couch clutching his chest and gasping for air. He'd seen me in a controlled panic on the phone with Dr. Goodman, Gene, and then our neighbor Judy. He still remembers the scene vividly to this day. It was a frightening scene to him at the time because he'd never his father in such pain or me in such a controlled panic but still, at the age of nine, he couldn't fully comprehend the gravity of it all. I doubt many nine-year-old kids are really able to grasp the concept of their father dying. Our neighbor Judy had stayed with him until Gene arrived. I had no idea how long Gene would take, given the snowy weather.

Finally, the bus came to a stop, and I got off. After a mile-long walk in the snow from the bus stop to our house, the thought of a nap crossed my mind but, knew right away I wouldn't be able to so. Jason needed to go out anyway, so I put on a pot of coffee and grabbed his leash. While Jason and I walked in the woods behind my mind was spinning like a top! I was delirious with fatigue, fear, worry, doubt, and questions. I was thinking about all the things that could wrong and all the good things that could happen simultaneously! What was the surgeon doing for my husband? Would it work? Would he die on the table? Would it make him like a new man?

That last thought gave me hope. Maybe Fred would come out of surgery with a new lease on life. As Jason and I followed the path the tears began to well up, the pressure of the past day, the past several weeks began to seep out of me. I found myself pleading out loud to no one but a dog and the snowy woods around me that he would survive and stay with me for a very long time. He was only forty-two years old! I wouldn't wish this kind of anguish on my worst enemy.

I sat in the dining for hours with a cup of coffee and staring at the phone. Finally, a few days after Fred's surgery, I was allowed to see him. Don had spoken to his parents, and they were more than happy to let Freddy stay with them for a while. Freddy really liked them, and he was allowed to watch a lot more TV with them than he was at home, so it was kind of a treat for him, especially after I told him his father was going to be ok. I knew I was going to be going back and forth to the hospital for at least a couple of weeks by bus and would only be home often enough to feed and take the dog out and sleep. For two weeks every morning, I walked to the bus stop on Mountain Rd. a mile from our home and caught the bus into Baltimore and came home on the same bus every afternoon. I was determined to see my husband in the CCU every moment I could. Fred had undergone a triple bypass. Three of the major arteries around his heart had become virtually useless. I believe collapsed is the word the doctor used. They had taken an artery from his leg to use for the bypass. The technology and the recovery time were nothing at all in 1976 like they are today. Fred was told at the time that this procedure was good for about ten years. The recovery time was months. He wasn't allowed to do much more than walk from the couch to the bathroom for a month after leaving the hospital.

The first week or so in the CCU Fred was pretty out of it. He was conscious but not altogether there. The morphine made him easily irritable, a common side effect I was told so I was careful of what I said. He slept a lot. The following week he was more alert and in better spirits. He was grateful to be alive and thanked the surgeon warmly every time when he would come to Fred's room to see him. To say I was relieved is putting it mildly. Actually, there are no words for the crushing weight that had been lifted from my shoulders. Living with a heart patient that can drop dead on you at any time is indescribable stress. I knew Fred had a long recovery ahead but that was a welcome challenge compared to worrying about when the next heart attack is going to happen! Fred's arteries had been replaced and in time he'd be relatively healthy again. Fred was finally allowed to come home sometime in March and during the next few months, while he was recovering, I got busy with the list of things I was determined to do including giving this home and the property around it a serious makeover!

The first order of business was solving the lack of storage due to the lack of a base-ment. The house had a crawlspace under it, with approximately three feet of space from the ground to the floor above. After some thought, I looked at the dirt floor of the crawlspace and decided there was only one cheap, immediate and practical way to make it useful to my satisfaction. I started digging. It took me a few days but, I dug and shoveled soil out of that crawlspace until I had dug a space about fifteen feet wide, twenty feet long, and almost deep enough to stand up in. Then on either side of my dug-out space, I covered the ground with extra thick drop-cloth plastic that I bought by the roll at Hechinger, and voila, I had my basement. I put what I wanted to be stored in boxes wrapped in heavy-duty green trash bags and lined them up on the plastic sheeting I'd laid out. Problem solved, except now I had a huge pile of soil behind my house I didn't know what to do with.

On Park Avenue, we had beautified our courtyard. On Joyce Lane, we'd had our breeze-way and a porch. With this house, we had none of the above. It was literally a rancher on a dirt lot with a cement driveway. For a few days, I looked at the huge mound of soil that I had shoveled out of the crawlspace, wondering what to do with it. I decided to make a patio out of it. I got the idea from how we had made the gardens at Park Avenue with the bricks and plastic liners filled with soil.

We went to Hechinger's and bought a lot of landscape ties and a lot of bags of the large nugget pine bark mulch. All the while sitting in a lawn chair, because that's all he was allowed to do, Fred instructed me on how to measure, cut, and nail together the landscape ties into a three-sided frame directly off the back of the house. With shovel and garden rake I spread the soil evenly within the frame and covered the soil with a thick layer of mulch. On our budget at the time, this was as close as we could come to an outdoor patio, and that's what it served to be for the next nine years. It actually looked very nice when it was finished. Now that I had a usable basement of sorts, I was able to transform the third bedroom from a storage closet to an office for Fred. I spent the rest of that spring and much of the summer landscaping. Using the same type of landscape ties that I'd used to make the patio, I built flower beds around the whole house. This was especially fun because when I went to turn the soil, I discovered all sorts of building material garbage buried right there beside the outer walls of the house! For days I was pulling chunks of cinder block, shingles, nails, empty caulk tubes, and pieces of black tar paper out of the ground. He has a real green thumb too. Eventually, all around the house, I had flower beds rich with new potting soil inside of landscape tie frames. Don came to visit several times with the trunk of his car full of potted flowers, shrubs, and ferns. Don has a real green thumb and together we filled the flower beds. In the front yard bordering the street, I set up my rock garden with the rocks Don and Gene had moved for me from my rock garden on Joyce Lane. Don placed the rocks for me, and we mulched and filled that garden with a variety of flora. With another trip to Hechinger, I completed the patio behind the house with a full set of the redwood lawn furniture and outdoor cushions that were so popular in the '70s. We also bought a wooden picnic table and benches at Hechinger so we could eat outside on the patio in the summer. Over the years we entertained all of our friends many times on that patio in the summer months.

Eventually, Fred was allowed to go back to work but the several months of recovery time had cost us a substantial amount of income and he spent long, long hours in his home office on the phone and on his drafting board designing store after store after store. His energy and vitality had returned, and even though he was still on a variety of medications he was back to his old self. I changed my way of cooking to a more heart-healthy diet with more dark green leafy vegetables and lean meat and fish. He lost weight, and even though he didn't entirely quit smoking as he should have, he started smoking an ultra-low tar and nicotine cigarette brand that was new at the time called "Now". He had been smoking a 12 mg tar cigarette and Now's were less than 1 mg tar, quite an improvement! He drank less alcohol and began to lay off the liquor altogether in favor of red wine.

Even with all of the extra work Fred was putting in for Baltimore Display, money was very tight, and we had to economize in numerous ways for quite some time. Christmas was especially lean that year. The only gifts we bought that year were a few things for Freddy. Luckily, he was easy to please. In those days his favorite toy was those Matchbox cars that were really popular at the time. They were only a dollar or two apiece, so he got a stocking full of them. For some reason, he was never interested in the plethora of cheaply made plastic toys that are typically broken within a few days after Christmas.

That first winter in Pasadena was an especially cold one for us. The house had oil heat just like we'd had on Joyce Lane, except the price of fuel oil had increased considerably that year. Instead of the $400 it cost us to fill our 300-gallon tank the year before, it cost us over $600 to fill the same size tank just one year later. A $200 increase may not sound like a lot now but, if you're old enough to remember, the purchasing power of $200 in 1975 was equivalent to the purchasing power of $1,000 today. Typically using almost three tanks of fuel oil per winter, that meant an extra $600 for fuel oil that winter that we did not have. Again, adjusted for inflation, today that would be an extra $3,000! That first winter, we never set the thermostat above 60 and when we went to bed, we threw a big log into the woodstove and shut the oil heat off. Believe it or not, we actually got through that first winter with a tank and a half of heating oil!

The following winter was even worse. The winter of '76/'77 was one of the coldest winters on record. People still talk about the winter of 1976/77. It was so cold people were driving their cars on the Chesapeake Bay it was frozen so thick. We decided to have a wood stove insert for the fireplace installed right away. Simple math told us the initial investment for the wood stove insert was much cheaper than trying to pay for expensive fuel oil all winter, especially when the average nightly temperature for months was quite often in single digits. That stove and firewood saved us a lot of money over the years. In the eight years we lived there, we saved at least $5,000. Beginning with the first winter we lived in Pasadena, Freddy and I made regular weekly trips into the woods behind the house with a bow saw and ax to cut, gather and split wood for the stove. At ten years old my son was hauling cut deadwood out of the woods with me and swinging a ten-pound maul splitting logs with an iron wedge for the woodstove. He got good at it too! By the time spring came, I had developed such muscles in my back and arms from gardening and hauling firewood for our woodstove that I had developed forearms and biceps like a man! After seeing how much money we saved that first winter, gathering and maintaining a stockpile of firewood for the woodstove in the winter became an annual routine. In the fall of 1977, Fred bought a chainsaw, a new ax, a new maul, and splitting wedges and on the weekends, he and Freddy would head into the woods together for firewood. Fred taught Freddy how to use all the tools, including the chainsaw. At the age of eleven, my son was handling a chainsaw and splitting logs like a 30-year-old lumberjack! Fred and I both felt, as parents, it was our job to teach our son how to do things for himself. Both of us had grown up in a world where you had to know how to do things for yourself.

The summer of 1977 saw the beginning of an annual family tradition, camping. At first, we tried a campground but found out that campgrounds can be quite busy, especially on weekends. If your intention is to commune with Mother Nature in total peace and quiet, away from other people and any hint of civilization, the typical campground with facilities such as bathrooms, showers, covered trash cans, numbered sites, and park rangers probably will not work for you. A car full of hard-drinking college kids or an RV with Mom, Dad, and eight young children can bring an end to peace and quiet quickly, just an FYI. Still, we had a nice enough time that first summer. The weekdays were quite peaceful. We even came home with a puppy. One night, hours after sundown, as we sat around the campfire, an odd caterwauling came out of the pitch black of the forest. Fred and Freddy went into the woods with flashlights but didn't see what the noise was coming from. Then, suddenly a small black ball of fur came running out of the woods right into our campsite. It was a puppy! By that time Jason was ten years old and fast asleep in the tent. Oddly enough, this puppy had very similar coloring to Jason's. We took him home with us, of course. Looking so similar to Jason we named the puppy "J.J.", for Jason junior.

The following summer, we returned to Otter Creek. We spent the first day getting set up, had dinner, and went to bed early looking forward to the next day. The next morning, we woke up to rain. No problem, we were prepared for a little rain! The tent had been oiled and waterproofed. We had big, heavy-duty ponchos, with hoods and waterproofed boots. Fred and Freddy had put up a large tarp, high above the fire and tied off to trees. We had coffee and cereal and took off into the woods to go hiking. The first day was alright. We had fun, hiking and then huddling by the fire under the big tarp that night after Fred made dinner. We figured rain was just a part of camping, right? The morning of the second day we awoke to the same rain and the morning after that, and the morning after that! The morning of day five we gave in to nature. Fred announced, "That's it, let's go home." Freddy and I didn't protest one bit! We had all tried to tough it out, but this was ridiculous! Waterlogged and defeated we started packing up. It wasn't fun anymore. Everything was wet. The tent had become saturated, our boots were soaked through. Everything inside the tent was wet including the sleeping bags. The dogs were miserable. We were miserable. We threw everything wet and muddy as-is into the car. Fred and Freddy knocked down the tent, rolled it up soaking wet and muddy, tied it down on top of the car and we drove out of Otter Creek. We were all very quiet for a time, depressed that our trip was rained out. We had driven for about a half-hour when it suddenly stopped raining. Ten minutes after that, the sun came out. All of a sudden, Fred slowed down and while looking in his rearview and side-view mirrors muttered to himself, "I wonder where that goes." I didn't know what he was talking about. I hadn't seen anything, but after driving hundreds of thousands of miles in his life, Fred was pretty observant on the road. He pulled over on the shoulder, made a U-turn, and in a few seconds, we were looking at a big wooden sign back off the road quite a ways that read, George Washington National Forest with a narrow dirt road next to it. Fred stopped on the shoulder by the sign, looked down the dirt road, and looked at me with a boyish grin. I knew exactly what he was thinking! I said, "OK, why not?"

Not knowing what to expect, Fred pulled onto this narrow, winding dirt road, and we went downhill . . . down, down, down, Fred's station wagon bouncing up and down the whole way. The road kept going and going and we started to wonder. We had to keep going though because the road was so narrow there was no way to turn around. Finally, almost an hour later, the road leveled out and led us to a spot that you still will not find in any camping/campground brochure. The dirt road led across a short wooden bridge that crossed a shallow river. Maybe 500 feet past the little bridge was another small road on the right. Actually, it was more like a path just wide enough for a car. Fred steered the car onto it. It was so narrow the limbs of saplings along it scraped the sides of the car. Two hundred feet later we saw the camping spot that primitive campers dream of. The only evidence that anyone ever camped there were a couple of small fire pits here and there that clearly had not been used for a long time. Besides that, the area was naturally pristine and primitive as primitive gets. The only other evidence of civilization was the dirt road we'd driven on to get there. There were no facilities at all, nothing but a cool, crystal-clear babbling, rocky river about a hundred feet across and two to three feet deep, and forest. We didn't know it yet, but we had discovered the "Pedlar River", one of several small mountain streams and rivers that lead to the Lynchburg reservoir. To us, it was absolute perfection! It just doesn't get any better. Here we had a clearing, right next to a crystal-clear water source, forest, rocks, and literally nothing else! There was even a small sandy beach by the river. I knew it before a word was said, we weren't going home now! NO way! It took us a day or two to dry everything out. There was a large sunny spot by the river where we strung up a clothesline and had everything hanging up to dry for two days. The first night was a little rough because everything was still wet but, after that, we had a blast!

For the next six summers, that spot beside the Pedlar River was for all intents and purposes, our own little private camping spot. Every summer we went back, we expected to get there and find that someone had discovered our spot, but no one ever did. Year after year, until Freddy graduated high school, we had the place all to ourselves.

With not even so much as even an outhouse, we were truly primitive camping . . . but we did it in style! We went camping very well prepared. We started prepping and packing for our annual camping trip three or four days before we left! We always brought three or four large coolers stocked with everything you could possibly want. We packed steaks, chicken, pork chops, Eckrich kielbasa, ground beef, corn on the cob, onions, potatoes, tomatoes, eggs, bacon, sausage, cans of hominy, grits, Bisquick, syrup, bread, rolls, mayo, mustard, Tabasco, powdered milk, cereal, bananas, boxes of Kraft mac 'n cheese, crackers, cheese, smoked oysters, sardines. You name it, we had it. We ate like kings when we went camping. Of course, I packed the bar too! I brought a few gallons of wine, red and white, wine glasses, a gallon of gin, a few two-liter bottles of tonic, plenty of limes, and our Tervis Tumblers. It took a couple of hours to get everything set up just right, so all three of us got busy with different tasks to get it done asap. First, Freddy helped Fred set up our big 12' x 12' canvas tent and put all the cushions and sleeping bags inside. Fred was always the camping cook, so he would get busy "designing" his custom fire pit to his liking, and he had it down to a science.

He moved rocks around like puzzle pieces until they fit just right and then searched for a big, thin flat rock to balance on one side of his fire pit to use as a shelf. It would get hot, of course, so it was a shelf that doubled as a surface to keep food warm on. He had a big three-foot-wide, thick metal grate that he'd taken out of an old, broken down, 60's model refrigerator specifically to use on his camping fire pit.

High above his firepit, he'd stretch a tarp tied off to trees so even a heavy downpour wouldn't disturb the campfire. I would set up the kitchen and the bar in the back of the station wagon. I organized all the food, dry goods, utensils, cutting boards, cutlery, washbasin, paper plate baskets, etc. for quick and easy access.

After the tent was set up, Freddy would head into the woods with an ax and bowsaw to collect the firewood supply and, I'm not talking about a stack of twigs. No, I'm talking about a real stack of firewood! Just like he did in the winter at home, he cut and carried ten-foot sections of fallen trees into the campsite, cut them into logs, split them, and stacked them. He was very selective too. He'd learned to find dry, well-seasoned downed hardwoods like hickory, oak, and maple, never pine. Seasoned hardwoods are best for open-fire cooking. Seasoned hardwoods give meats a nice flavor and burn slowly. Pine flame does not give meats a nice flavor at all, and it burns very quickly. We had a dozen old-school oil lanterns set up all around the camp and a five-gallon, thick, soft plastic water bag with a spout that we would fill up and hang from a tree branch. We even had a heavy-duty doormat in front of the tent. Our complete setup was so nice, we could have camped there comfortably for months!

We usually woke up very early, not long after sunrise. The morning dew, clean crisp air, and early morning songbirds are natural break-of-day alarm clocks. My husband was always the first one up. The first thing he did was drop some wood on the coals still smoldering from the night before and within minutes had a hot steaming blue kettle of cowboy coffee ready. By cowboy coffee I mean the coffee scooped right into the water and brought it to a boil. As soon as it boils, you take the lid off, give it a good stir, let it boil for maybe another minute, and then set the kettle aside for about five minutes until the boiled grounds settle to the bottom of the kettle, that's it. Pour gently. After coffee, Fred cooked us a big hearty breakfast to keep us fueled up until lunch. Hiking in the mountains was our favorite activity. After our breakfast settled a bit, I packed each of our day packs with water and a light lunch and we spent the rest of the day, usually until around 5:00 pm, hiking one of the dozens of trails nearby. Depending on the trail, we'd hike anywhere from as little as five miles to as much as ten or twelve miles. There were several mountains surrounding our campsite. Two of them had elevations of 2,600 feet. The others were between 1,400 and 1,800 feet. When hiking in the mountains, there are a few hiking basics that are important to be aware of before you start. You should know the difficulty and distance of the trail and whether or not there is a water source available anywhere along the trail or if you need to carry all the Some trails ran straight uphill for several miles.

Others run along the side of the mountain and a much lesser incline. Trails with mostly steep inclines are a grueling workout! Hiking directly uphill on a mountain trail at a steady 45-degree angle for even two miles in the summer heat is physically challenging. Walking back that same two miles downhill is one hell of a workout on the knees! Your hiking speed will depend greatly on the incline. On a trail with a mostly steep 45-degree incline, you may travel as little as one mile an hour. On a moderate incline of 25 or 30 degrees, you might manage 2 mph. Most people average 3 - 4 mph on a flat surface. It's also important to carry enough water. Water weighs 8.34 pounds per gallon. With only moderate activity in moderate temperatures, the body requires at least 2 pints of water per hour. With strenuous activity in the summer heat, you should drink at least a quart of water per hour. Based on those figures, for five miles of steep incline mountain hiking, you should have at least a gallon of water available to you. You don't want to get halfway through 5 miles of a steep incline, strenuous hike in the heat, and run out of water. Unless you're in very poor health, chances are you'll survive the second half of the hike without water, but you'll be damned thirsty, you'll most likely experience a significant loss of energy, maybe get lightheaded and, you almost certainly will not be having any fun.

On our first camping trip to Pedlar River, we explored the river, and a few hundred yards upstream we discovered a spot where the constant flow of water over a large boulder in the middle of the river had created a large, wide pool that was well over six feet deep. Perfectly situated right next to it was a huge flat boulder big enough for three adults to sunbathe on! It was so perfect, it looked as if Mother Nature herself had looked upon that very spot and proclaimed, "Let there be a pool deep enough for them to swim in with a nice flat rock next to it for them to sunbathe on!" Once or twice during our stay, we would opt for a lazy day at the pool and sunbathing rock instead of hiking, especially if it was really hot and humid.

Whatever we did with our days, every night Fred cooked an incredible dinner. Fred was an incredibly talented camping cook and most nights a couple of hours after dinner Fred would break out his favorite dessert . . . Krispy Creme glazed donuts warmed over an open fire!

The forest had been my only source of solitude as a child during the war and, it stuck with me for life. Fred, having grown up in the city, took every opportunity he could to get out to the Skyline Drive in Virginia when he was younger, and he too loved it for life. Freddy fell in love with it quickly too and waited all year for those two weeks roughing it in the Appalachian Mountains every summer. We loved camping so much that we were always sad on the way home after our two weeks in the woods were up! Communing with pure nature for two weeks is an experience like no other!

We did have a lot of fun in the summers in Pasadena. Just six doors down the street from us was the Magothy River. There was a small community beach we used quite often. Fred bought a twelve-foot-long aluminum Jon boat and a 7 1/2 horsepower outboard motor for it so he and Freddy could go out fishing and crabbing on the weekends. In those days the Magothy was loaded with fish and crabs. Unless it was raining, we had dinner outside on our patio in the summer almost every night and, quite often dinner was whatever Fred and Freddy had caught that day. Fred had built a grill right next to the patio and would steam blue crabs or cook the fresh perch, croaker, or rockfish he and Freddy had caught right on the grill. Circle Rd became the summer meeting place for all of our friends and all through the late '70s and early 80s, every summer we had several parties on our homemade patio. We even hosted the company picnic for Baltimore Display one year.

Sometime in the late 70s, I joined the Mountain Club of Maryland, aka., MCM. The MCM was a group of forest lovers like me that got together on Wednesdays and Saturdays to take day hikes in the numerous parks and state forests in Maryland. Each hike had a leader and co-leader that mapped out the hike beforehand to calculate distance, hiking difficulty, etc. I was a faithful member of MCM for over twenty years. Before long I became one of its most avid leaders. Over the years, Fred and Freddy went with me many times on the weekends and we made quite a few good friends in the process. Every two years MCM holds a marathon, all of the Appalachian Trail in

Maryland in one day. It is thirty miles of trail from Penn Mar to Harpers Ferry. I never did it, but Freddy did in 1979 and came in second place. Not bad for a 13-year-old! The MCM was very important to me. It was my weekly solace, so to speak. By the time I joined MCM, Freddy was in junior high school and as kids do, was becoming busier and busier with activities at school and, of course, his friends. Fred was also very busy with a big contract he had landed with all of the US military exchanges nationwide. He was constantly designing the interiors of military exchanges and his income began to show it with considerable increases in his commissions. Baltimore Display was making a lot of money from Fred's military contracts, A LOT!

Since my son was approaching his teens and busier with his own interests, Baltimore Display was keeping Fred busy and, I had already done pretty much everything I had intended to the house, and I was now involved with MCM every week, I decided it was time I get my driver's license. Fred had already been teaching me how to drive occasionally on weekends, so after a few more lessons with my former driving instructor husband, I took the test and passed on the first try. When Fred asked me what I had in mind for a car he was stunned by my answer. I said, "Can I have yours?" Now, mind you, I know almost nothing about cars but, I loved Fred's company car. At the time Fred had a metallic forest green 1977 Chevy Malibu Classic station wagon. It was a 3-speed automatic on the column with a 400 cubic inch small block V8 and a 4-barrel carburetor, powerful. It was a beautiful color, comfortable, had all kinds of room in it, rode so smooth it was like driving on glass and . . . it was FAST! When you floored the pedal in that car it took off like a rocket! Fred laughed and said, "Most women would want something like a sporty convertible, not my wife, she wants my Chevy station wagon." So, Fred told his boss the next day that he needed a new company car because I wanted his. Fred's boss had become very willing to keep him happy so without another thought, he sold Fred the Malibu for $500 and told him to go to the dealership and pick out whatever he wanted for another company car. I drove that car for another 12 years.

Life continued on rather uneventfully for the next few years. Fred's good health continued as well as his prosperity with Baltimore Display. His contract with the military went global and his designs for their exchanges were incorporated into all US military base exchanges worldwide, Army, Navy, Air Force, and Marine Corps. When that happened, Fred's military contracts became the lion's share of profit for Baltimore Display and he finally had the income he had always wanted for us, as well as being the star of the company. He even purchased the small piece of property right next to our lot. It was too small to build on and had been unused since the day we had moved in. So, Fred found out who owned it and purchased it to increase the size and value of our lot.

Freddy graduated high school in 1984 and even though he had been accepted to several different colleges within Maryland he decided instead to go to Anne Arundel Community College the following fall. His high school sweetheart had decided to go there as well, and he didn't want to leave her and go to a four-year college several hours away. They both were sure they'd be together forever of course! Less than two years later they were both dating other people. Alas, the naive decisions we all make when we are young and inexperienced! After a couple of semesters in college, Freddy got a job waiting tables in a nice restaurant and was making such good money in tips that he decided to venture out on his own and rented a place near his school with a few friends. For the first time in 19 years, Fred and I were alone in the house.

Then, about a year later, the most extraordinary thing happened . . . something both of us had dreamed of many times but never in a million years expected to come true!

CHAPTER 12

RETURN TO JOYCE LANE

•••

Early on a Saturday afternoon in January of 1986, while Fred was in his office busy creating another floor plan for a department store on his drafting board and I was in the kitchen starting dinner, the phone rang. Fred answered it, it was usually for him anyway. At first, I could just barely hear Fred's end of the conversation. My husband was not an easily excitable man. He generally carried himself with a kind of quiet dignity. Normally he spoke deliberately but quietly. He was rarely loud, but after a few moments, I heard him exclaim, "You're kidding?!", followed by, "Am I interested?!" and then, "Yes, YES . . . absolutely I am interested, yes, thank you very much!" "Who in the world is he talking to?", I thought out loud. My curiosity was killing me, and I was about to drop what I was doing and walk down the hall to see who had called when Fred came walking into the dining room and then just stood there, looking at me with shocked eyes and an ear-to-ear grin lighting up his face as if we had just won the lottery! He stood there still grinning at me for another moment and then said, "Guess what?!" "What?", I asked. He said, "That was Mr. Mylander, 244 Joyce Lane is for sale!" I couldn't believe what I had just heard. I was speechless with shock! Our little dream home on Joyce Lane that we'd sadly had to move out of ten years ago was now for sale! Mr. Mylander told Fred that we were his first call, knowing how sad we had been moving out of it the first time! Of course, we were his first call for that property! Mr. Mylander was selling the house with two acres of land for $100,000. Fred sprang into action immediately, called our realtor, Anne was her name and told her to put our house on the market immediately. Then he went to our bank the next day and took out a bridge loan for the down payment to buy the house on Joyce Lane before we even had an offer for the house we were still in! Fred was worried Mr. Mylander might change his mind for some reason. He wouldn't have changed his mind but, my husband was not a man to leave anything to chance if he could help it. When it came to business, Fred never left that till tomorrow what he could do today. The bridge loan was a risk but, a calculated one. Pasadena had become a desirable location. Much of it was still quite rural and its close proximity to Baltimore and Annapolis had more than doubled property values since we got there in 1975. Believe it or not, we bought the house for $32,000 in '75. I believe we sold it for close to $100,000 in 1986. Today, the estimate for the exact same house and property, with the only improvement being a small deck added to one side of the house, is $350,000! Even though it was the dead of winter, it was evident that we had landscaped around the home beautifully, and with the many improvements we had made to the place, such as putting in the fireplace and buying the small piece of property next door, it sold rather quickly. I don't think I showed our house a dozen times before we had a buyer. I found out that if I was ever so inclined, I could possibly make a living in sales. I didn't just show our house. I sold it! I promoted it. Anne always came with the prospective buyers, but I was so eager to sell it and move back to Joyce Lane, I did all the talking. She said I was a natural.

I pointed out all of the wonderful perks, the schools, the beach right down the street, my gardens, the large lot, all of the shopping that was close, Down's State Park a few miles away, and so on, and so on.

As soon as we had the opportunity, we drove to Joyce Lane to have a look at the quaint little cabin we had left ten years before. Nothing could have prepared us for what we saw when we got there! I thought I was looking at a small slice of poverty-stricken Appalachia! Any semblance of our gardens or landscaping we had done was long dead and gone. The grounds all around the house had been reduced to dusty soil and clumps of crabgrass. Off to the right of the house was a bench seat from the inside of a car positioned on top of four cinder blocks with a round, cinder block fire pit in front of it. Not far from the car seat, all down the backside of the hill behind the house were literally hundreds and hundreds of beer bottles and beer cans, years worth! The windows were filthy with years of grime. The roof was missing shingles. It was an absolute horror, and we hadn't even gone inside yet! There was a half-rotted with black mold, rusty hulk of what had once upon a time been a boat in the garage along with mounds of trash, old paint cans, more beer cans and bottles, and rusted remnants of old tools. The kitchen had years of grease stuck to the walls, stove, oven, and cabinets. The living room had a few pieces of moldy, moth-eaten furniture and a very large, tattered Confederate flag was nailed to the wall. Each of the two bedrooms had a disgusting, stained mattress on the floor. All of the screens on the porch were either torn or just missing altogether and the basement was a wet, moldy mess of trash and debris as well. Mr. Mylander was completely unaware of all of this. By 1986, he was well into his eighties and had given the task of managing his rentals to his son many years before. Clearly, his son had not taken the job very seriously. Mr. Mylander was a very kind, honest man and a gentleman. His son . . . not so much!

After we had walked through and seen exactly what we were getting into, Fred looked at me with eyebrows raised and said, "You sure you wanna do this?" He was joking, of course. Structurally, the house was fine. The only repair the house needed was a new roof.

Needless to say, Fred and I had our work cut out for us. If you've read this far, I'm sure you can already guess, that didn't scare us one bit. Hard work never did. Unless you're born with a silver spoon in your mouth and inherit the family fortune or win the lottery, there's one rule that almost never fails. You'll get out of life what you put into it. If you want a lot out of life, you will almost certainly have to put a lot of work into it. No matter what it looked like, we got our dream house back. The rest was just going to take a lot of elbow grease and creativity.

It took us several days just to collect all of the garbage inside and out and have it hauled away. It took several more days and a few gallons of Spic and Span, Windex, and Pine-Sol to get it clean enough to actually move into. To tell you in detail everything we did to that house over the next decade would be a separate chapter in itself. I'll try to give you the gist of it in a paragraph . . . or two.

Some projects were ongoing, such as landscaping. It took me years to cultivate the gardens to what they are today. First, Fred treated the whole interior of the house with antiquing oil. The wood had been neglected for years. What followed was, (and not necessarily in order), we took out the drop ceiling, turned half of the attic into a loft bedroom, installed two big skylights, replaced and insulated the roof, had a pond built, closed in the breezeway, and the porch with glass sliding doors, turned the cement floor garage into a family room, (which Fred jokingly renamed the North Wing), with a hardwood plank floor with decorative natural rope inserted and glued between the planks, removed the garage door, replaced it with sliding glass doors, replaced most of the wall on the other end of the garage with sliding glass doors, installed a pellet stove in it, installed a huge Hunter ceiling fan, replaced a great deal of the wiring in the house, built flagstone paths in the front of the house and out to the gardens, built a parking pad for both cars with landscape ties and had it filled with stone, bought a wooden shed that matched the house, stained the outside of the house, installed a water softening system, replaced the old wood cellar doors with new metal doors, remodeled the bathroom with all new tile in the shower, new shelving and vanity and painted the wood a light gray, and had a new well dug due to some new county zoning regulation which then made it necessary to relocate the driveway one hundred feet further from the house! We had to literally turn the old dirt driveway into a front lawn and gardens . . . and with everything I just listed, that isn't half of it. Of course, we didn't accomplish all this in one year and, certainly not without life dumping a few more challenges in our laps along the way!

Late November of 1986, I was leading a hike with the Mountain Club on a trail just outside of Hagerstown, MD, and Fred was my co-leader. It was a cold cloudy day and there were several inches of snow on the ground. As hike leader, I was at the head of the group and Fred brought up the rear. About a mile into the trail, Fred, informed a couple of the hikers at the back of the group that he wasn't feeling well and to tell me that he was going into Hagerstown to do some Christmas shopping. I had no idea. I was a hundred yards ahead at the front of the group. Of course, they didn't think anything of it, and I didn't get the message until they caught up to me several minutes after we broke for lunch. I was concerned right away, of course. It was out of character for Fred to just abandon a hike like that unless something was wrong, especially since he was my co-leader. We were several miles into the woods, no one had cell phones back then so all I could do was hope for the best. When we arrived back at our cars later that afternoon two Park Rangers approached me and told me that two hikers had discovered Fred lying in the snow about a mile from the trail entrance. One of the hikers had run back down the trail to the Ranger station. Park Rangers had to carry Fred out on a stretcher a few hundred yards to a fire road that was accessible with a park service four-wheel-drive truck that took him back down to the parking lot where an ambulance was waiting to take him to the hospital in Hagerstown. Apparently, Fred had been conscious and at least able to speak because the Rangers knew my name, who to look for, and approximately when I would return from the hike. My heart sank. All the fears I'd felt through the first three heart attacks came rushing back to me. For ten years I enjoyed life with no cardiac induced terror, no phone calls from ICUs, no trips to the hospital at 3 am. I swallowed hard, caught my breath, jumped into the car, and drove straight to the hospital in Hagerstown. By the time I got there, Fred had been in the ICU for several hours, stable and sedated. The cardiologist on duty told me that had it not been for the fact that Fred was lying in several inches of snow and the sheer luck that other hikers came by soon after, Fred would probably not have survived. He was scheduled for several tests the next day. I'd been here before, so I knew he wasn't going anywhere any time soon. The doctor let me into the ICU to see Fred but, he was completely sedated.

I was scared to death, again . . . and there was nothing I could do, again. He was in the doctors' hands. I reluctantly drove home with that damn lump in my throat the whole way, again.

Fred was in the ICU for a little over three weeks this time. I made the three-hour round trip to see him several times. The longer Fred was there the more depressed he got. Seemed like every other day his doctors were performing some kind of test or procedure, or testing a new medication, so many I can't remember. It all got so confusing. By the end of the third week, Fred was worrying about being home for Christmas. His doctors had developed an entirely new medication regimen that seemed to be working very well. He had so many new medications, I can't remember them all now thirty-five years later. Halfway into December, Fred's doctors were still reluctant to discharge him just yet, although they were very getting very concerned about his deepening depression.

A psychologist came to speak with Fred and called me shortly after. After speaking with Fred, it was his opinion that it was both psychologically and medically better for Fred to go home as soon as possible for Christmas. I didn't have a discharge date yet but, I knew it would be soon. I got busy decorating the house for Christmas, bought a tree, dragged it into the house myself, and decorated it. I wrapped every present we had and put it under the tree. A few days later, Fred was discharged just a week before Christmas, and I drove to Hagerstown to get him. The psychologist had been absolutely correct. Between all his new meds and his joy at being home for Christmas, he was just like his old self within a few days. We had a wonderful Christmas. Every

I don't know why but, Fred never had another heart attack. Maybe it was the improvements in medications over the years or maybe the drastic improvements in his lifestyle, quitting fatty foods, liquor, and cigarettes were a major contributing factor. Maybe it was the fact that we now owned our dream home. Maybe it was a combination of all the above but, life did carry on for quite some time after that cold day on the trail in November of 86. During one of his checkups with his cardiologist in 1987, the cardiologist saw something he didn't like, and Fred was hospitalized for two days and given a temporary pacemaker. After two days Fred came home but, his cardiologist strongly suggested that Fred consider a permanent pacemaker. Fred said he'd think about it. After a few days of recovering and taking it easy, Fred was up and around and back to it.

I think it was late in '87 that J.J. was outside with Fred one afternoon and suddenly took off down the hill chasing a fox. At the bottom of the hill, the fox ran across Joyce Lane, J.J. followed and go hit by a car. Fred heard the car's tires screech to a stop, and he ran down the hill. J.J. was alive but his front legs were badly broken in several places. Fred scooped him up and rushed him to the closest animal hospital. X-rays showed several fractures in both legs. The Vet told Fred he could save J.J. and his legs but it would require surgery. J.J. was eight or nine years old at the time but still very energetic and in perfect health so, Fred asked the vet to do the surgery. Fred loved that dog so much, the $6,000 it cost for the surgery didn't mean beans to him. For his dog, money was no object. Recovery was a challenge too. J.J. had casts on both legs for a long time, a couple of months at least. Fred made a harness to put under his chest and hold his front feet off the ground when he took him out. J.J. did recover. The surgeon had done a wonderful job of putting J.J.'s leg bones back together. The surgeon showed us the after-surgery X-rays. J.J.'s leg bones had several plates and small screws in them. J.J. walked again just fine, although he didn't do much running anymore. He lived another three years. In the end, he developed cancer and Fred took him to the vet to end his pain. We were both horribly depressed and tearful when we lost J.J. He was such a special dog. Both of us were holding back tears for days. On a Saturday, less than two weeks after, Fred came driving up our driveway, came running into the house, and said I had to come with him right away. He drove straight to an SPCA dog shelter where our new fur baby was waiting. We came home with an eight-month-old, blonde lab mix. Fred named him Sonny, or maybe the spelling was Sunny. Fred said that he was like a sunny day after many dark and gloomy days.

Sometime in 1988, Baltimore Display got a particularly large, expensive order from one of his long-time clients, Jos. A. Banks, for Christmas. When Fred got home, he told me all about it. The order was, 100 six-foot garlands, 50 wreaths, and 50 sprays, each piece decorated with lights, balls, burgundy berries, babies' breath, and hand-tied burgundy ribbon bows, for EACH of their five stores and, they needed it all delivered by the first week of November. It was late July. Fred's boss, Lee, accepted the order, of course. Baltimore Display was widely considered the very best commercial display company on the entire east coast. He would never turn down Jos. A. Banks but, he wasn't completely sure who was going to do the labor. He was short two employees. One was on maternity leave and, another had just quit. Lee asked Fred if he had any ideas and Fred said, "I'll bet Toosje can do it." Fred knew I would take the order and he knew I could do it too.

Mind you, this was 1,000 separate pieces, each piece hand-decorated with five different items. This is slow, time-consuming, and monotonous work. Fred and I did some quick math. I knew I would need a helper. The minimum wage in 1988 was around $3.50 an hour. I got a helper and paid her cash, $5 an hour, $200 a week for 12 weeks, $2,400. I know, you're thinking $5 an hour?! Doesn't sound like much but you have to remember, it was 1988. Adjusted for inflation, $200 a week (cash) in 1988, equals $461 dollars a week (cash) today. To illustrate it a bit further, today, your hourly wage (before taxes) would have to be roughly $17.50 to net that $461 dollars a week. Fred thought $12,000 for the entire job was a good price. I said, "Tell Lee I'll do it for $12,000". We figured $1,000 a week, minus what I paid my helper, and minus gasoline, I would net about $9,000. Again, $9,000 adjusted for inflation is about $26,700 today.

We knew Lee wouldn't argue the price. He was going to make at least ten times that on the entire order, minus Fred's commission. Before he called Lee, Fred asked me, "Are you sure about this?" I said, "For $9,000, damn right!" For the next three months, I drove to Baltimore Display, five days a week, and worked from 9:00 am - 5:500 pm on the second floor in their hot warehouse, put together each piece of that order by hand. That warehouse wasn't air-conditioned either, only the first floor was.

No matter what, it was well worth it. That wasn't the only time I did work like that for Baltimore Display either. That job and many others like it paid for a lot of things we wanted to do to the house.

Sometime in the late '80s, Fred struck an incredible deal with a carpenter named Marty that handled carpentry work for Fred several times for Baltimore Display clients. Marty was newly married, and he and his new wife had bought a very old house they intended to gut and remodel. Marty was a talented builder, but he wasn't a designer. We wanted a deck built around our house. Marty needed an interior designer to turn his old, gutted house into the home he and his wife had envisioned. It was perfect. Marty had already gotten estimates from a few other designers and was daunted by their cost, so he offered to build us a deck that wrapped around three-quarters of our house if Fred would just be his designer start to finish. Done! Fred spent a lot of time designing Marty's house. I lost count of the Saturdays Fred spent between Marty's house with a measuring tape or in his home office bent over his drafting board but, when it was all said and done, we had a gorgeous retaining wall behind the house and a big, beautiful deck and the inside of Marty's house was exquisite. Ok, I am bragging a bit but, Fred was simply a genius at what he did. He really was. I heard his customers say it all the time! If the laws of physics and space allowed for it, Fred could design just about anything people could imagine, he was that good. All the builders had to do was follow his drawings or blueprints and, they were very detailed. Fred was quick to be on-site too if the builders ever had a design question. Marty was impressive too. He never had a helper, and he could build more all by himself in one day than most builders with a helper could in two days, and his work was impeccable. With the deck complete, and the house pretty much redesigned to our liking, we had a new meeting place. For many summers to come we entertained our friends, family, coworkers, and my fellow hikers and bikers many times on that deck.

For years I had wanted to take Fred to Holland to meet my family and of course, to show him where I grew up and now, we had the time. Fred's success in his career not only resulted in more income, but he also had more free time and in 1989 we decided to go to Holland for three weeks. We made all the arrangements well ahead of time, bought the airline tickets, and notified all of my family in Holland well in advance of when we would be arriving. It took several phone calls to tell them all.

Not long after we made all the arrangements to go to Holland, I went for my regular annual checkup and mammogram. There was a lump in one of my breasts. I went home, waiting for the results of a biopsy hoping for the best but, no such luck. The biopsy showed it was malignant stage I. Cancer! Just the mention of the word induces fear and foreboding. I was scared, very scared. Cancer ran in my family. My parents, aunts, uncles, all had died of cancer.

For years and years, I had worried over my husband's mortality and now it was my turn to worry about my own! I had never really feared for my own life before, but I must admit, the worst-case scenario of dying from cancer was a bit terrifying. My oncologist wanted to schedule a lumpectomy the following week. Fred and I were supposed to be boarding a flight to Holland in a few days. I thought about it for all of maybe five minutes and then called my oncologist back and told him I was going to Holland for three weeks and I'd take care of it when I got back. That put it off for about five weeks. My oncologist protested vehemently and told me the lump could possibly grow considerably in 5 weeks and I could not only lose the breast but if the cancer was very aggressive it could even get into my lymph nodes. I was 57 years old and the odds of a lump growing that fast at that age were minimal so, I decided to take my chances. Fred started to try and convince me to have the lumpectomy immediately, but I insisted I would not do it right away, and that was that. There was no arguing with me, and he knew it. I said, "NO, we're going." I wanted Fred to see Holland, with me for three weeks and there was no way I was not going to do that! I had watched my husband work his ass for over twenty years, and aside from the camping, (which is a lot of work), he'd never had a real, honest to goodness, carefree, stress-free vacation. Fred had suffered several heart attacks since 1973 and had a triple bypass in 1975 that we were told, at the time, was good for about ten years, possibly fifteen, if we were lucky! I didn't know if I would get this chance again to take Fred to Holland and there was no way I was going to pass it up.

We had a fantastic time. I showed Fred all of Holland, he met all the family and they adored him! Fred was particularly fascinated with the history and especially the old architecture in Holland. It was three of the best weeks of his life. We bicycled across the Dutch countryside, went to museums, had the finest food and wine, and we had a ball!

When we got back, I saw my oncologist asap. The lump had increased to stage II. He started to explain that he could still do a lumpectomy followed by radiation but . . . I put my hand up and stopped him right there. I said, "Just take it off." I had read all about breast cancer recurring after stage II lumpectomies. I told my oncologist, "My boob is not more important than my life, and besides, my breastfeeding and modeling days are over." Enough said. I had a modified mastectomy followed by some chemo and really good reconstructive surgery and haven't had cancer since. I've seen a few female friends and acquaintances go through psychological hell with breast cancer and the thought of losing their breasts. At first, it was the idea of cancer itself that terrified me, not losing my boobs. Given the choice, I would rather have kept them both, of course, but at the age of 57, they were quite simply a body part I could do without, especially to save my life. Life can and will burden us with very, very difficult choices, but at the end of the day, as they say, the most important decisions we ever make are the ones that protect LIFE itself. To wake up and see the sunrise another day is, after all, the most important thing . . . is it not? Human aesthetics are only important to the living. I think, if one truly considers the vast multitude of reasons for living, physical appearance becomes rather insignificant. The war had influenced my attitude on appearance. As a child during the war, I had witnessed some beautiful people doing some very vile things. That alone influenced me to look for people's inner beauty as well as the beauty in Mother Nature.

Princess died late in 1989. Although Fred had been the one and only person that ever bothered to look after her and take her in as a member of his family, it was amazing how many people came out of the woodwork claiming to be close to her! They all walked away disappointed. Princess died with close to a million dollars in her will which was strictly allocated to certain organizations and schools. Princess left Fred in charge of a sizable trust specifically designed to fund private colleges that did not receive any state or federal funding. Fred traveled several times to visit many of these schools to decide if and how much the fund would donate to them. Of course, Princess made sure that a percentage of this trust was allocated to Fred for his efforts.

Through the rest of the '80s and into the 90's I began to hike less and less and bicycle more. Not only had I hiked just about every trail in Maryland and was getting a bit bored with it, but Fred and I had purchased a pair of Trek hybrid bikes and had enjoyed some long rides together. We outfitted both bikes with panniers and for one trip we spent several days riding the C & O canal path. Bicycling was a lot easier for Fred than hiking, especially bike trails on level ground. We did several trips together. Most of them were short enough we could do them over a weekend because Fred was still working, albeit a lot less.

The ongoing remodeling of our house continued. That was kind of never-ending. Fred was always coming up with new ideas for different projects and different things to do inside the house and over the years we transformed the house into an immensely improved and almost unrecognizable rendition of the simplistic cabin it had been.

Sometime around 1990, a good friend of ours became a bike trip leader. Throughout the 90's I went on several of her trips. Some for a day, some for many days. For instance, we did all of the C & O canal, up and then back, 369 miles. I think it took us eight days riding an average of 46 miles a day. Lodging was pre-planned and we stayed in a motel every night. I did quite a few trips like that. Some trips were tenting trips where we carried everything in panniers and popped a tent every night. I only did a few of those. One of those was the absolute hardest ride of my life. In 1994 I decided to participate in the CAM, "Cycle Across Maryland". I was 63 years old. The CAM was over 300 miles and started at Leonardtown, MD and, ended at Berlin. It took us 7 days and was without a doubt the most grueling trip I have ever done. First of all, it was July, so it was hot. At the end of each day, we stopped at a designated school because the event organizers had gotten prior permission for us to use the big grassy sports fields schools have to set up hundreds of tents, port o pots, food services, etc. The problem was if you weren't riding in or at least near the front of the group, you're evening would not be fun at all. The later you arrived the farther your tent was from the water, port 'o pots, and the food, and there were hundreds of riders so there were hundreds of tents. Twice I arrived so late, almost all the food was gone. I had to rehydrate so I drank a lot of water but then several times I had to walk 100 yards to the port o' pot to pee. I was surrounded by tents just a few feet away so, there was no alternative. Most of the participants were much younger than me so I almost always arrived much later than they did. Still, I loved the ride and was up to the challenge. I can say I did it! The best part was when we got to the Bay Bridge, Governor Schaeffer was there to greet us. He had ordered one lane of the bridge closed so we could ride across. There were lots of TV cameras and there were bagpipes playing as we rode by. All I can say is I made it. I don't know how but, I made it to the end.

One day in early Spring of 1997, late in the afternoon, I saw a big GMC van towing a pop-up camper behind it coming up our driveway. I looked out the kitchen window wondering who the heck it was and saw Fred behind the wheel of the van. He had left that morning in a Chevy station wagon company car. He came into the house and asked me to sit down in the dining room. I didn't ask questions. I knew he was about to explain all this so all I said was, "Ok.", sat down and waited for what was coming. He paused for a moment, collecting his thoughts, and then he said, "I retired today. I figure . . . by now, whatever we don't have we don't need. All my life I have wanted to see my country, and now we can! We can go anywhere we want to go!" What could I possibly say? He stood there looking at me, waiting for me to say something and all I could say was, "OK." All through our marriage, we always discussed important matters together before making a decision, including large purchases. There was nothing I could say. I loved the idea. I was thrilled he was retired. I was thrilled we were going to travel all over the USA. Most importantly though, to me . . . I knew it was my husband's heartfelt wish and desire to see as much of his country as he could while he was still alive. He'd worked his ass off for 50 years! He deserved this. We spent the next couple of months preparing. Fred spent at least a month mapping out the whole adventure complete with all the stops we wanted to make. We thought of every potential problem that could happen to us during the trip and planned ahead for them. We spent the majority of the next two years on the road.

To describe the trip in any substantial detail would require another book. In short, I can say there that there are so many places in the USA that are so beautiful they simply take your breath away. From mountains so high that they disappear into clouds to canyons that are so immense, and deep that the sight of it makes you feel utterly insignificant! We drove from MD to FL, across the US via the southern route to California, then north to Washington State, and then east across the northern USA, all the way back to the east coast, stopping at every attraction that Fred had mapped out to see. On the second-year trip, we did much the same just an entirely different route that took us through a great deal of the Midwest, all the way to Nevada.

What I can tell you is this, aside from a few exceptions like the day we got married, the day Freddy was born and the trip to Holland, I had never seen my husband happier on a consistent basis day after day, and his beloved dog, Sonny was with him every single mile of it. Fred just loved that dog!

On a personal note, during our cross-country trip, I found the American people, from every last part of the country you can imagine, to be the warmest, friendliest, giving people I have ever had the pleasure of meeting in my life. Everywhere Fred and I stopped, we met and were greeted by very nice, gracious, down to Earth, wonderful helpful people. Trust me when I say, we live in the most wonderful country on Earth! Cities are cities, for the most part, but . . . rural America is wonderful like no other place on Earth. I can say with confidence, you could travel from state to state for years exploring rural America and never find enough time to experience it all. I'll take the US over any country in Europe any day!

Fred loved his country, more than any American I have ever known to this day. He knew everything there was to know about American history. He had studied it on his own in his younger years. Fred believed that this was not only the greatest country in the world but more importantly, the greatest idea. He was a firm believer in our Constitution. It upset him immensely how more and more, year after year it was increasingly being disregarded and corrupted. He always loved to point out that no other nation ever in history has accomplished so much in only two centuries. There is a very good reason for that but, that conversation is a different book. If you're as patriotic an American as Fred was and I became, you probably already know what I mean. He also believed it was a beautiful country, and he was determined to see as much of it as possible before he died.

We ended our cross-country adventures in the fall of 1999. During the last months of our time on the road, I noticed Fred was becoming less energetic. He became fatigued more easily and started foregoing walks. Many nights after I had gone to bed in our pop-up camper, Fred was still outside, sitting in a lawn chair, always with a glass of red wine, gazing at the stars. When I would ask him to come to bed, he always said, "I'll be there in a minute." Some nights, minutes became hours. I think he was intent on enjoying the beauty around him and the joy of being alive within it while he still could.

When we returned home Fred got busy right away getting all of the photos we had taken during our tour around the country organized into photo albums. He took literally hundreds of photos. It took him weeks to organize them and write captions for each one. When it was all said and done, we had five albums of photos. The albums Fred made were gorgeous. It always amazed me how creative and artistic and detailed Fred was. Throughout the holidays that year, friends of ours would spend hours poring over the photo albums Fred had put together. For months to come, Fred and I delighted in explaining the details of the trip to friends and family. There was so much to tell, so many different stories of places and people we encountered all across the country. It was truly one of the best times of his life, and I was grateful that he had been able to do it and I got to do it with him. There were so many things my husband told me he'd wanted to do in life and didn't get to. I'm sure that happens to a lot of us. How many of us get to do everything we want to do in life? That's why I was so happy he got this wish.

Life is short. So many of us don't realize that until the hourglass is almost empty. It's been said in many different ways by many different people, but, I believe it to be true, at the end of life, the biggest regrets we have are the things we didn't do, the paths we didn't take, the things we didn't say, the people we didn't touch . . .

CHAPTER 13

LOSING FRED

••••••••••••••••••••••••••

I awoke around three in the morning, as usual, to shuffle half-asleep to the bathroom and then back to bed. As I slid back under the covers, my left arm pressed lightly against Fred's back, and even semi-conscious with sleep, I suddenly became eerily aware of how eerily cold his skin felt. I gently placed my hand on his shoulder, and he felt so cold. I shook him gently asking, "Pope, want me to get you your other blanket"? He didn't respond. I shook him again a little harder . . . again, no response. I laid there for a moment, staring through the darkness at my husband's back while a painful knot of dread, the likes of which I'd never felt, grew in my throat. Slowly I pulled the covers back, stood up, and stepped apprehensively around to Fred's side of our bed. I bent over slightly and looking into his face shook him again and said, "Popeke?!" Nothing. I began to tremble as I stood there in dreadful, quiet panic and denial, looking down upon his motionless form for a moment, trying to swallow the painful lump of panic in my throat. I knelt down slowly to the floor and leaned forward until my face was just a few inches away from my husband's. An overwhelming finality began to permeate every ounce of my soul. I laid my hand gently upon my dear husband's kind face one last time as I spoke his name louder, desperately . . . "Fred"?! With one final wave of irrational denial, I was hoping he was just in a deep sleep and hadn't heard me, but I knew in my gut that he would never respond ever again. The skin on his face was cold and rigid, and I knew the absolute worst fear in life had finally befallen me. My beautiful husband was gone. The love of my life, my soulmate, the only man I had ever truly loved with all my heart and soul, had fallen asleep beside me for the last time. Never in all my eighty-nine years have I ever felt as defeated and alone and in the bowels of abject despair as I did at that moment. I can't tell you how long I knelt there, sobbing by my husband's bedside, staring through my tears at his still face but, I do remember the anguish was so painful and powerful I was paralyzed with it.

Something must have finally willed me to stand, what I don't know. I only know I did because I remember shuffling numbly out to the dining room in a shock-induced trance, sitting down at the dining room table, and then staring blankly at the dark of night that was just beyond the glass doors. Sonny had woken up and followed me, sat at my feet, whined, and looked up at me as if he knew what was happening. Actually, I'm sure he did know. In my temporary stupor of incredulity, my mind entertained, for just one brief moment, the wishful thought that this was all just a bad dream. For one fleeting moment, just a few seconds, I was joyous! Oh, what a relief! Just the idea of it being just a very bad dream washed over me, and in that split second of delusion and denial, I almost stood up to run back to the bedroom, but a sliver of the customary practicality with which I'd lived most of my life, usually out of necessity, returned and kept me in the chair. As I was pulling Kleenex out of a box, the room filled with the song of the Tufted Titmouse, and my attention was drawn to the bird clock Fred had given me for my birthday years before. That clock is still in the same spot.

Each hour on the clock is a different bird and bird song and the Tufted Titmouse is at five o'clock. It was five o'clock in the morning. I stared at the clock. I couldn't move. I couldn't think, and again I felt my sanity slipping into the cloak of a surreal nightmare. My mind jumped from one thought to the next, who to call first, who would be up, where's our personal address/phone book? Is it in the kitchen? I couldn't maintain a single thought in my head for more than a few seconds! Then, all of a sudden, as if I had been slapped awake, some semblance of logic and calm returned to me, and thinking out loud I said, "It's five o'clock in the morning, everyone's sound asleep." It occurred to me that there was absolutely nothing I could do at five am that couldn't be done after nine am. The situation wasn't going to change in the next four hours. It was at that moment that I accepted and surrendered to the unequivocal absoluteness of the moment.

I sat there, slumped in the chair, motionless and defeated, staring through tears, blankly out at the black of the night within the forest that surrounded our home. It was still very dark and perfectly quiet outside. Even the very early morning birds that begin singing just before sunrise were still fast asleep.

With Sonny sitting between my legs looking up at me, I rested a hand on his head and slumped back into the dining room chair gazing achingly in the direction of the bedroom where my dear husband lay lifeless, under his favorite quilt, in the same exact spot where he had lovingly kissed me goodnight just hours before and I felt the very first gut-wrenching pang of contemplating life without him.

I bent over to comfort Sonny, kissed the top of his head, and together we sat staring through sliding glass doors at the almost silent and peaceful darkness outside, quietly waiting for the dawn to bring the first day of the rest of my now incomprehensible life.

* * *

Eventually, a few hours after sunrise, I forced myself to stand. As if on some kind of autopilot, I numbly opened our personal phone number/address book, picked up the phone, and made all the necessary phone calls to family, friends, the funeral home, and our doctor. I honestly can't recall much of that day. It's like the blur of a bad dream you know you had but the details have faded into obscurity.

Fred did not want a funeral. He always thought that the whole traditional process of embalming, a casket, a viewing, and then a funeral was morbid and a waste of money. He had already arranged for a simple cremation by a local funeral home and asked me to sprinkle his ashes in our garden.

One of our dearest friends, Peg, arranged to have a wake for Fred in a private room of a very nice restaurant in Annapolis that her son worked for and two of our closest friends, Gene and Alan paid for all of it. Gene and Alan both loved Fred very much.

Only our closest friends were there. Fred was loved, respected, and cherished by everyone in attendance and each of them spoke of Fred in their own way when their time came. Fred had touched each one of them deeply. My husband was a very passionate, deep feeling and sincere man. I've never known another human being like him ever in my life. Fred didn't have any superficial relationships, ever. When he chose a friend, it was for life because he saw, admired, respected something wonderful in that person that enriched his own soul, and everyone in that room was there because Fred had enriched their lives as well. My son wrote a wonderful and poignant eulogy, that only he could have written. There wasn't a dry eye in the place.

It was a modest, yet elegant ceremony, sincere, intimate and unpretentious . . . just what Fred would have wanted.

CHAPTER 14

DECISIONS

....

Several weeks after the initial shock of Fred's death had subsided and I was more capable of logical, coherent thought, my mind began to tumble around the same question over and over. Now what?! Losing my husband was devastatingly confusing. It suddenly occurred to me more than ever that although Fred and I had been an excellent team in life throughout our marriage when it came to complex legal, financial, or business-related matters, Fred had always been the primary problem-solver, so to speak. We had always discussed matters of importance first, of course, but I knew very little of the intricacies of such things as finance or real estate, etc.

Dutch girls in the 1940's were taught how to be homemakers and good wives and even though I was taught mathematics in school as a child I was horrible at it. Never in my life have I had any interest in legal or financial matters. Fred tried to teach me all about bank accounts, checkbooks, and more but I never wanted to learn it. That would be my mistake. As in many marriages, each of us had settled into a role that we happily took responsibility for, and now, suddenly, the legal/financial mastermind half of us was gone. So, I called a good friend of ours that had been our attorney once and she agreed to help me with all of the legal and financial matters, including the stocks and trust on a permanent basis.

For months I went through the motions day after day. I was there, but, not. The house was too damn quiet. Except for the bird clock, every hour, the house was silent most of the time. It was hard to sleep because there was nothing next to me. For 37 years there had been a warm body next to me and now it was a cold empty space. Mornings were the worst because we always had coffee together and talked. My counterpart was gone. I felt as if half of my being and my soul went with him. All I had was my dog, Sonny. I could see he missed Fred terribly too. There were certain playful things that only Fred did with him. My neighbors Suzanne and her husband George kept an eye on me, tried to cheer me up. On the other side of my house was an older couple I didn't see much. Their son Tom, and his wife Stephanie, live there now and have become close friends. I went hiking a few times with my mountain club friends but without Fred Sonny was home alone all day when I did. I couldn't do that to my dog.

I pondered the idea of selling the place and buying some sort of condo or apartment in a senior community of some sort. I vacillated back-and-forth between selling the whole kit and kaboodle but not wanting to move out of our little dream home. Fred and I had worked so hard for so many years to acquire it and then restore and remodel it together.

A hiking buddy of mine had sold her home after her husband died and had bought a condo in an upscale 55+ community in Annapolis. I called her and explained to her what was on my mind, and she graciously invited me to come for lunch the next day so she could give me a personal tour of her condo and surroundings. The next day as I drove into my friend's condo community my immediate impression was pleasant enough but far from love at first sight. It was tastefully landscaped with colorful gardens and lush shrubbery but had too much of a manicured look to me. Her condo was obviously of high-quality construction and featured all the perks that come with that, such as crown molding, polished hardwood floors, granite countertops, top-of-the-line appliances, and solid hardwood kitchen cabinets. All of the common areas were of the same quality, tastefully decorated with professionally framed artwork, large, plush, colorful potted plants, and expensive cherry and mahogany furniture. I'm sure most people would have found the whole place quite lovely, and it was but, it wasn't me.

It wasn't Joyce Lane. I knew right then and there I could never be happy there or anywhere else for that matter. I knew it would never feel like home. What was I thinking?! In that instant, my mind was made up. I was going to stay in our home for the rest of my life.

For a few days, I mentally put together my "to-do list". I set about researching what it was I needed to be self-sufficient and safe in the home. One of the problems we had experienced many times over the years was losing our electricity during bad storms, so I bought a big Generac generator and a 500-gallon propane tank that would run the generator for two weeks. I paid for the lifetime maintenance plan as well. I still had the big van and a pop-up camper Fred and I had traveled with. I knew I would never use the pop-up camper, so I sold it. Word to the wise, find out what things are worth before you sell them. I found out a few years later from my son that the pop-up was worth about $3,000 used. I sold it for $500. Yeah, Freddy did a real face palm on that one! I didn't want the van either and Freddy's car had died so I gave him my Chevy Cavalier wagon and traded the van in on a brand-new Subaru Outback. That I did do research on. What a great car! I bought it in 2000 and I still have it, 21 years later! I should do a TV ad for Subaru. The last thing I did was have an air conditioning unit installed on my back porch, so I had a place to escape to on the 95 degrees, humid, dog days of Maryland summer.

In time I was going through the day efficiently like my old self physically, albeit not quite yet mentally. I still thought of Fred a thousand times a day, but eventually learned how to live with it. Pain like that doesn't magically go away without any effort. It's actually very difficult to put into words but, managing grief, I discovered, requires a great deal of mental effort. I had to literally relearn how to live. I had woken up every day with my soulmate for 37 years, and suddenly, that was all gone. Eventually, I learned to think more and more about the wonderful memories that were created in our lives together and less and less about the pain of the loss. There is nothing we can do about death. It is absolute. There is something we can do about being alive, and I had a treasure trove of wonderful memories Fred and I had created in our 37 years together to carry me through, day after day.

CHAPTER 15

LIFE WITHOUT FRED

....

Now that I had the business aspects of my life taken care of, the business of the rest of my life was at hand. There is no manual for this. It is slow and painful and scary. Just when I was beginning to be able to wrap my head around it all, another blow. I got up one morning, shuffled to the bathroom, and then to the kitchen to turn on my coffee pot like I did every morning. Then I went to the dining room, opened the sliding glass door, and called for Sonny to go out and pee. He didn't come. Right away, that rush of fear swept over me and the lump in my throat appeared. I called him again, but I already knew. I walked over to his bed where he lay perfectly motionless. He had died in his sleep. I knelt down and pet his head one last time, tears welling up, and felt myself beginning to come apart. I stood up, grabbed my cordless phone, ran out to the porch and called Suzanne. She came over, collected Sonny, bed and all, and took care of everything. I couldn't handle one minute of it. It was too much. I sat on the porch and cried for some time, thinking, "Now I'm really alone!" I was still drying my eyes when Suzanne returned. She sat on the porch with me for a long time, trying to comfort me. I don't know what I would have done that morning if Suzanne hadn't been there. I mourned Sonny for several weeks. I loved my dog and I missed him terribly. It was all the more painful because Sonny and Fred had been so incredibly close, almost like a unit. It was as if in losing Sonny I was losing the last bit of Fred that I had to hold on to.

I must say, I have the most wonderful neighbors. Suzanne and her husband George and Stephanie and her husband Tom have kept a close eye on me since Fred died and have helped me in many different ways. My son promised me not long after Fred died, when I was ready, all I had to do is call and he would move in immediately and take care of me. He would have come that day if I asked but, except for the three months recovery from a hip replacement in 2015, I have been more than capable of taking care of myself and my house in every way. Freddy's lovely wife, Laura, is a nurse, a BSN/RN, and stayed with me all through the recovery of my hip replacement. It's been necessary for my own happiness these past 20 years to live alone, completely independent as long as I possibly can be. Freddy knows me. He understood that. He knows me better than anyone alive now. Through the kindness of my neighbors, I've been able to live alone, independently, in my own way for twenty-one years.

When the grief became manageable and I was able to think somewhat clearly again, I began to weigh my options. I was still alive. What was I going to do? Even in mourning, that thought constantly lingers. Now what? What am I going to do? It lingers even subconsciously. I found myself many times sitting and staring at the wall, not knowing what to do with myself! Since I had already decided to stay in the house, the gardens, all my bird feeders, the pond, and maintenance of the house itself kept me busy part of the time but not nearly enough. I considered getting another dog but then it occurred to me that I had been hiking and biking just months before. Another dog would keep me at home.

I didn't have the heart to leave a dog alone for more than a few hours.

That alone made my choice pretty clear. I needed a new goal, a new reason for living, a new . . . passion.

I had done some bicycling in the late '80s and early '90s. Then Fred and I spent a few years planning for and then traveling all around the US. In 2000, I really started cycling avidly, almost weekly for years. I was only 69 years old and still quite capable of riding a bicycle, with loaded panniers all day long, fifty, sixty miles.

I went to The Bike Doctor in Arnold, the only bike shop Fred and I had ever used, and bought a brand-new Cannondale hybrid bicycle, panniers, helmet, lights, everything I would possibly need.

Freddy did the math (he's good at that), and calculated that for fifteen years, from 2001 - 2015, I pedaled approximately 40,000 miles. That is a conservative estimate. During my 70's, in 2001-2011, I was able to do long trips of 300 miles or more, and I did A LOT of them.! One of the longest of these trips was all of the C & O canal, both ways, over 600 miles. I did that ride three times in my 70's. The long trips were either tenting trips or pre-planned with stays at motels or B&Bs along the way. The CAM (cycle across Maryland) was a tenting trip, of course. I believe 1,400 people participated in that ride. Normally the long rides I did were 5 - 7 days, usually over 300 miles, and with a group of about a dozen ladies. Most of these ladies I saw again and again on these trips, so we became close friends over the years. Most trips were pre-planned with bookings at B&B's at night, but quite a few over the tears were tenting trips. Another memorable trip was a three-hundred-mile tenting trip in Canada I did with one of my regular riding buddies, Ellen.

I joined a group called Cycling Seniors. They were very organized and arranged dozens of trips, some of which lasted as long as ten days. Several times a year they picked a central location to stay at for a week or so and we would spend every day cycling all day, different routes and trails around it. In the evening after "Happy Hour", of course, we'd have a fine meal and go to bed early so we could get up at dawn and do it all over again.

Of course, I did not invent "happy hour", but . . . I did make it a tradition in every cycling group I participated in. Before I joined these cycling groups, at the end of the day's ride, they would all head off to their rooms or tents or showers, etc., and we wouldn't see each other until dinner or sometimes not until morning. I changed all that. All of our marriage, Fred and I had "happy hour". This was the one hour (or two), after he came home from work, that we would pour a drink, sit down together, and talk about the day. It got so that "happy hour" occurred pretty much no matter where we were, camping, on business at a motel, on a cycling trip, etc.

So, after my first trip with my fellow cyclers, I planned a surprise for the second time. After the first day's ride, when we stopped, without any fanfare, I set up "happy hour". I pulled out a box of wine, plastic glasses, some hors d'oeuvres, laid it all out, and announced "happy hour".

Of course, they all just stood there and looked at me for a moment like I was nuts, 'til they all thought about it for a minute. I could see on their faces they were all thinking, "Why not?" Many of them did this at home, why not after a day of cycling? And so, the tradition was born. Every trip I went on for the rest of my life with all of my cycling friends included Happy Hour. Some happy hours were very elaborate and part of the planning of the trip included who was bringing which wine and which hors d'oeuvres. Year after year, especially with cycling seniors, we had some of the most fun times in a variety of locations. We traveled to places like Martha's Vineyard, Rhode Island, Rock Island, Williamsburg, Greenbriar, Chestertown. Chestertown was an annual, ten-day trip around Labor Day. We always looked forward to that one. It was like a ten-day cycling/party.

I cycled avidly and consistently until about 2015. In 2015 I was cycling with a group in Oxford, MD, and was involved in an accident. Some obviously inexperienced goofball right in front of me slammed on his brakes and stopped his bike right in the middle of the path, on a dime . . . a big NO-NO when you're riding in a group! Never, ever stop suddenly on a bike path for any reason, group or not. Steer your bicycle OFF of the bike path (lane) and then stop. I had no time to react and slammed right into him, the biker behind me slammed into me, and so on. I went to the ground and another biker landed on top of me! I was 84 years old. I was tough but not that tough! Not long after that, I began developing lower back pain that worsened slowly over the next few years. I still cycled but not nearly as much and pretty soon I stopped the long trips altogether. I dealt with the back pain for a while but after many months an x-ray revealed 2 cracked vertebrae in my lower back. I had to wear a lower back brace and not do much of anything for about six months. After 2015 my left hip began to cause me pain as well and eventually in 2019 a hip replacement was necessary.

Needless to say, after 2015, my cycling career slowed down considerably until I was relegated to riding on the B & A trail near my home for maybe 5 - 10 miles, and only when I felt up to it.

I was also a member of the International Women's Group. A few years after Fred passed away, a friend of mine invited me to take a look at it and I was immediately interested. In addition to being a supportive group, they occasionally volunteered for certain events or causes and organized trips to museums, opera, concerts, etc. I had a great time with them quite often over the years and made a lot of new friends there as well.

Don is still a lifelong friend and we've done many things together. We both have an appreciation for classical music and have been to the Meyerhoff in Baltimore for concerts. I still see Don every holiday, Thanksgiving, Christmas, our birthdays and quite often he just visits for happy hour and dinner.

The truth is, I have never gotten over the death of my husband. To this very day, it doesn't take very much for me to dissolve into tears when discussing my husband. Sometimes I hear a song or read a poem he loved and feel the tears begin to well up.

Freddy and I both have shared tears during this project of my memoirs. I think most people are familiar with the term "soulmate". Fred and I were true soulmates, in every sense of the word. We shared everything: our thoughts, our dreams, our aspirations, our likes, dislikes, our philosophies, our opinions, our hopes, and our fears . . . everything.

We shared almost every decision. Occasionally, if one of us had to make a quick decision without the other present, each of us could answer for the other without worry as we knew each other that well. From the moment we fell in love, our priority was each other. Everything else was secondary.

For twenty-one years now I have kept my mind and body occupied in one way or another every day. Whether it be working in my garden, cleaning my pond, filling my bird feeders, cycling, hiking, spending time with my women's group, reading, simply watching TV, or watching my birds from my glassed-in porch, I keep myself occupied. I have never gotten over losing my husband. He was my soulmate, the love of my life. Without him, a huge part of who I was, the most important part of my life was gone. I merely learned some ways to live with the loss.

Oddly enough and, this is very difficult to explain but, a melancholy peace of mind came over me after Fred's death. The fear that I'd felt for years was gone, albeit replaced with crushing grief. For much of the previous twenty-five years, I had essentially lived in a quiet yet consistent state of apprehension, just plain fear. I went to bed a thousand times and kissing him goodnight, secretly prayed to myself that he would wake up with me the next morning. Sure, there were distractions, but I'd seen him collapse and end up in an ICU so many times, I never knew how much time I had left with him! The thought, the idea that I could lose Fred at any time without warning was always lurking somewhere in the back of my mind. Living with that kind of apprehension day after day, year after year is very stressful. Suddenly that fear was completely gone.

How cruel of a trade-off . . . to become free of years of fear only to be stricken with years of abject grief in the same instant!

When the time came that I was mentally able to enjoy being out cycling with my friends, something happened one day that had not yet occurred to me. I had been bicycling with a friend of mine all day and when we got back to the parking lot where we'd parked our cars, she said, "Hey, want to go downtown and have a glass of wine, maybe an appetizer?" Immediately, I started to say, "Oh, thanks, I'd love to but, I have to go home and . . . . . . "

What was I about to say? Go home and get dinner ready? Take the dog out? There was no dog and no one to cook for.

I had to learn to live with that too, living with just me, myself, and I! Maybe relearn how to live is a more appropriate phrasing. I had not lived alone at all, for any considerable length of time since I had my apartment at the Hamiltonian back in 1962. For a long time, life without Fred, and Sonny for that matter, was more than just uncomfortable. I felt like I was adrift in a sea of confusion and grief, unable to communicate with myself.

With my passion for cycling, nature, my close friends, and the care of my home, my gardens, and my birds, eventually, I was able to salvage some joy in my life after losing Fred.

I knew how much Fred valued each day of his life and our life together, how much he loved the world, his friends, and all of nature's creatures and creations. I knew in my soul that he would want me to continue appreciating each day, making each one count in the same ways we did together. Every day that you see the sunrise is a gift.

I learned when I was very young during the war how precious and precarious life is, and how easily and cruelly it can end in an instant, without warning. From then on, I saw each day as important, valuable, and not to be wasted. Fred felt the same way. Perhaps that was one of the many reasons we fell in love. I never knew my husband to squander time, waste a day doing nothing. Even with his free time, he made sure it was used to do something he or we would truly enjoy. That concept is one I think is wise to embrace, the value of time. I've said it all my life, "This is not a rehearsal." It's not! We get one life, one shot, one chance to do something meaningful or valuable with the lives we are given, whatever that may be. That's why I say, each day is important, because none of us ever know how many we have. I have been fortunate. So far, I have had 32,850 of them, give or take . . . and the meter is still running!

As this is being written, I am weeks away from my ninetieth birthday. Naturally, like most people that have lived this long, I have an urge to pour out pages of advice and lessons I have learned in my life. I've already voiced quite a bit of what many might consider advice within the pages of this book.

I would like to say this . . . above all, no matter what life throws at you, BE TRUE TO YOURSELF. Be your own best friend. If you don't love yourself, how can you expect anyone else to? Embrace who and what you are and live your life, your way, as long as it doesn't cause harm to others. The only one on Earth that you cannot lie to is yourself. Embrace your failures as well as your triumphs and trust yourself. If it feels wrong to you, or unfair, or unsafe, or cruel . . . it probably is. Finally, do not fear adversity, pain, discomfort, or hardship. You're going to experience all of it to some degree, whether you want to or not. Instead, meet the hard, painful parts of your life head-on, just as you meet the joys in life. It is very true, what does not kill us makes us stronger in so many ways, ways that we may not realize until years later.

Be open and accepting of life's experiences. Every single thing we experience in life, good and bad, contributes to who we are as individuals, our character, our beliefs, what we become and, what we do.

One more thing, stay active. The body deteriorates much more quickly from lack of use than it does from use. Keep moving. My cycling friends got sick of hearing it, but it is very true, motion is lotion! Regular physical activity keeps the joints and muscles in condition.

Today, I lead a quiet life. I am grateful for all I have had and all I have learned and done. I've had a full and eventful life. I have lived honestly and loved truly. These days I am perfectly happy tending to my gardens, my pond, watching my birds, and seeing my friends. Above all, I am most grateful that I have no regrets. I've taken stock of my life and can't recall anything I would change, even if I could.

Ultimately, I truly believe that my life unfolded exactly as it should have.

Again, I sincerely thank you for taking an interest and reading this memoir of my life. It is truly humbling. I sincerely hope something within these pages was beneficial to you and your life. I wish you, my dear reader, the best in life always and sincerely hope that you live a long, happy, fruitful life.

By the way, I went for a fifteen-mile bicycle ride just last week.

AFTERWORD

After all that I have done in my life, my greatest reward I see every day is the wonderful shrubbery and tall trees that I planted when they were so small. They surround and protect my cabin and when I sit on my porch enjoying my feathered friends on the bird feeder, I am so glad that I'm still here to enjoy the simple things in life that I always felt close to.

Catharina 2021